The Future of Christian Ethics

Ronald H. Preston

THE FUTURE OF CHRISTIAN ETHICS

SCM PRESS LTD

British Library Cataloguing in Publication Data

Preston, Ronald H.
The future of Christian ethics.
1. Christian ethics
I. Title
241   BJ1251

ISBN 0–334–00526–4

First published 1987
by SCM Press Ltd
26–30 Tottenham Road, London N1

Typeset at The Spartan Press Ltd
Lymington, Hants
and printed in Great Britain by
Richard Clay Ltd
Bungay, Suffolk

Contents

Epilogue

Preface

The chapters in this book took shape in the years 1980–86, though some of them existed in a preliminary form before that. They have a similarity in approach and subject matter. There are a number of minor overlappings, but the only major one is between chapters 8 and 12, where points made towards the end of the former are developed more fully in the latter. Chapter 2 originated as a paper written for a consultation in Oxford in the spring of 1984 between some theologians of the Church of England and some from the Lutheran Church in Germany. The fact that it was written for a German constituency affected what I thought needed explaining, but not the substance. Chapters 3 and 4 were given as public lectures in the John Rylands University Library of Manchester; the first was published in the *Bulletin* of the Library Vol. 67, No. 1, Autumn 1984, and the second in Vol. 63, No. 1, Autumn 1980. Chapter 5 is new, and is needed because of the change in the theme of the study work of the World Council of Churches from 'A Just, Participatory and Sustainable Society' to 'The Integrity of Creation'. I have raised the question whether the change was premature, not in any way suggesting that the latter is not an appropriate theme on which to work. Chapter 6 was given as a public lecture in Hull University in the Autumn of 1985. Chapter 7 is based on a lecture given twice to a conference of those working for the three-year Extra-Mural Certificate in Religious Studies in the University of Manchester. Chapter 8 was given at a conference on the theme at New College, Edinburgh in February 1985, arranged by the Department of Christian Ethics and Practical Theology in the Faculty of Divinity of that University. Chapter 9 appeared as part of Occasional Paper No. 14 of the William Temple Foundation, Manchester. It has been included, together with another review-article (Chapter 14, written for private circulation to the members of a Working Party) because they deal with two issues which have forced themselves into the forefront of public attention in the last few years, and are very likely to remain there for some time. Chapters 10 and 11 are new, but they go back to work in a third-year undergraduate special subject seminar which I held for four years, 1976–80. Chapter 12 started as a lecture to an inter-faculty audience at Christchurch, New Zealand in July 1983, but it has been considerably revised. Chapter 13 originally appeared in _The Coming Penal Crisis_ (ed. A. E. Bottoms and R. H. Preston, Edinburgh, 1980), which was based on an interdisciplinary consultation on the theme held in Manchester University. I have included Chapter 15, after some hesitation, as it gives a short account of the context in which work in Christian Ethics is carried on at University level, which I think may have a wider interest than the experience of one person. It originally appeared in _Crucible_, the Journal of the Board of Social Responsibility of the Church of England, January–March 1982.

The bibliographies are selective. They could have become very extensive, but I hope they are enough not only to refer to the main sources drawn on, but to help anyone who wants to follow up any of the themes to find their way into them. I have for the most part excluded references to pamphlets and to articles in journals.

It remains to thank Mrs Brenda Cole, who was a tower of strength in the Social and Pastoral Theology office in the Faculty of Theology in the University of Manchester from 1975 to 1986, for bearing the brunt of coping with the manuscripts in her spare time; and Mrs Kathleen Petch of the office of the William Temple Foundation who has also helped. As always thanks are due to the editorial and production staff of the SCM Press, with whom I have had ties over the years which have meant much to me. In the case of this book, special thanks are due to Miss Jean Cunningham for detailed assistance and for preparing the index.

I should perhaps add that in recent years I have become much more aware of the desirability of inclusive language; here I am afraid inconsistencies remain.

St David's Day, 1986   RONALD HAYDN PRESTON

1

Introduction: The Future of Christian Ethics

The Christian life is one of being and doing. Christian Ethics has to study both. We need to act from the right motive and to find the right content of actions in particular situations in terms of our fundamental beliefs and attitudes. How we move from one to the other is itself a major matter to investigate.

Our basic Christian insights need cultivating in the context of Christian worship, and in fellowship with our fellow Christians and a sharing of minds with them. This involves drawing upon the help which comes from what theology traditionally calls the 'means of grace', prayer and sacrament and Bible study in the community of Christians; and living with the tensions which inevitably result from the differences of outlook between Christians of very different background, experience, and temperament, as they try to grow together into a greater maturity of discernment in thought and action.

This book is not concerned with what we might call the 'formation' of right motives, but with decision-making. It draws upon the Christian faith for an attitude to men and women with which someone who believes that they have all been created in God's 'image' and can be (indeed are being) re-created in Christ, should approach problems of decision-making; and it explores to some extent how far such basic attitudes might be shared by believers in other faiths and ideologies. But its preoccupation is with certain key areas of ethical choice where decisions are called for. Its underlying theme is that we cannot move directly from basic Christian insights to these areas without some kind of empirical investigation, with its inevitable hazards of incomplete information, uncertain interpretation of it, and hidden ideological distortions. The more detailed one becomes at the level of specific policy recommendations the more hazardous it is, and the more Christians who are equally committed to a general direction of policy may come to different conclusions as to the best detailed way to pursue it.

The suggestion is that because of these uncertainties progress is best made by working in groups, in which relevant but differing experiences are checked against one another and expert opinion evaluated. No one is wise enough on his or her own to arrive at a cogent conclusion. A further suggestion is that progress is best made to see if agreement can be reached at a middle level as to the *direction* in which churches and individual Christians should strive to see policy implemented: a level between generalities and detailed proposals. This may not be possible if the divisions of opinion are so sharp that no agreement as to general direction can be reached. In highly polarized situations this is indeed the case; and it then behoves Christians to listen very carefully to what questions other Christians who are deeply divided from them are putting to them, and to find means of keeping contact, even if the practical necessities of decision-making drive them conscientiously into opposing sides. If the situation is not so polarized the search for a majority consensus at the middle level is a good way of proceeding (there will usually be some minority which disagrees), in the effort to help Christians to a more informed judgment.

Of course detailed proposals may also be put forward for discussion; or more than one set of proposals for implementing an agreed general direction may be indicated. These are better put in an appendix. William Temple did this in his *Christianity and Social Order* in 1944, whilst, to take a contrary example, those who worked on *The Church and the Bomb* report in 1982 took a different line: they included only one way of implementing their general conclusion about policy directions involving British nuclear weapons, and they included this detailed policy in the main body of their report. It is worth asking the question whether they might not have had more effect in producing a better informed public opinion and General Synod debate if they had followed Temple's example.

I

Work in Christian Ethics is carried on in different settings and at various levels.[1] In all of them the situation has improved in the last thirty or forty years compared with the doldrums that existed before. Apart from the USA, Christian Ethics has been a much neglected discipline in the English-speaking world. It is interesting to reflect why this is so, and in a fuller study it would be necessary to do so. English people are in fact intensely interested in ethical questions; and so among them are church congregations if a way can be found of involving them in reflections on an ethical theme. There are four main settings. (1) Certain universities and colleges of tertiary education; (2) Seminaries or theological colleges for training 'professional' Christians, mostly ordained; (3) Interdisciplinary working parties and special agencies; (4) Lay groups, either on a professional or congregational basis.

A slow improvement has been seen in the number of professional teachers of the subject.[2] This has led to the establishment of a Society for the Study of Christian Ethics, though it is not yet so well established as to be considered essential to attend if one is teaching in the field.[3] In Roman Catholic seminaries, where Moral Theology was always taught (and for present purposes I am making no distinction between Moral Theology and Christian Ethics) the situation has vastly improved since the Second Vatican Council with the discarding of the old manuals, which were mainly concerned with the precise demarcation of sins and their level of seriousness, with the confessional in mind, and the recovery of a method much more related both to the heart of the gospel and to a serious encounter with the data of the modern world.

Anglican theological colleges have improved too, but for different reasons. From 1959 to 1964 Christian Ethics was cast out of the General Ordination Examination (as it was then called). Anglicans are notoriously willing to pay for only a comparatively short period of training for the priesthood, a legacy of the time when it was assumed that a classically educated English gentleman was naturally fitted for the priesthood with scarcely any preparation at all. There was a complaint that too much was being crammed in to the time available and a demand that the examination load be lightened. The Bishops were offered the alternative of removing either a third Old Testament paper or the one on Christian Ethics. They chose to remove the latter. At that point I received a letter from Canon J. S. Bezzant, to the effect that a body of men who made such a decision needed their heads examining. The loss was not in fact as great as it appeared because the subject was so badly taught as to be derisory. However, after a while the absurdity of the situation was realized and Christian Ethics was restored. Furthermore an effort was made to help those who had to teach it by the production of a handbook to guide them, later entirely rewritten and much extended.[4] There is still too much to cover in the time allowed, and there is rarely a staff member who has good qualifications to teach it, or who stays long enough to acquire one.[5] Roman Catholic diocesan seminaries have something of the same problems, though the Religious Orders are better at maintaining continuity.

The members of staff of Free Church theological colleges stay much longer, but they are not an exception to the fact that on the whole seminaries and theological colleges do not foster scholars who make a major contribution in the field in the way that they have on occasion done in the case of Biblical or Doctrinal studies.

A further question is whether any of this 'academic' theology faces up to the challenge of Political and Liberation Theology as discussed in chapters 10 and 11. In my judgment it does so only to a small extent.[6]

There has been much more activity in organizing working parties on particular themes or particular issues. I am thinking, for instance, of the British Council of Churches, the Board for Social Responsibility of the Church of England, the Division of Social Responsibility of the Methodist Church and the Catholic Institute for International Relations. Indeed all the mainline churches are involved in such activities. Compared with a generation ago the increased effort in this respect is striking. A problem is rather the extent to which the work, when completed, is fed into the life of local congregations and regions, and how far their capacity for dealing with it and their rate of absorption can be enhanced. Beyond that there is the question how far through them, or directly, it influences the general public. On occasion it obviously does. The Church of England report *The Church and the Bomb* of 1982 aroused so much attention that the debate on it at the General Synod was televised. So much attention is rare. However in my judgment the greater production by the churches of well-informed and reasoned material, free from pious platitudes, is slowly producing a more aware Christian constituency. Those who allege that it is all 'unspiritual' and not the churches' business are still vocal, and have to be combated, but the presumption is not in their favour.

There has been a growth of special agencies in the field of Christian Ethics which warrants a special study of their initiation, finance, characteristics, successes, failures, difficulties, and relation to the wider church structures. Examples would be the William Temple Foundation, The Christian Medical Fellowship (an evangelical body), now paralleled by the Linacre Centre Institute for the Study of Ethics in Health Care (a Roman Catholic one), an Institute for Church and Society based on Oxford, and a Marriage Research Centre based on London. In 1982 Francis McHugh produced for the Christendom Trust a Directory of them and of Christian Social Action groups under the title *British Churches and Public Policy*.

As far as lay groups are concerned it would need a very extensive enquiry to know how far they are increasing, for they can be very varied.[7] They can be made up of Christians from the same profession or job. Teachers are the commonest example of these. There are some medical groups. Industrial Mission has promoted some at both management and trade union level, as well as joint ones. Or they can consist of Christians from different occupations, and the unemployed, gathered in a house group, or more formally. Again they can be drawn from one congregation or from several, and from the same confessional tradition or be ecumenical. The possibilities are many. And when I refer to them as 'lay' I do not mean that ordained men and women are necessarily excluded, but that their orientation and direction is lay. They are part of the slow movement to promote full lay participation in the life of the church, in its internal structures and in the realization that the vast bulk of Christian witness comes through lay people in their families, their jobs and as citizens. The movement is a slow one because church structures are heavily influenced by the power of the professionals, and most of these are ordained.[8]

Greater activity has meant more books. Forty years ago there was not much choice in trying to find a competent survey of the field that came from a British background. Peter Green's *The Problem of Right Conduct* appeared in 1931 and was widely read for some time; it is not to be dismissed, but was hardly adequate to the scope of the subject. Then Sydney Cave's *The Christian Way* had a spell of use from 1958. Now there is no lack of them.[9] Even more is this the case with respect to particular issues. Sexuality used to be the only area always covered, but even that was partial. For instance, when I began teaching there was nothing on homosexuality besides sections in traditional manuals, left in the decent obscurity of Latin, and concerned with the confessional. Now there is an abundance of material. A host of issues which are either new or were not thoroughly thought through before are seriously studied. *The Dictionary of Christian Ethics* which made a pioneering start in 1967, and has had imitators, needed to be almost completely rewritten and much enlarged when it appeared again in 1986; 'new' had to be added to the title. No one can complain of lack of material. The problem is to keep pace with it.

II

Some questions emerge from this activity which need attention. Inadequacies of teaching in the past mean uncertainties among Christians in the present. In the Roman Catholic Church an excessive reliance on the authority of the *magisterium* has meant that many are uneasy with the more relaxed tone, except on questions of sexual ethics, which has prevailed in official teaching since the Second Vatican Council. And because they held unreal expectations of the certainty with which ethical dilemmas can be answered, they are at a loss when these inevitable uncertainties are stressed in the Pastoral Constitution of that Council, *Gaudium et Spes*.

In other mainstream churches uncertainties are due to lack of systematic teaching. Churchgoers do not have a method for dealing with ethics. So they lack confidence, or are unwarrantably fixed and dogmatic. They are not clear on so basic a matter as the nature and authority of conscience. Like many Roman

Catholics they hanker after a fixed and clear conclusion to a moral problem, and do not realize that it is rare to find one clear cut 'answer' to it; or they find that this is so, but do not understand why it is so. They may know in theory that one walks by faith and not by sight, but they do not like it applied to ethics. Some indeed have the same attitude to doctrinal issues. They can hardly not be aware of doctrinal differences within Christendom, but they assume that their position is right and all others are wrong, and may even be heresies. But others who have learned to live with a doctrinal pluralism (though realizing there must be some limits), are disconcerted when they find the same thing in ethics. It is common to find an assumption that Protestant morality is one of obedience to arbitrary divine commands.

Christian Ethics involves holding together three sources of moral illumination: (1) the Bible; (2) the Christian doctrinal and ethical tradition; (3) moral reasoning in a contemporary context. As I mentioned at the beginning of this Introduction, there is a widespread desire to move directly from either the first or the second directly to a detailed conclusion on a contemporary problem, without any intermediate step involving some element of empirical judgment. Yet even if a general principle is drawn from the Bible or tradition rather than a specific text, the problem comes with its detailed application. As an illustration we can take the principle of 'the sanctity of (human) life'. We do not consider human life in all circumstances to be absolutely sacred, because on occasion we think it justifiable to take it. And we have also to resolve conflicts of life with life. The extent of the proper protection to be given to the human embryo and at what stage in pregnancy from conception onwards, has been so much discussed that it led to the appointment by the Government of the Warnock Inquiry.[10] Christians are divided on this. Some argue that it should be given the protection proper to full human status from conception, others that a progressive protection is called for. The Board for Social Responsibility of the Church of England has produced a report which puts forward both views as plausible, and rather weakly says it cannot resolve the issue.[11] It has, however, shown that it cannot be settled by the Bible. Can it be settled by tradition? Tradition changes and develops, as it has for instance on slavery or usury or religious liberty, so that it is always possible to ask of tradition, Is it plausible? That leaves us with moral reasoning. Here Christians have to use the same canons of consistency, and power of reasoning, as anyone else. Driven back from the Bible and tradition some Christians take refuge in a self-evident proposition. The trouble then is that there are rival propositions. In the Warnock case some think it evidently absurd that a human foetus from the moment of conception should be given the protection appropriate to full human status, others say that it should. How can the discussion be advanced? Only by getting behind these two positions and asking why they are thought to be so clear. Are there hidden presuppositions? In this case there seems to be one concerned with the status of 'nature', as we experience it, in relation to our belief in God. How fixed is it? How far is it to be modified under God in aid of greater human flourishing, as far as we can judge the matter? So moral reasoning leads us back to a doctrine of God; behind, that is, the biblical evidence from which it is derived and how it has been, and is to be, interpreted. The appeal to nature is a tricky one. St Paul was caught out on the question of hair lengths for men and women, mistakenly thinking that a current social custom was a fixity of 'nature'.[12] Christians have not regarded 'nature' as fixed. If it is to be thought so in the case of the human embryo we have to ask the questions, Is this plausible? Is it consistent with other views we take of medical interventions? We are back to weighing evidence. In fact we continually move to and fro between Bible, tradition, and moral reasoning (the latter including elements of empirical judgment on contemporary data). One hopes that in due time a consensus will emerge among most Christians. But also one hopes it will emerge in time to be of some influence, and not tag along after the issue has for all practical purposes been settled, as happened in the case of usury. At least the churches are much better informed, as a result of the greater activity I have been discussing, if they choose to use what is available. It is no use addressing an imagined situation which has already passed.

The Bible and the doctrines drawn from it give us our basic orientation towards human kind and towards nature. Detailed ethical precepts in the Bible have to be seen in their context, whereas the truth about the kingdom of God brought out by, for instance, the parable of the Good Samaritan is perennially relevant. Our basic orientation has to be brought alongside the data of contemporary moral issues. The fixity for which Christians yearn must be found in the right place. That is living in the church in which Jesus is worshipped as Lord, in which we are the heirs of the first disciples, all strictly monotheistic Jews, who found themselves driven to worship him, shocking as it must have been to their previous most basic presupposition. From this base we bring our total understanding of life alongside the empirical date of our own day.

From Jesus comes our fundamental motive, 'Freely you have received, freely give.'[13] That is the basic motive of gospel ethics. It has a kind of unconscious spontaneity. Subsidiary to it is the cultivation of Christian graces within the Christian community, with the aim of growing together towards our full maturity in Christ. The first is grounded in the past, in the new life brought by Jesus, as it tackles the issues of the present; the second looks to the future as it does so. Some Christians, reacting from the complexity of moral issues, and wishing to differentiate the Christian rather sharply from any other ethic, want to remain closely within the Christian fellowship at the expense of commitment in the structures of the world. Stanley Hauerwas has recently criticized a concentration on moral quandaries, ambiguous situations, and hard cases; after a stress on the autonomy of moral judgment and a needed universalizability in moral judgments he thinks Christians end up with the same conclusions as non-religious moral philosophers.[14] This does not seem necessarily a cause for worry. It would be odd if they were greatly at variance with the range of opinions among moral philosophers, if moral reasoning is one of three basic elements in Christian ethics. Also his concentration on shaping our desires and aspirations within the context of the Christian community makes it hard for Christians to participate in public dialogue on moral issues with those of other religions and secular persuasions. A balance has to be kept between the two approaches. The first sentence of this Introduction expresses both.

I have several times stressed the necessity of taking empirical evidence seriously, but a caution needs to be uttered. It is necessary to examine it critically in case there are hidden ideological presuppositions in it which are unsatisfactory from a Christian viewpoint. For instance, latent in all work in the social sciences is a doctrine of the human person which may or may not be acceptable to a Christian, and which may affect what is considered as significant evidence and what weightage is to be given to it. Contrariwise new evidence may lead to the modification of hitherto accepted Christian positions. There is a reciprocal relationship here. The same considerations apply to evaluating expert evidence. It is often indispensable, but experts differ, and may have their own presuppositions and interests which need evaluating. Medical ethics has become far too important to be left solely to medical folk, but it cannot be studied at all without them. That is why theology has to be related to all other disciplines, and not just Arts subjects, as I have argued in the last chapter.

I draw three conclusions from these reflections.

1. We need to work ecumenically. All the main confessional traditions include a spectrum of views, though it is harder for the Roman Catholic Church to admit this officially than it is for others to do so. All these traditions have had too fixed a view in the past, and have to learn to cope more adequately with social change. They can help one another by doing so, and they can avoid a wastage of scarce resources. In practice they do so fitfully, but not of set purpose nor as a matter of course.

2. We must not constantly be searching for something so distinctively Christian as to say that no one else could have arrived at it. There is an exaggerated fear of merely echoing some form of humanism. In fact some humanists are very close to a Christian outlook; it would be surprising if it were not so in a civilization drawn both from the Judaeo-Christian and classical humanist traditions. But other humanists are not. On the other hand there are some strange elements in the Christian spectrum! Christians should welcome allies wherever they can find them. It is very important in a plural society that they should do so, and that they strive for maximum public consensus where legislation is involved. There often is no peculiar, specific, detailed Christian contribution. In the ethics of distributive justice three criteria have been much discussed; right, merit and need. Christians have not ruled out any one of the three altogether, and they have not produced a fourth. In the ethics of corrective justice three criteria have been much discussed; retribution, deterrence and reformation. Christians have not totally ruled out any one of them, and have not produced a fourth. Their methods and procedures are not essentially different from ethical reasoning as

done by others. What they do bring with them is a perspective derived from their worship, which provides certain presumptions with which they aproach ethical questions in looking for and weighing evidence and criticizing ideologies.

3. Group work is indispensable if we are to cope with the rapidly changing scene and establish some division of labour. But we also need to give as much attention to the means of communication and dissemination of the work when completed as we give to its production.

I see no reason why the gains of the last few decades cannot be consolidated and built upon, and a constituency increased which is alert to issues of ethics, looks for work to be done on them, and is prepared to work at them itself.

*Christian Ethics
in an Ecumenical Setting*

2

The Development of Social Ethics in the Church of England in the Twentieth Century

Theological development cannot be fruitfully considered without reference to the social, economic and political milieu within which it takes place. This is particularly so in the case of social theology and ethics. Therefore, it is wise to begin with an analysis of the general as well as the theological position of Britain and the Church of England in 1900. This is the theme of the first section of this essay. In the second I deal with the development of social teaching in the Church of England since 1900: in the third I make some general reflections on the organs for expressing social teaching, and on the situation today.

I

In the year 1900, Britain had had about 130 years of rapid industrialization and urbanization, in which processes it had been the world's pioneer. It was still probably the most powerful state economically and politically, and this was reflected in the atmosphere of imperialistic presuppositions of which the Boer War at the turn of the century was a symbol. However, Britain was being rapidly overtaken by other states, though she was slow to realize it. The Empire Exhibition at Wembley in 1923 and 1924, to which I was taken as a boy of ten, still reflected this atmosphere, as did the ethos of the schools I attended. The British public had not realized the loss of power occasioned by the 1914–18 war; and they also took some time to realize the much further loss of power occasioned by the 1939–45 one. Indeed, the recent Falklands war indicated that it is by no means generally accepted: there was considerable approval of the sentiment that it had put the 'Great' back into Britain. In this connection the distancing of the churches, including the Church of England, from such an attitude is a measure of the change in its social ethics since the Boer War. We shall refer to this again later. Meanwhile, there is much truth in the remark of the American statesman that Britain had lost an empire and failed to find an alternative role, as the centre of power in the 'Western' world has shifted from Europe to the USA.

It has not been two world wars alone that have produced great changes during the years 1900–1984. Allied with them, because of the amount of resources devoted to military research and defence, but also operating independently, have been immense technological changes which have brought social and economic changes in their wake. A notable result of these have been, for example, a doubling of the standard of living in the first twenty-five years of the reign of the present Queen, with a consequent increase in expectations which it has produced, and of disgruntlement when they are not realized. In 1900, the average weekly wage earner had to spend over 90 per cent of his income on the basic necessities of food, clothes and shelter; now it is no more than 60 per cent. Though this increase in affluence has been checked since 1973 through various factors of which the oil price rises of OPEC have been a major one, it is still likely that the general trend (or 'secular' one as the statisticians call it) will be upward, though not at the rate of the pre-1973 years.

The two wars and modern technology have greatly accelerated social and geographical mobility. This has been particularly marked in the case of women, reflected for instance in the way they dress. Far more go out to work if they can; and it was their work in the factories in the 1914–18 war which accelerated the process, and also secured for them the vote. Developments in transport have transformed physical mobility, and those in the media cultural mobility. The first mass daily paper was Lord Northcliffe's *Daily Mail* in 1896; and in this century we have had the cinema, and then the radio and then television. Leisure time has been transformed, cultural horizons widened, and it has become much easier to participate vicariously in a life-style of which one has no direct acquaintance, and to live in a fantasy world.

Since the 1939–45 war, urbanized Britain has become a plural society, made obvious by the number of people with black and brown skins (not so many yellow) seen in the streets. The effect on the religious balance of the country is noteworthy; for instance, Methodism, which has been the strongest noncon-formist church in England since the Industrial Revolution, is now outnumbered by followers of Islam.

Since poverty is a relative term and not an absolute one, the increase in wealth has not removed problems of poverty. In the year 1900, the country was still in the shackles of nineteenth-century *laissez-faire* thinking, according to which each adult should be responsible for his own life and circumstances and as independent as possible from others. Foreseeable mis-fortunes should be provided against in advance; unforeseeable ones, if they were beyond the resources of the individual to deal with, should, if at all possible, be alleviated by private benevolence, and only in the last resort should the state be involved. If it were, the conditions of relief should be made sufficiently uncomfortable to give the person or family concer-ned a strong inducement to get themselves out of it. The gen-eral assumption was that if you were poor it was your own fault, and the onus was on you to show you were not at fault. Much effort was given to separate the 'deserving' from the 'undeserving' poor. The twentieth century has seen an under-mining of this whole approach until the election of the Thatcher Government in 1979, since when there have been signs of a return to it in the guise of advocating a return to Victorian virtues. The undermining was begun by the publica-tion in 1909 of the Minority Report of the Royal Commission on the Poor Law. It was written by Sidney and Beatrice Webb, who were to devote their lives to social investigations. No one remembers the majority report, but the minority one laid the foundation of the Welfare State, begun by the Liberal Govern-ment before the 1914 war. (Bismarck was ahead of Britain in this respect.) During the second world war, a notable enquiry by William Beveridge on Social Insurance and Allied Services set out a programme to combat what he vividly described as the Five Giants of Want, Disease, Ignorance, Squalor and Idle-ness. He greatly influenced the policies of post-1945 govern-ments. The Welfare State was seen as providing to a citizen help in coping with the hazards of the life cycle by right and a basic living standard below which he or she would not be allowed to fall. Its development was aided by the rapid economic growth already mentioned. One result was a younger generation which had more community resources devoted to it than any previous one in British history; and it was noticeable, at the time of the student 'revolt' of 1969 and after, that even the most radical student 'drop-outs' took it for granted.

No one thought that the Welfare State was working as smoothly as it might, or that it could not be sharpened and improved, but there was quite a broad consensus on it between Conservative and Labour. Expectations became greater, and the experience of trying to run a state based on welfare capitalism (what in Germany is called a social market economy) revealed complexities arising out of the vested interests of rival groups, rigidities which hindered adaptations to new situations, and contradictions occasioned by the vulnerability of Britain to international economic pressures (particularly because of the dependence on the strong USA economy) which could not be avoided but which politicians did not like publicly to admit. These developments have eroded some of the former consensus, and we have seen recently a backlash on the part of the political Right and the political Left. The Right has seen a return to an individualistic philosophy and allied with it, although ultimately incompatible with it, a return to an hierarchical and paternalistic picture of society; on the Left there have been demands for a purer socialist policy, hedged about if necessary by strong nationalist protectionist policies. What the outcome of these contending views will be *vis-à-vis* the previous policies of welfare capitalism is quite unclear.

These various social, economic and political changes have had their effect on the churches. I do not think it is possible precisely to determine how far theology is an independent variable and how far it is conditioned by these factors. It is certainly not *determined* by them. But I think it is a mistake to argue as if there is a residual core of distinctively theological reflection unaffected by these cultural factors (using the term in the broadest sense); and it is equally a mistake to assume that theological considerations can be dissolved without remainder into changing cultural factors, as sociologists of religion often do – whether overtly or covertly. The two have a reciprocal relation to one another; and to my mind this is a better term than dialectical, with its Hegelian and Marxist associations.

In addition to these social factors, Christian theology had to face the challenge of Darwinism in the nineteenth century, and in the twentieth it has not been able to ignore Marx, especially since the Russian Revolution of 1917, and it has had to cope with Freud and the movements of thought in the area associated with him. Putting it more generally, we have seen vast developments in the human sciences of individual and corporate man. All these developments have led to the secularization thesis of dynamic sociology, according to which there is an irreversible movement in advanced industrial societies away from the ecclesiastical control of human institutions, the Christendom situation, to the erosion of religion until it disappears or, perhaps, remains a socially insignificant hangover from the past.[1] Its 'plausibility structure' is undermined; perhaps a minor role of 'cognitive dissonance' may remain, but that is all.

I do not think this thesis is plausible. Neither psychology nor sociology has produced a plausible general theory of the origin, development and future prospects of religion as such, or the Christian religion in particular. Moreover, with the intellectual tools appropriate to them I do not think it is possible for them to do so. However, the decline of ecclesiastical control and the social prestige that went with it is indisputable, and has been much accelerated in this century. One of the problems of the Church of England, with its particular form of Establishment, is that it retains the outward appearance of the old Christendom situation when the inward reality is almost gone. Its leaders and members can thus easily deceive themselves about its position and tasks.

Along with these changes, has gone a secularization of the European mind, well portrayed in an earlier stage in Owen Chadwick's study of the nineteenth century.[2] This is to use the term secularization in a different sense, to cover the way in which nature, man and God are thought of both separately and together. The result is that even if doctrines are verbally expressed in the same way they are thought of differently, so that a vast amount of doctrinal reconstruction is perforce going on. However, this is not our present concern.

Ethically, there is no doubt that all the churches, and certainly the Church of England, lost a lot of moral authority as a result of the 1914–18 war. It had allied itself to such an extent with the most jingoist and naive expressions of the national cause that when the post-war economic and political malaise exposed the hollowness of the talk of 'a war to end wars' and of making 'a land fit for heroes to live in', the resulting disillusion rebounded against the church. In the 1939–45 war the churches made an effort to avoid the same mistake and to a large extent succeeded. But they have never recovered their pre-1914 position.[3]

As an established church, the Church of England found itself in 1900 in a situation when half the churchgoers in the country dissented from it. There had been a substantial dissent ever since the settlement of 1662 which failed, indeed hardly tried, to accommodate the Puritans. This had been greatly increased by the evangelical revival, mainly Methodist, which accompanied the early years of the Industrial Revolution. To this was added the influence of Roman Catholic Irish labourers and their families, especially after the potato famine of 1845. From about 1840 the Church of England had somewhat recovered its position as against the Free Churches, but the quarrels between them in the nineteenth century over power and prestige were a melancholy side issue to the intellectual, social and evangelistic tasks occasioned by the Industrial Revolution. It produced a new type of civilization in the history of the world with which the church, with its roots in the agricultural past, has found it hard to come to terms.

The Church of England claimed pastoral responsibility for all (or sometimes for all those who did not expressly repudiate it), but in fact it was on the way to becoming a denomination – but emphatically not a sect. There is no sectarian strain in Anglican ecclesiology or social ethics. In practice rural areas were vastly over staffed as against the conurbations, and in them the local squires had a very strong influence over the churches. Even so, many churches had to be built in towns and cities, but few in working-class areas were well attended; and where there were strong congregations, they tended to have a paternalistic and archaic atmosphere. Such radical Anglican social thinkers as there were tended to be middle- or upper-class. However, it is important to note that they, and still more some Baptists and Primitive Methodists, had enough contact with working-class life to give the characteristic nineteenth-century working-class institutions – Trade Unions, Co-operatives and political groups – a Christian or quasi-Christian flavour. Because of this there has not been in Britain the division which has characterized some countries of Western Europe between 'Christian' and 'secular' social democrats, the Christians being right wing and the secularists being on the left and anti-clerical and often anti-Christian; nor have we had 'Christian' Trade Unions as against 'secular' ones. Another effect has been that the influence of Marxist categories has been small in British working-class organizations; it has been chiefly found among intellectuals.

The Church of England played a full part in the vast amount of voluntary philanthropic activity which characterized the Victorian age; we often call it 'ambulance work'. It was very much *de haut en bas*. Good was done to the poor but there is little evidence of their voice being heard or their participation called for. The leadership of the church was entirely in the hands of the small privileged group with access to the ancient Universities of Oxford and Cambridge.

In 1900 there were not many resources for a social ethic available to the Church of England. The traditional Anglican and Puritan Moral Theology had collapsed at the end of the seventeenth century. This is dealt with in R. H. Tawney's classic study, *Religion and the Rise of Capitalism*, which appeared in 1926. The church was too corporate for an age of increasing individualism, and intellectually too lethargic to cope with the rapid economic and social changes which were soon to begin. There was no Lutheran 'two realms' doctrine indigenous to the country. What was left was the individualist version of the Calvinist work ethic, of which the basic study is still that of Max Weber.[4] This persisted well into this century.

Moreover, there was no tradition of teaching Christian ethics, personal or social, in the Universities. One Chair in the field had recently been founded in Oxford but that was all. And that remained the situation until recently. British Christian culture was Protestant and expressed itself in a biblicist individualism which called for consecrated individuals who would give personal obedience to certain God-given prescriptive regulations found in scripture, mostly in sexual matters, and by doing so would earn a heavenly reward. No attention was given to social values and social structures, or to the questions raised by the exercise of power in society, other than support for the national sovereign state.

The one exception to this lack of resources for a social ethic was the legacy of the Christian Socialist Movement of 1848–54, associated chiefly with the name of the theologian, F. D. Maurice. It was from this that the development of social thought in this century sprang. It had faded temporarily after 1854, but from 1889 was taken up again, largely through a society called the Christian Social Union. The legacy chiefly took the form of a basic critique of the theory of competition and the free market, expressed in the term *laissez faire*, in so far as it was seen as an overall theory of how God intends human beings to relate to one another in society. The CSU was entirely Anglican, mainly clerical (strongly supported by a number of bishops), and with a membership of up to 10,000, not one of them being working-class. It talked of the need for 'the formulation of a Christian political economy', but never tackled it. It did, however, campaign against particular social abuses. The CSU was the most important group concerned with Christian social ethics in 1900, but they were all somewhat vague in their social and economic analysis. Theologically it was nearly always to the doctrine of the Incarnation or the Body of Christ to which they appealed, not – for instance – that of justification by faith. The appeal was to the more Catholic rather than to the more Protestant elements in the Church of England. Indeed the Protestant element in the Church of England played no part in developing a social theology at this time.[5]

II

The war of 1914 marked the first watershed of this century. Until then, the tendencies and activities present in 1900 continued. As an indication of their influences it is worth noting that in 1907, the convocation (of clergy) of the Province of Canterbury passed a resolution that a 'living wage' should be the first charge on the profits of an industry. (There was a parallel to this in the first modern social Papal Encyclical *Rerum Novarum* in 1891.) This was a frequent element in Christian social thought, and it is still heard. It represents an insight that there is something wrong in treating labour, the labour of human beings, as a factor of production in exactly the same way as land and capital, as the pure theory of capitalism does. But it is not enough to chip away at one main element of the theory without spelling out the implications of this for the working of the whole. This was never done, probably because it was thought to be too near party politics to do so.

A major intellectual contribution in the pre-1914 period was a symposium on *Property: its Duties and Rights*, edited in 1913 by Bishop Charles Gore, a leading Catholic Anglican. It included an essay by the liberal humanist social philosopher, L. T. Hobhouse, which distinguished between property for use and property for power, developing more precisely the traditional Christian defence of private property made by St Thomas Aquinas. The implication of that defence was that everyone should have private property; it should be widely distributed. Modern capitalism had developed quite differently. Clearly the very different types of private property need differentiation. And if the role of property – and profits – in capitalism had been more closely examined, a useful distinction between profit as a directive and profit as an incentive could have been made. (This is a distinction which, applied to the Soviet type of economy, could rid it of much of its sluggishness and could lead to some *rapprochement* to a reformed welfare capitalism.) But Christian thinkers shied off economics as an academic study.

A year before the war ended a private group of eleven members, the Collegium (of which William Temple was a leading member), produced a book on *Competition: a Study of Human Motive*; and in 1918 some of them, including R. H. Tawney, brought out *Christianity and the Industrial Problem*. This is known as the report of the Archbishops' Fifth Committee of Enquiry. These Committees were set up following upon a largely abortive National Mission of Repentance and Hope which the two Archbishops, of Canterbury and York, had instigated. The Fifth Report was weighty and had a good deal of influence. Again, there was stress on a 'living wage'. But many other matters were stressed, including the right to strike. There had been in recent years an emphasis, particularly in certain Roman Catholic circles, on Distributism, involving a society of small property owners (the link with medieval teaching on private property is obvious). Also Guild Socialism had been widely advocated. This would be roughly the same as Producers' – as distinct from Consumers' – Co-operatives, in which the work force would own and manage the undertaking. It had affinities with the medieval guilds. It was with these that the Christian Socialists had experimented in 1848–54. The Fifth Report was influenced by this, in that any alternative order of society to that of capitalism which it envisaged was of that kind. Not surprisingly, the members were divided on the issue. One can see in all these thoughts the effort to draw upon a tradition of Christian social ethics from the medieval past, but it did not come to terms with the realities of the capitalist system as it had by then developed. There is a place for Producers' Co-operatives (it has worked best in agriculture), but it is not a structure which solves all problems, if only because it gives power to the workers but, unless other structures are created, not to the consumer or the community at large. In the event the cause of Guild Socialism faded away in the post-war deflation of 1921 and its aftermath.

In 1920, the world-wide Lambeth Conference of Anglican bishops met. These ten-yearly conferences have no executive authority but are for the mutual building up of the bishops. However, they are a significant test of opinion. The eighth committee of the conference referred once more to the 'living wage', and contrasted the spirit of co-operation and sacrifice found in the trenches in the war with that of the self-interest and unrestricted capitalism in industry. It spoke against 'mechanical laws' (ie. *laissez faire*), and favoured Industrial Parliaments (an idea Mussolini was to take up in the Fascist corporate state), so that workers should have 'a share' in the control of working conditions. In an encyclical letter the bishops wrote of 'the necessity of a fundamental change in the spirit and working of our economic life. The change can only be effected by accepting as the basis of industrial relations the principle of co-operation in service for the common good in place of unrestricted competition for private or sectional advantage.' This is a good example of the alternative social teaching in the Church of England to biblical individualism. But it is basically slipshod. It challenges the basis of *laissez faire* with an utopian principle, and then softens the impact by the indefinite 'unrestricted'. No indication of how this might work out was, or could be, given without coming to grips with the basic economic problems of production and distribution, saving and investment, which any society has to solve, and this was never attempted. Probably it was thought too divisive, and a 'politicization' of the faith, to use a term recently come into favour. At all events, this was the social theology preached between the wars by most in the church who preached one at all. The main organ was the Industrial Christian Fellowship, which had absorbed the Christian Social Union. It was dependent on voluntary subscriptions from parishes and individuals, and the vagueness of the message meant that there was some truth in the remark that it raised money from bourgeois parishes on the grounds that it was a weapon against red atheist revolution, and spent it in factory meetings in advocating social change in dramatic but vague terms.

1923 saw the first Labour Government in the history of the country. It was a minority one, but even so it was a potentially alarming prospect for an established church, so that a message of general good will sent to the Prime Minister by an *ad hoc* group of 700–800 clergy was significant. In the same year, the National Assembly of the Church set up a Social and Industrial Committee. In practice, the industrial side was left to the unofficial Industrial Christian Fellowship. The next year saw the interdenominational national Conference on Christian Politics, Economics and Citizenship (COPEC) in Birmingham, with William Temple as Chairman.[6] It was a conscious prelude to the 'Universal Christian Conference on Life and Work' at Stockholm in 1925, where the British found themselves, as was often to be the case later, midway between the 'social gospel' outlook of most Americans and the transcendent emphasis of most of those coming from continental Europe.[7] I mention these to remind us that there is a certain artificiality in considering the Church of England on its own.

However, the next development was a purely Anglican one. Some Catholic Anglicans became dissatisfied with both capitalism and the collectivist socialist alternative and set out to develop a 'Christian sociology'. It became known as the Christendom Movement. It looked back in a general way to medieval thought on society, and to natural law in the sense of a source for the derivation of *a priori* Christian principles (a sense which has been so much criticized in recent Roman Catholic moral theology). It was good, particularly in the person of its leading thinker V. A.

Demant, on the basic moral virtues on which capitalism depends for its working, which it presupposes but has hardly thought about, and in practice tends to undermine rather than to foster. This is the theme of his book *Religion and the Decline of Capitalism* (1949), in which he carried on the work of Tawney by subjecting the current state of capitalism to theological scrutiny. But the positive proposals of the Christendom Movement were very weak. It talked a lot about economics but never studied it, and therefore adopted an absurd monetary theory called Social Credit, invented by an engineer, C. H. Douglas. To my mind it reveals a weakness in theology to think that the root of human woes in the social order can be corrected by a manipulation of the monetary system. A better theology would not have been taken in by Social Credit. There was also a good deal of economic nationalism in the Christendom group, partly in order to return to a more self-sufficient economy free from the entanglements of international trade. Natural law thinking also led them to some quixotic conclusions. Artificial manures were branded as 'un-natural' in favour of compost heaps, and artificial insemination of cattle likewise on the ground that it deprived them of the pleasures of courtship.

Christendom thinking had a good deal of influence between the wars, many being taken in by its false air of expertise, and it had the effect of deflecting the social thought of those impressed by it from reality. However, the economic crash of 1929 onwards and the rise of Fascism and Nazism were leading to a greater realism. The theologians of the 1930s were Barth, Brunner, Berdyaev, Maritain and Reinhold Niebuhr, none of them Anglican or British. Their effects on the Church of England were minor and diverse. For instance, those influenced by Barth tended not to be interested in social theology and ethics. William Temple was the main figure, and in general he continued in the outlook already referred to, but as the decade wore on he became increasingly influenced by Niebuhr. Much ambulance work continued, particularly for the unemployed, and there were some imaginative church housing projects. But there was no inter-war successful synthetic Church of England social theologian. William Temple came nearest to one. A quick summary of the reasons for this inter-war weakness would include clericalism, ignorance of the social sciences, partisanship among different church groups, and a return to a more transcendent emphasis as against both liberal Catholicism and liberal Protestantism.

A search for greater social competence began to grow. This was chiefly due to ecumenical influences in the preparatory work for, and the subsequent influence of, the second Life and Work World Conference, at Oxford in 1937, with the title 'Church, Community and State'. There was a social-theological input to this which has not been excelled since. It was mainly due to the perceptive thought and organizing capacity of the Anglican lay theologian, J. H. Oldham, and is best expressed in his section of the preparatory book for the Conference, *The Church and its Function in Society* written jointly with W. A. Visser 't Hooft, who was to become the first General Secretary of the World Council of Churches. This greater competence was not seen at first in the Church of England. The Conference which William Temple called during the war, in 1941 at Malvern, was a throwback into a sterile debate between those in the *a priori* natural law tradition and those in a simplistic Christian socialist one, which ended in confusion.[8] But greater competence was seen after the war, particularly in the area of sex ethics, which of course, has great social importance and is very relevant to our subject.

In 1939, the National Assembly of the Church had established a Moral Welfare Council to co-ordinate work previously divided between two bodies, one which had been started to combat the idea prevalent in Victorian times, that men could not be expected to keep the standards of continency required of women, and the other to undertake ambulance work with ummarried mothers. There had been little new thinking on human sexuality, except that in 1930 the Lambeth Conference of Bishops had given a very cautious acceptance to contraception. It was said that the married lives of the bishops who did not accept it greatly influenced the majority to do so; and they were the first representative Christian body which did. It provoked a sharp reply from Pope Pius XI in the Encyclical *Casti Connubii*. It was held that the Anglican bishops had given way to modern sensuality. (It was the comparatively recent date of this encyclical which was the main reason why Pope Paul VI rejected the majority report of his own Commission and issued *Humanae Vitae* in 1968.) As the 1958 Lambeth Conference approached, the Archbishop of Canterbury, Geoffrey Fisher, thought that the situation had moved considerably since the cautious position of 1930, and appointed a Commission to examine the issues. The result was a major report, *The Family in Contemporary Society*, which appeared in 1958. For the first time a Church Commission had the advantage of the services, for twelve months, of a senior and respected academic, in this case a sociologist. The theologians and others of the Commission had access to much expert evidence. Traditional thought and empirical evidence were brought to bear on a new moral claim, the relational value of coitus. When the bishops met, they were well briefed, and produced a cogent report, which within a year or two had changed the whole Anglican climate of discussion. (Other members of the World Council of Churches, except the Orthodox, were to follow a year later.) This section of the Lambeth Report was in marked contrast to the International Section, which by comparision was feeble because it had had no such expert briefing beforehand. This was the pioneer of church working parties which were interdisciplinary, including experts and informed 'lay' persons with relevant experience, but not amateurish. It has been followed by others in this area (and in other areas I shall mention) such as *Abortion: an Ethical Discussion* (1965) and *Putting Asunder* (1966), which was an effort on the part of the established church to suggest a better divorce law for the state.

In the case of contraception, lay people had gone ahead and demonstrated the responsible use of it in marriage. The theologians caught up afterwards. Was this a surrender? Sociologists of religion who have a model of an authoritative church in mind, with rules handed down from above, and often take medieval Christendom as a norm, are apt to say that this is the abandonment of the faith in favour of pragmatism and social utility. Some traditionalist church folk agree. I think this is a mistake. It is the fixed understanding of humanity and 'nature' which has proved incapable of coping with the rapid social changes of recent centuries, which it seems clear we shall continue to experience. The church was archaic and ignorant. Recent work has been designed to bring it up to date, to find out what is going on and subject this, when it has been identified, to a theological critique, and one which allows the empirical data to raise questions for the received theological tradition. The whole procedure has its problems, which this is not the occasion to discuss, but the upshot is that the church is in a much better position to exercise such influence as it is proper for it to exert corporately, and through individual members in their jobs and as citizens, because it is informed and up to date.

One area in which there has been the biggest change in recent years is that of industry. The church has begun to take seriously the actual problems of industrial management and work. The pioneering was done at Sheffield from the end of the war by E. R. Wickham, later to become Suffragan Bishop of Middleton in the Diocese of Manchester. There are now over 400 full-time Industrial Missioners, the great majority Anglican. Various motives led to this state of affairs, notably: (i) the perception that political democracy should have some counterpart in industry which is apt to operate in an authoritarian way, (ii) evangelism, because the church had little contact with the industrial worker where he lived, (iii) a servant model of the church rather than a triumphalist one, (iv) a holiness model of the presence of Christ's representative in the working world (this particularly influenced priest-workers, but there have not been many of these in England, unlike France, except a number of non-stipendiary clergy, who are mostly working in education), (v) a mission of the church to the 'principalities and powers' of the world, in this case to industrial management and to a lesser extent Trade Unions (this was particularly the case with Wickham). It has been part of a much stronger stress these days on the role of the laity, though in fact the personnel of Industrial Mission has been overwhelmingly clerical.

One of the gains in the struggle for competence has been the acceptance of conflict as an integral part of corporate industrial life. That is why the sentiments of the Fifth Report of 1918 seem so vapid now. Conflicts arise out of divergencies of interests, and industry is not a unitary organization but a coalition of interests. Conflict can in fact be an industrial lubricant. A theology of power and conflict has to work here in the same way as it had had to do in the issues of war and peace and, as in that case, relate it to love and justice, in the effort to see that conflicts are handled creatively and not merely destructively. Struggling with collective morality is not easy for those brought up in an individualist ethic with a biblicist flavour. The General Synod, which has replaced the National Assembly, for instance when faced with the issue of the 'closed shop' is still prone to think that its main contribution is to urge the exemption of individuals who consciously object to this on religious grounds.

Meanwhile, Industrial Mission is becoming more issue-based and less work-based (as it is in France and Germany). Group work relating to it has led to a number of competent church reports, recent ones including *Work and the Future* (1974), *Understanding Closed Shops* (1977), *Winters of Discontent* (1981), largely on strikes, and *Growth, Justice and Work* (1985).

III

What have been the organs for developing and expressing a social ethic? There were the National Assembly, and the Convocations of clergy of the Provinces of Canterbury and York, now for practical purposes united in the General Synod. There were Diocesan Conferences (now Synods), and area Deanery and Parish Councils. How much thought at the centre reaches the parishes is uncertain, and much depends upon the activities of unofficial church societies, like the Industrial Christian Fellowship between the wars, or the Mothers' Union, the most persistent and largest of these societies. Since the last war, official Boards have been set up, of which that for Social Responsibility is the one that covers the area of this essay, and most dioceses have local equivalents. Then there are unofficial bishops' meetings, as well as the ten-yearly Lambeth Conferences of all Anglican bishops, which are occasions of opinion-forming among the episcopate. From time to time pressure groups are formed on particular themes or issues, but these are rarely purely Anglican; though a recent example of one which is solely Anglican is the Jubilee group, which is a recall to the Christian Socialist tradition; and there is an Anglican Pacifist Fellowship, though this is weak as compared with the Christian section of the Campaign for Nuclear Disarmament, which includes all churches. Another technique which has been frequently employed is for the two Archbishops, or one alone – usually Canterbury – to appoint a Commission on a particular issue. What advice they take beforehand is not known and probably varies a lot. These usually produce well-argued reports which have a good deal of effect on church opinion.[9]

The areas of expression have covered sexual questions, racial ones, economic, social, political and international ones, and since the unravelling of the genetic code a number of new questions in medical ethics. The church also takes a lot of interest in education because it controls so many private ('public') schools, mostly for the children of the wealthy, and local primary (and a few secondary) schools in villages and (mostly) in working-class areas of towns and cities.

In international affairs, church support for the League of Nations was very strong, but its thinking was as woolly on international as on economic issues. This woolliness was finally expressed by the reaction to the Munich agreement of 1938. The search for more competence in this area produced a more cautious attitude in the 1939–45 war, but only Bishop G. K. A. Bell in the course of it drew upon the resources of the Christian tradition to advance a critique of some of the strategies pursued in waging the war itself. After it much church opinion thought he had been right, and this in turn has gradually built up a sustained reflection on nuclear warfare which is critical of NATO's strategy of the first use of nuclear weapons if needed to repulse at attack in Europe. A recent report expressed this and was widely discussed.[10] There has also been a good deal more realism in support of the United Nations and in understanding the inherent limitations within which it operates but which make its existence possible. On the whole, church opinion is now getting beyond merely the support of 'ambulance work' in the case of international disasters like famines, and is seeing the necessity of long-term policies, not least in trade as well as aid, to prevent them happening in the first place; but this is very much an ecumenical phenomenon and not particularly a Church of England one.

The upshot of the search for greater competence has been the recognition of diversity of opinions and options, and the realization that there is not one 'Christian' answer to the various issues that have been mentioned. Few today would talk of working out the features of 'a Christian economy'. However, it is possible that Christian opinion may rule out certain particular policies: it looks as if capital punishment may come into this category. Also on occasion organs of the church may come to a detailed conclusion, whilst usually operating in a middle area between general sentiments and detailed policies. In 1981 the General Synod condemned some clauses in the Government's Nationality Bill as racist, by 198 votes to 1; it has since returned to a strong attack on the Act now in force, with no one voting for the Act. In general, however, the collapse of an *a priori* deductive method, and the investigation of issues by a varied team leads more to clarifying issues and options than to firm and authoritative prescriptions. Moreover, the General Synod is more aware of its own social conditioning, because of its middle-class and professional composition, and is more hesitant to talk about Trade Union and working-class affairs than it was. If it is unrealistic on any matter, one of its own Boards will find a way of pointing this out. On the whole, episcopal leadership is reasonably informed and perceptive, at least as compared with 1900, but it is not always followed. Many churchgoers are inherently conservative in every sense of the term and have to be coaxed into the late twentieth century. Further, the church is too much centred on the Oxford-London-Cambridge axis, the traditional source of influence. But it is certainly more socially aware than it was in 1900.

The situation today is that many of those in the evangelical tradition are developing for the first time a social ethic which takes structures as well as personal attitudes seriously. Also they are more influential than they were, because of the collapse of traditional Anglican-Catholic theology in the light of the changed emphasis in the Roman Catholic Church since the Second Vatican Council. Lacking any live indigenous social theology of their own, some have turned to Dutch neo-Calvinism.[11] I do not think they will find much permanent help there, and it is uncertain what they will then do; but if they turn to the sources already mentioned, we may see some interesting convergences. Moreover the ecumenical movement is influencing everyone. Evangelicals still have some difficulty in coming to terms with the modern study of the Bible; but in many ways, the rest of the church is also unclear when it comes to using the Bible in relation to ethical decisions. There is still a yearning for the textual injunction. Homosexuality is a test case; there are many who think the ethics of it can be settled by quoting St Paul. Official Roman Catholic teaching, at least on sexual questions, tends to operate with the same method, but also with Natural Law and Papal statements, drawing teaching from both these and Bible texts (though most Roman Catholic moral theologians have moved away from this method), and this creates some difficulties in what is otherwise increasing co-operation with that church.

When William Temple wrote *Christianity and Social Order* in 1942,[12] he felt he had to spend quite some time in defending the right of the church to 'interfere' in that sphere. This has been more and more granted, though lately it has begun to be challenged again as 'politicization', if it is critical of the government, but not if it supports it. In fact, the official church has become more distanced from the government than has probably happened before, certainly from a Conservative Government, whose philosophy of possessive individualism and lapses into jingoism grate on many Christian ears. An instance of this is the successful protest by the churches – all of them – against the original ideas for the service at the end of the Falklands war; and I have already mentioned the Nationality Act. It is now jokingly said that the Established Church, instead of being the Conservative party at prayer, is now the Social Democratic party at prayer. It has been said that the traditional stance of the church *vis-à-vis* the government of the day has been that of 'critical solidarity'. Over the four hundred years since the Reformation there has been much more of solidarity than of criticism, but recently the balance has become more even.[13] Evidence shows also that members of the General Synod are more 'progressive' than public opinion in general on many issues (and probably more so than the majority sitting in the pews on Sundays), except on economic issues, where their attitudes closely correspond to what their class position would lead one to expect. How these changes will affect the establishment remains to be seen.

However, one urgent issue is arising in our society. In the early stages of industrialization and urbanization, evangelicalism provided the internal controls for many, and this greatly helped to ensure that the rapid social changes were relatively trouble-free. Today our society lacks any similarly powerful incentive to moral cohesion and public order, and is becoming increasingly hard to govern. Beyond its perennial evangelistic task, can the church foster, together with any allies she can find among those of other faiths and philosophies, sources of disinterested concern for the common good?

3

The Future of Protestant Ethics

I find that in the *Dictionary of Christian Ethics* there is no article on Protestant Ethics. Nor is this surprising. There is no single Protestant ethic but several of them. Moreover, it is not possible to write about their future without some reflection on their past, as it appears to us as we look back on it from our understanding of the present. It is on this basis that we can attempt to look to the future, realizing that to do so is a hazardous business, not least because the future is likely to surprise us. Thinking about the future is rather a conservative activity, because we can only extrapolate upon what we grasp of the present, and the experience of recent centuries suggests that we are likely to be surprised by novelties; indeed, one feature of the Christian faith is that it should prepare us to live with, expect, and evaluate new features in human life.

One of the characteristics of all forms of Protestant ethics (as indeed of Catholic ethics) is that they came into being in a time of *relative* cultural stability, at least as compared with what has come since. Of course there was social change, but it was not so rapid that the son did not live in a substantially similar world to his father. This is no longer so. The great intellectual change between the modern world and its predecessors began with the foundation in Britain in 1662 of the Royal Society for the Advancement of Science (with its motto *nullius in verba*). A century later the technological and social fruits of this began to be seen with the advances in agricultural techniques which, in turn, made the Industrial Revolution possible, again beginning in the British Isles. Ever since then their effects have become more and more global, the rate of technical and social change has become faster, and there are no signs of this ending (short of the mass destruction brought about by a nuclear war).

Not only have all forms of Christian ethics to cope with this, but they have also seen the critical intellectual movements which have accompanied them pose serious challenges to hitherto accepted Christian positions. Scientific methods of an appropriate kind came to be applied to the study of the human past, and history as the discipline we know today came into existence. Sacred books, like the Bible, and sacred institutions, like the Church, could not be exempt from critical study. The result has been the breakdown of traditional authorities in Christian ethics as they have been appealed to in the past; the Bible (which particularly affects Protestants), the Church (which particularly affects Roman Catholics), and Natural Law (which affects Protestants least, Anglicans next, and Roman Catholics the most). Added to this, the old 'Christendom' position has broken down also. The result is that all traditional confessional traditions are in some disarray, and it is precisely out of this situation that the Ecumenical Movement has developed. We must not fall into the trap of discussing traditional Protestant ethical positions as if they could any longer be thought of as being able to proceed self-sufficiently within their confessional boundaries.

It is against this broad perspective that I turn to consider various expressions of Protestant ethics, on which I need hardly say there is an immense literature.

I

The Lutheran ethic has been particularly associated with the doctrine of the two realms or kingdoms, that of God's right hand and his left hand. Of course this was not in essence a new idea. Its roots are in the two ages or aeons of the New Testament, developed in the two cities of St Augustine, and in the medieval notion of the two swords. Luther wrote of two realms, two governments and two laws; and fine distinctions can be made between them but, with respect to all, he wrote of true Christians who do not need the governments or laws of this world, but become subject to temporal authority and accept callings in civil government, solely for the sake of their neighbour, to restrain wickedness by Wrath. Luther takes no account of the fact of sinful Christians, even though he admits true Christians are rare. He goes on to make a distinction between an office and a person holding it, and thinks a Christian rule can be only by love and is therefore impossible. Justice is not considered as a direct concern of Christians.[1]

The importance of Luther's conception was that it attacked the ideas of the omnicompetent Church which in the last resort claimed to control both realms, and confused spiritual and political powers. It allowed for the legitimate autonomy of different academic disciplines studying different areas of human life, as the medieval synthesis broke up. No longer could ecclesiastical persons tell scholars what to think and men of affairs what to do. Conclusions could not be prescribed in advance. This has been of importance as the natural and human sciences have developed in the centuries since the Reformation. There has been a price to pay, it is true. The sciences have become more and more specialized and sub-divided, so that we have experts who are in command of a small field and can hardly talk to each other, much less to the general public. Worse, they can be so uninformed about the common affairs of men that they are gullible outside their expertise, and a potential menace as citizens. Also there are often implicit (and sometimes explicit) value assumptions in the work of scientists in both the natural and human sciences which are not necessary to the discipline and may be gravely defective from a human, and particularly a Christian, point of view. Too rigid an adherence to a two realms position can lead to the lack of a critique of these disciplines just where it is needed. But these dangers can be corrected without abandoning the important and liberating contribution of the two realms doctrine to Christian ethics.

Luther himself lived at the beginning of a new intellectual and social ferment of which he had little knowledge. His own attitude in economic and social matters, for instance, was for the most part medieval. He had no understanding of the crumbling feudal economic order of his time, nor of the reasons for the rapid inflation which was upsetting established social structures and making social change faster than was customary, though not particularly fast by our standards. He wrote and said a lot about it, but the upshot was what R. H. Tawney called 'the occasional explosions of a capricious volcano'.[2] However, another of his contributions was of permanent importance, his bringing of the notion of Vocation or Calling (*Beruf*) out from the monasteries and nunneries into the market place. No longer were monks and nuns to be called Religious with a capital R, as those called to a special vocation to follow Counsels of Perfection (poverty, chastity and obedience) as against the Precepts binding on all Christians. This has been of quite fundamental importance, not least in the development of the 'Protestant Work Ethic' (now increasingly called in question). It has led to a much better theology of the laity; and especially of human sexuality and marriage as no longer an inferior way of life to that of the celibate. The full harvest of this is only now being gathered. Only in the last decades has a renewed theology of marriage thoroughly worked this out, and only since the Second Vatican Council has the Roman Catholic Church practically abandoned the double standard understanding of the call to join a Religious Order.

Unfortunately, however, the doctrine of Vocation in the world has been perverted in much of Protestantism by equating it with professional and bourgeois occupations, and not with skilled – still less unskilled – labour in manufacturing and commerce. But this cannot be blamed on Luther, who saw clearly that if one is a cobbler and a Christian one is a Christ to one's neighbour if one cobbles his shoes efficiently, and that there is no higher vocation than that.[3] Also, the notion of vocation has been interpreted in an individualistic sense from Luther's time onwards. However, in principle it is a flexible and profound understanding of man in society, which has potential fruitfulness in our advanced industrial societies which are moving to a narrower and more productive manufacturing base on which a more service type of economy can be built. Vocation must not be identified with one particular type of job for each person for life; much greater flexibility will be required. What the doctrine of Vocation did not do was to provide a theological basis for leisure and the contemplative side of life. The only role of leisure was to fit one for work by a necessary rest. Resources from Catholic tradition are needed to correct this.

Lutheran ethics is also always associated with the phrase *simul iustus et peccator*, which certainly frees the Christian to live boldly amid the moral perplexities of life, with the freedom of one who knows he is held in the gracious love of God. It is a recovery of the gospel from a distortion of it as it came to be perceived in the later Middle Ages, when the exhortation to Christian living seemed to amount to (1) try hard to be good, (2) do penance when you sin, (3) depend on the merits of the saints, which can be appropriated by Masses with the required intentions. It is vital that the doctrine of justification by grace through faith be brought to bear on ethics as well as doctrine. However, there has been a serious under-playing of sanctification in the Lutheran tradition, as generally received, arising from a horror of returning to a religion of works, of earning one's acceptance by God. Theologically this horror can end in de-humanizing man, as when persons are compared to tubes or channels through which God's grace can flow to the neighbour (as in Anders Nygren,[4] going back to Luther). Something has gone seriously wrong when human beings are compared to tubes. The fear of a religion of works shows itself in the difficulty ethical writers in the Lutheran tradition have had with the problem of working at how to implement the Christian ethic in particular cases, or casuistry.[5] To this I shall return.

The Calvinist ethic has shared many of the characteristics of the Lutheran in its departure from medieval doctrine and ethics, but it has proved much more dynamic in practice. One reason has been its stress on the third use of law as a guide to personal and civic righteousness. Luther had stressed only two uses of law, political (to ensure order in human life) and theological (to convict men of sin).

Perhaps, too, the stress on the sovereignty of God allowed the Calvinist to be less afraid of sanctification, of stressing good works; these might be a means of making one's calling and election sure, but could not be thought to be trying to influence God's changeless decrees. To Calvin the two kingdoms or governments both have a positive meaning. The temporal, political realm is a gift of God's providence, apart from the Fall, for Christians have need of civil government which educates man for the duties of humanity and citizenship. God rules the outward order through the civil rulers, but on the model of the absolute sixteenth-century French state, so political action is not for the private citizen – he is to leave it to the magistrates. At all events Calvinism has had a profound effect on both the political and economic realms.

It has often been pointed out that the seeds of modern Western political democracy are found in the century after Calvin in the intense debates in England after the execution of Charles I, in the army, in Parliament, and in the left-wing radical groups – all of them in the Calvinist tradition.[6] It seems that stress on Christians as the people of God, and on the sovereignty of the people of God under the sovereignty of God, led to an assertion of the equality of each member of the elected people of God, since God might have a word to say to his people through any one of them, and so all must be listened to. Of course it was not worked out neatly, quickly and consistently but the radical seed was there. In the end it proved impossible to concede liberty to the 'saint', especially in the gathered congregation, without conceding it to the 'sinner' too in a wider context, and so by several secularizing steps we arrive at the outlook behind the constitution of the USA, with all that has flowed from that, and at the 'one person, one vote' of Western political democracy.[7] I am aware, of course, of other ingredients in this, such as the thought of the French Enlightenment in addition to the Calvinist contribution to it. Neo-Calvinism also fostered voluntary associations in the middle area between the family and the state, which are indispensable in our Western type of democracy; they are a major means of self-giving, providing psychotherapy and sociotherapy vital for the common good of persons in community.[8]

In economic life we come to the famous thesis of Max Weber concerning the relation of the Protestant ethic (particularly the Calvinist) to the spirit of capitalism.[9] The immense discussion provoked by this does not die down, and it has become difficult to recover what exactly Weber maintained. Putting it briefly, it was that there was an 'elective affinity' (to use his phrase) between some leading Calvinist ideas and the motivation needed to make the new, dynamic capitalist system work. The hard work, thrift (to save and acquire capital and put it to use), and sustained pursuit of wealth, combined with restraint in consumption, all required an asceticism of the market place which was new in human history. Weber never crudely maintained that Calvinism caused capitalism; in fact he was trying to assess the variety of factors which led to this startling change in economic life in the Western world. One of them was some aspects of the Calvinist ethic. I think he made his point.[10] The upshot is that both in politics and economics Calvinism has had a dynamic effect, and in ways which would have seemed strange to Calvin himself.

Anglican and Puritan ethics continued until the end of the

seventeenth century in the style of Catholic Moral Theology, though modified in some particulars, when the tradition died out for reasons which have never been fully explained. It had certainly become somewhat archaic and unable to keep up with economic changes. Perhaps the eighteenth century was so pleased with itself that it had no time for serious reflection on cases of conscience, and was happy to let Protestant individualism run riot, tempered by innumerable appeals to individual charity in the Sermons which were a feature of the age. However, the previous century saw some notable moralists, Perkins, Hall, Ames, Sanderson, Taylor, Baxter and Sharp, to name seven.[11] Their views rejected three elements in the Catholic tradition of moral theology: (1) it was no longer tied to the confessional; (2) the distinction between Precepts and Counsels of Perfection was denied; every Christian is called to the perfection of holiness; (3) the distinction between mortal and venial sin was denied; all sin is serious. The result was to link moral theology closely with ascetical theology, and to give it a distinctly rigorist note. The call to holiness was taken very seriously. There was a danger that a religion of works could develop, that growth in holiness would be required before we could be sure of divine acceptance, but this was to a large extent avoided by the style of devotion taught along with the moral theology, where the note of justification by faith is strong. Worship and ethics were held closely together.[12] Within this framework the English moralists were ready to discuss in detail cases of conscience in the whole range of personal, domestic and public issues. Baxter, the Presbyterian, was almost the last. In them conscience is broadly understood as it was in Aquinas, as man using his reasoning powers on moral issues.

For the next two centuries England was left to the ethics of Protestant individualism, and these were the crucial centuries of the development of industrialism. The church has not yet recovered the lost ground. When moral theology was taken up again later in the nineteenth century, it was under the influence of the Oxford Movement. It was related once more to the 'cure of souls' in the confessional; post-Tridentine Roman Catholic manuals were adapted for Anglican use.[13] It was not until after the first world war that Kenneth Kirk set out to broaden the whole approach, but he did not get far beyond more personal and churchly issues. He had not much to say on the economic and political questions which several centuries before were freely discussed, putting them under the heading 'cases of doubt'. But his method was potentially liberating.[14] Anglican ethical thinking since then has (with one or two exceptions) been taken up into that of the Ecumenical Movement.

There remains to mention the ethics of the Protestant Sects, the left wing of the Reformation, who had their precursors in the previous centuries and have had many and varied successors since. Both Luther and Calvin formed their ideas partly against the Anabaptists' rejection of Christian involvement in civil government. Sects have fascinated sociologists of religion. Bryan Wilson of Oxford University has produced a sevenfold typology of them.[15] They vary from the 'respectable' Quakers to bizarre communes. Most are preoccupied with an ethic of perfection and not an ethic of responsibility. Most of them are transitory. The enduring ones have been the historic peace churches, best expressed in thought to-day by the USA Mennonite, J. H. Yoder.[16] Indeed, the question of whether pacifism is a literal rule required by the gospel in the behaviour of Christians and, still more, of states epitomizes the issues raised for Christian ethics by Protestant sectarianisms. There is no sign of their position gaining any more general theological assent than it has ever done, though perhaps mainstream churches are more open to possible initiatives from them, and more ready to defend a space in which the public authorities will allow them to operate.

II

As I have mentioned, all the classical Christian ethical positions, those of Protestantism included, were worked out against what was assumed to be a relatively stable order, at least as compared with anything we have known in the last two centuries. And with the exception of some forms of sectarian ethics there has been a marked tendency basically to accept the social order as found. Luther thought it far on in the history of the world; it would be impious to try to change it radically; only heroes bring about change and only then by special divine guidance, and the best we can hope for is that God's providential care will prevent disintegration. There has been a marked tendency to see criticism of the authorities as a politicization of the church and the acceptance of them as being suitably unpolitical.

Moreover, I repeat that discussing Protestant ethics solely within traditional confessional divisions can be misleading. All have changes in common because of social changes. In particular Liberal Protestantism and Pietist Protestantism have developed in all three of them, whilst the shock of the French Revolution reinforced a doctrinal conservatism to defend the old order. Liberal Protestantism was a theological expression of the social and cultural confidence of the nineteenth century, the Protestant century. In its immediately optimistic form it canonized the philosophy and institutions of *laissez-faire* capitalism; in its penultimately optimistic form it critized these institutions in the name of social justice, particularly in the 'social gospel' movement in the USA, but saw no reason why society should not progressively evolve into the kingdom of God seen as a kind of co-operative commonwealth.[17] Pietist Protestantism developed in eighteenth-century Lutheranism and Moravianism, through which it influenced Methodism and subsequently spread in many directions, notably various Holiness Churches, but affecting large numbers of ministers and laity in all the main Protestant confessions. Charles Wesley wrote more than 6,000 hymns. They explore almost every facet of the relation of the individual to God but have nothing on the public and corporate aspects of human life and Christian responsibility; and Methodist hymns have had an enormous influence on Anglo-Saxon Protestantism. However, much the same can be said of the most used Anglican hymn-book, *Hymns Ancient and Modern* (1861), which predominantly represents mid-Victorian individualist piety with monastic overtones. Moreover, pietist ethics was often allied to a Fundamentalism which was a mistaken response to the rise of critical and historical studies of the Bible; and much of what is now called the 'conservative evangelical' position is a mixture of doctrine and ethics of this individualist type, which appeals to the Protestant Reformation but which is quite alien to what either Luther or Calvin stood for. (One of the more encouraging signs in Britain at the moment is the break-up of this monolithic position, so that there is now no issue on which evangelicals all agree, and in addition there is the beginnings of a serius social theology among them.[18] There is a similar situation in the USA, but the experience of three 'born again' presidential candidates in the 1980 election, and the activities of the 'Moral Majority', are not encouraging.)

In recent years some Protestants have been much influenced by existentialist thought, for instance Barth and Bultmann in their different ways, and this has reinforced tendencies to think of the Christian life as a moment-by-moment existence, living like an extemporary speaker under the command of God, and thus to give little or no attention to ongoing thought on the content, as distinct from the motive, of ethical decision. For instance, the sum total of Bultmann's contribution to Christian ethics seems to be that in order to love our neighbours as ourselves we should put ourselves in our neighbour's position and then we shall simply know what to do.[19] A position like this has deep Protestant roots. Calvin, for instance, seems to have assumed that Christians would just know what to do to fulfil the law.

It is these individualist strains in Protestant ethics which had led to the continual polarizing of the question whether Christians should set out to change persons or systems. Individualistic Protestantism has said that all that is necessary is to produce 'converted' or 'consecrated' persons; 'changed' in the vocabulary of Moral Rearmament; they will then behave in a Christian way and social problems will be solved. Catholic ethics has never made this mistake. This position was nicely illustrated in England in 1975 when, owing to an initiative from Donald Coggan, the Archbishops of Canterbury and York issued an appeal to the nation which focused on two questions, 'What sort of society do we want?' and 'What sort of people do we need to be in order to achieve it?', and omitted a third question, 'What sort of social structures do we need to help people to be what we need them to be?' In reaction to all this, Protestantism has thrown up a minority of politically radical Christians who have seen the fundamental question as the overthrow of unjust social structures, and often tacitly assumed that it is only because of these structures that people behave badly. The polarization of the issue as one of changing persons or changing structures is a false one; both need changing. And it is a serious deformation of Christian understanding to assume that the church and the Christian are only concerned with the first.

There are, in fact, two aspects of Christian ethics. The first is to act from the right motive. This is a basic matter of Christian formation. How is Christ to be formed in us? How are we to build one another up to our full stature in him so that Christlike graces, the gifts of his Spirit, multiply in the world? This is what our drawing upon the resources of Christian faith in prayer and worship and fellowship together can hope to foster. It is concerned with the development of ongoing Christian character with a deepening capacity for moral discernment. The second aspect is to achieve the right content in action. This is where so much Protestant ethic has been so weak in virtually abandoning this side of the moral life, half of it in fact. It will not do to dismiss this whole aspect as 'legalism' and talk disparagingly of casuistry. Casuistry got a bad name at the time of the Counter-Reformation because of its misuse.[20] But we cannot avoid the necessity of systematically bringing to bear fundamental moral insight in particular cases. Traditional moral theology on the other hand has operated through the centuries in too *a priori* a manner, deducing rules from alleged self-evident premises, and then developing subtle arguments to resolve difficulties when in particular cases rules conflicted or were uncertain in their application. The intention was noble, to be certain that one could find the Christian way to act in any circumstances (as Jewish casuistry in New Testament times tried to bring Torah to bear on every detail of life), but it wanted to be too secure in the inevitable complexities of moral decision and was not willing to live by faith and not by sight. However, there has been a remarkable revolution in Roman Catholic moral theology in the last twenty-five years; the old manuals are cast out and a new, far better, moral theology has been born. Let Bernard Häring's recent three-volume moral theology, *Free and Faithful in Christ*, stand as an example.[21] It is true that the *magisterium* has not yet caught up with all of it, particularly in sex ethics, but that is another matter.

The point is that bad casuistry must be replaced by good. The problem of bringing a general understanding of Christian ethics to bear on particular cases involves all the questions of the formation of conscience. How to use the Bible? What are the resources and what are the mistakes in the Christian tradition? What relevant 'secular' knowledge is needed? Are experts needed? What are the limits of their competence? How to evaluate when experts differ? Is relevant lay experience being drawn upon? What kind of group reflection is the best help towards clarifying ethical decision making? All these questions require expansion; suffice it here to say that the aim is to bring the qualities of Christian discernment to bear upon particular issues, calling upon all relevant help from any source, to answer the question 'What is going on now?' Only then can possible courses of action be explored. Quite often it will be seen that some courses of action are ruled out; sometimes a broad agreement will emerge as to the general direction at which to aim, even if there are differences about the detailed route; sometimes there will be agreement on details (the General Synod of the Church of England in 1981 condemned details of the Government's Nationality Bill by 198 votes to 1); sometimes there is no agreement, and in that case Christians who take any one particular position can be faced by searching questions put to them by Christians who take a different one. (This has happened in the debate in the World Council of Churches on violence, non-violence and the struggle for social justice.)[22] Certainty cannot be promised. Moral judgment is the art of discernment. But a lot of positive help to moral discernment, and removal of obstacles to it, can be provided; and we can be helped to learn from experience. To repeat, we walk by faith and not by sight in ethics as in doctrine.

These various forms of the Protestant ethic can be brought alongside Richard Niebuhr's well-known fivefold typology in his *Christ and Culture*, since it is another way of relating Gospel and Law or Grace and Nature.[23] Of the five positions only the fifth, Christ the Transformer of Culture, is adequate to times of rapid social change (which is not to say that the other four have nothing to contribute). The Christ against Culture position is represented by pietist Protestantism and can come into its own in an alien environment, but even then should not be applied woodenly, as the history of the church in the different Communist countries shows. The Christ of Culture position of Liberal Protestantism – and the Byzantine position of classical Anglicanism – is not critical enough of its milieu, but there is often a case for it, for instance, in helping newly political independent African states to achieve a sense of nationhood as against tribalism. The Christ above Culture position of medieval Catholicism is only possible in a Christendom situation, which is decaying everywhere it existed, leaving impressive but misleading outward remains behind. The Christ and Culture in Paradox position of Lutheranism has creative potential but makes too sharp a separation between the two kingdoms. There remains the Christ the Transformer of Culture position, towards which the various elements in the traditions of Protestant ethic need to make their contribution.[24]

III

What is to characterize an adequate moral theology or Christian ethic, whether Protestant or Catholic? (There is no agreed difference in meaning between these two terms; if a distinction has to be made, I take Christian ethics to be concerned with the general character of the Christian way of life, and moral theology with relating this to particular circumstances, but I am not making anything of this distinction at the moment.) I mention three elements:

1. Moral theology must be rooted in the Christian tradition whilst being creatively selective amid the varying expressions of it. Its basis should be the words of the gospel, 'Freely you have received, freely give',[25] or, in other words, 'Live in thankfulness for the graciousness of God you have already known through Jesus Christ.' Realize that because you are justified by faith you are free to live boldly and joyfully, knowing that you cannot fall outside God's grace, not because of his power but because of his love. In bringing this gospel to bear on particular circumstances the traditional sources of authority, Scripture, Natural Law and the Church have all to be re-thought. There is no direct step from any one of them to a detailed ethical decision in the modern world; quoting general rules derived from any one of them (e.g., 'the sanctity of life') will not be itself resolve an ethical issue.[26] The conclusions on specific issues arrived at in the past, from the New Testament onwards, have all been to some extent conditioned, or 'time-bound' to use Barth's useful phrase. The simple type of Protestant appeal to Scripture, *sola Scriptura*, will not do; and there is some danger that just as many Protestants have become aware of the complex hermeneutical problems in the use of Scripture, Roman Catholics in their new and welcome zeal for biblical study may fall into traps of which Protestants are now

aware. Natural Law cannot any longer be used in the non-historical, physicalist way that was customary (contrary to the flexibility of Aquinas), but must be used to stress the dignity of the person, and that the realm of the moral is natural to man, and the basis on which he should operate in it. Official church teaching has to be set against the context in which it was given, including the knowledge available at the time.

2. Moral theology must be related to human experience in general. This is the more necessary because of the pluralism of most modern societies and the necessity that men of different faiths and ideologies find a way of living together in the world without destroying themselves. This reinforces the necessity for taking human moral life seriously, and persons as moral agents; and for shewing how persons should make moral choices. This brings us into the realm of moral philosophy. It is important to remember that the methods and procedures of Christian ethics are no different from the methods and procedures of ethics as analysed by moral philosophy. Here there is a deficiency in a good deal of recent Protestant ethics, which has not taken seriously the fact that though the Bible does not argue about these matters it *presupposes* them (as indeed it does God).[27] In considering questions of ethics Christians do not come to alien territory but to one already inhabited. There is a close connection between morals and religion, but they are not identical, and it is necessary to relate to, build upon, and deepen the moral understanding which is part of human life as given. It is not good enough if Protestant ethicists think it necessary to demolish the realm of the moral as the quintessence of sin. Brunner will tell us that 'in the last resort it is precisely morality which is evil',[28] that the sense of 'ought' is a by-product of sin because it means 'I can't', that conscience is to be interpreted purely as an experience of the wrath of God. Bonhoeffer will say that 'the knowledge of good and evil is separation from God',[29] and Barth that 'the general conception of ethics coincides exactly with the conception of sin'.[30] It is even said that the more a man desires God the more he must be evil since desire itself betokens a lack and is therefore bad. This is a foolish polemic. How perverse to see the sense of 'ought' as essentially a menace and not a vocation (though, of course, it can be a menace on occasions, especially in those

suffering from what is traditionally known as a 'scrupulous' conscience). More attention needs to be paid to the strain in Reformation teaching concerning civic righteousness in Lutheranism and common grace in Calvinism. There is, in fact, in man a capacity of moral judgment (which Christians, of course, think of as God-given, whether the human persons who possess it recognize its source or not), and it is salutary to realize that because of it those outside the Christian tradition can be quite capable of recognizing and identifying a legalism and a self-righteousness in Christians when they see it.

The contribution of the Christian faith to the moral life is to disclose the nature of *agape* as that of God himself, to see this as the basis of Christian motivation and as the criterion by which possible moral rules are arrived at, or the consequences of possible lines of action in a particular situation are evaluated. Christianity does not solve the problem facing any normative ethics, whether to decide in a particular situation by rule (deontology) or by estimated consequences of possible actions (teleology); that is where the art of moral judgment comes in. (This was the point of the Situation Ethics debate.)[31] Moreover it is the Christian ethic itself which should lead us to seek for a common ground at the level of an understanding of the common good, with those of other faiths and ideologies.

3. Moral theology must be able to cope with rapid social change. This has already been mentioned more than once. It is here that the Ecumenical Movement comes in. This has always been concerned not merely with the unity but also with the renewal of the church. If one looks at the fairly considerable minorities within the main confessional traditions who are anti-ecumenical they seem to be those who are anti-renewal, who are most satisfied with, and find security in, a received tradition from the past which in their view has nothing to learn from either the changing circumstances of the present or the experience of fellow Christians from a different confessional tradition.

In particular the Roman Catholic-Protestant division still has relevance, but much less than it had. How far are Protestants still merely reacting against Rome? The most substantial modern Lutheran ethic available in English is that of Thielicke. Much of his anti-Catholic, but temperate, discussion sets up a man of straw, though we must remember it was written before the Second Vatican Council.[32] In ethical matters the polemic against casuistry and legalism is misplaced, that against Natural Law is in danger of throwing the baby away with the bathwater, and that against the *magisterium* still has a point, but needs to realize how much is changing (as well as how much needs to change) in its practical working. The Political and Liberation theologians, and especially the latter, who have made an astonishing impact since about 1966, find the traditional Protestant-Catholic ethical and doctrinal divisions simply irrelevant. They get on together without them, and together call in question a great deal of customary politically 'neutral' church thinking and practice.[33]

Roman Catholic moral theology is making great efforts to escape from previous strait-jackets and cope with change, just as Protestants have found it necessary to move from the existential occasionalism which has characterized much of their recent thinking by, e.g., appeals to phenomenology and cultural anthropology (David Little),[34] character structure (Stanley Hauerwas),[35] trust (Knud Løgstrup)[36] or responsibility (Richard Niebuhr),[37] to name but a few.

To my mind there is in the Reformation doctrine of the Orders of Creation, never fully adumbrated, a source which could be developed to help Protestant ethics fulfil these tasks. Its strong point is that by showing how we are influenced as persons by the structures of life in which we find ourselves, without any choice on our part, long before we are able to make any critical response ourselves, it undercuts the characteristic Protestant temptation to concentrate only on changing persons. Persons are not *determined* by the structures; in due course they can partially transcend them and try to change them, but long before that they have been *conditioned* by them from infancy. Structures mould persons before persons can mould structures. The notion of Orders of Creation came into disfavour because they were interpreted in a static and paternalistic fashion, and in particular because they were misused in the Nazi period. In response to the Barmen Declaration of the Confessing Church in 1934, stressing the lordship of Christ, there were the Ansbach Proposals, written by Paul Althaus and Werner Elert, stressing nation (*Volk*) and blood.[38] On the Catholic side, although the extensive treatment of Justice in traditional Catholic moral theology did pay attention to structures, for the most part it tended to assume that the *status quo* was just.

The best account of the Orders is given by Brunner,[39] who is quite clear that we do not find them as God intends them but as deformed because of human sin; we cannot escape from life in them but must also reform them; like the church they are *semper reformanda*. Different names for them are used by different theologians. Barth, in spite of theological reservations, talks of 'provinces', Bonhoeffer of 'mandates', Thielicke of 'orders of divine patience', Wendland of 'institutions' and Künneth of 'preservation', while earlier Troeltsch talked of areas of 'objective' as against ones of 'subjective' obligations.[40]

What, and how many, are they and how are they established? Basically there appear to be four: (i) Some structure of marriage and family arising out of human sexuality; (ii) some structure of economic life arising out of basic human needs, and the division of labour; (iii) some structure of political authority because of the need for security; (iv) some community of culture because of human creativity. The first three are commonly mentioned but the fourth is often ignored. Brunner is good on it, and it is important because of the aggressive anti-culturalism of much Protestantism. It is impossible not to be cultural; even clothes, hair styles and household objects involve it. To ignore this is merely to arrive at poor cultural expressions, unworthy of humans. (Language, of course, is a cultural expression, and through it we express our whole perspective on life, including faiths and ideologies through which we interpret life in the Orders in its very different manifestations in the course of human history.) These four Orders can be empirically established with reasonable certainty. One would expect the Bible either to presuppose them or to mention them explicitly. Exegetes move uncertainly at this point. Thielicke, for instance, makes an unfortunate distinction between Orders based on the Creation (marriage) and on the Fall (the state); all need to be seen from both angles. Note that nation and blood can neither be established empirically nor biblically, contrary to what Christian nationalists in most countries assume. Bonhoeffer and Brunner also bring in the church, but that is surely an Order of Re-creation; only by a paradoxical extension of meaning can we say that everyone is born into it *qua* human being. But, once in it, it functions in the new creation in the same way and with the same stipulations as the Orders of Creation; that is the justification for infant baptism, and also for seeing the church as *semper reformanda*.

The doctrine of the Orders of Creation avoids both occasional-ism (already mentioned) and the utopianism often found in sectarian Christian ethics, and also latent in a good deal of Liberation theology, where it derives from the utopianism latent in Marxism, whose claim to be a 'science' Liberation theologians accept too simply. The doctrine of the Orders does this by bringing home a sense of structure as necessarily involved if human life together is to be human and not anarchic. But it must be emphasized again that they need to be under constant critical scrutiny; they have not a fixed normative content, because human life and structures remain open to the future and we do not know all that they have it in them to be. It is in this connection that the theologians of hope rightly stress the importance of formulating goals for the humanization of life and not passively accepting things as they are.[41]

Large questions face us in each of the realms of the Orders. In so far as the Christian sex ethic was expressed in negative universal prohibitions regarding masturbation, intercourse out-side marriage, polygamy, contraception, sterilization, abortion, divorce, and homosexuality, little remains of it; and new issues like artificial insemination from a donor have arisen. As I have said, there has been better theological thinking on sexuality in recent decades than perhaps ever before, centring on responsibi-lity in sexual relationships. It needs developing and transmitting. In the area of economic life the Protestant work ethic is called into question through the productivity of modern technology and the disappearance of routine mental and physical 'dead end' jobs in which in the course of history most people have spent their working lives. A more corporate service society is needed, and the abandonment of the ethic of 'possessive individualism' which has had an unfortunate revival in this country and the USA recently.[42] As far as the area of state authority is concerned, issues of the character and theological status of nationalism are far from resolved. And there is the growing questioning of the 'established disorder' and demands for rapid, revolutionary change, by violence, if necessary, as a last resort; the disorders of the contemporary world are making us consider much more urgently the ethical issues of civil disobedience and rebellion. In the order of Culture the cultural poverty of much church and contemporary life needs attention. There is much to work on in all these questions, and I do not see any reason for confining ourselves within confessional boundaries in doing so.

I have omitted the Orthodox from this discussion, as marginal to it and presenting special problems,[43] but I see no reason why Protestants and Catholics should not more and more work on ethics together. I regularly attend meetings of Roman Catholic Moral Theologians and find them very valuable. It seems to me, therefore, that the most promising future of Protestant ethics is tied to the most promising future of Catholic ethics, and that our theme might best become the future of Ecumenical Ethics.

4

The Question of a Just, Participatory and Sustainable Society[1]

I

The rather cumbersome title of this lecture is taken from that of the present stage in the studies of current problems of Christian social ethics within the Ecumenical Movement. It is on these studies that I want to comment, but before doing so it is necessary to put them briefly into perspective.

Few will dispute the speed of technological change in the world today, and the profound social transformations it is bringing with it all over the globe. An entertaining insight into how far and fast things have gone in this country in my lifetime is provided by Laurie Lee's well-known picture of his youth in rural Gloucestershire in *Cider with Rosie*. This speed of change has proved difficult for the churches to cope with. They had built themselves into the *relatively* stable European culture, and its offshoots in other continents. They tended to take it for granted, and were caught unawares when the forces which we now call the Industrial Revolution initiated a much more rapid rate of change, a rate which increases and shows no signs of coming to an end. They had little or nothing to say about it. How were they to catch up and not talk to a situation either passing or already past?

Early in this century a movement began which was concerned both with the unity and renewal of the church: the Ecumenical Movement. It is usually dated from a Conference in Edinburgh in 1910. There are many accounts of it, and I do not propose to add to them. The point to notice is its double aim. It was clear that the fragmentation of the Christian church, however much it may have been a regrettable necessity in the past, was an anachronism and hindrance in the twentieth century, and so the goal of unity must be worked for. But it was also realized that the churches needed renewal; and it was in the search for renewal, through what was called the 'Life and Work' side of the Ecumenical Movement, as distinct from the 'Faith and Order' side (which was concerned with unity) that the recovery of a relevant Christian social ethic was pursued. The main landmarks in this recovery have been a series of carefully prepared major international study conferences of which there have now been four: (1) Stockholm in 1925, which faced the problem of being the pioneer, and met amid the preoccupations with German 'war guilt' which still hung over Europe.[2] (2) Oxford in 1937. This met in the shadow of the mass long-term unemployment in the Western world following upon the Wall Street crash of 1929 and also, and not unconnected with it, the rise of brutal totalitarian Nazi and Fascist regimes in Western Europe. The theme of the Conference was 'Church, Community and State', and it had a solid theological input which has not been equalled since.[3] (3) At Geneva in 1966 there was a major conference on 'Christians in the Technical and Social Revolutions of our Time', which was largely concerned with the economic and social questions raised globally by rapid social change, and where Christians from Third World countries were, for the first time, heard on a world platform demanding changes of such a radical nature and so speedily that the term 'revolution' had to be applied to them.[4] (4) In July 1979 at the Massachusetts Institute of Technology (MIT) the latest of these study conferences took place. Now the issues had broadened still further to include the basis and mode of functioning of the science which lies behind the technology which in turn had led to the rapid social changes. Its title was 'Faith, Science and the Future', but this was shorthand for its real theme which was 'The Contribution of Faith, Science and Technology in the Struggle for a Just, Participatory and Sustainable Society'. This is the source of my title.[5] Between the Geneva Conference and the MIT one the theme of a Just and Sustainable Society had emerged in the Ecumenical Movement, mainly through the sub-unit on Church and Society of the World Council of Churches (which is the successor to the old Life and Work side); and Participatory was added by the Central Committee of the WCC after its Assembly at Nairobi in 1975.

It is possible, therefore, to trace a continuous thread in

ecumenical social ethics, at least from Stockholm in 1925. The fact that the whole Movement was 'unofficial' until the World Council of Churches was constituted in 1948 made no difference. The pioneers had done their work so well that it was simply carried on. Its frame of reference, however, which had been predominantly Western, became global. Its confessional range expanded with the growing range of the WCC itself, notably the greatly increased contribution of the Orthodox from Eastern Europe and of indigenous churches from the Third World. Since the Second Vatican Council the Roman Catholic Church has had active participant observers in this part of the work of the WCC (and it is officially part of the Faith and Order side). The range of expertise called on has also widened, the latest being that of the natural scientists and technologists. This extension of range has been important. The world has become a smaller place than it was even twenty to thirty years ago. Phrases like 'a village world' and 'spaceship earth' are doubtless imperfect, but nevertheless they are vivid ways of drawing attention to the extent to which we are inescapably bound together in our small planet. Modern communications have made this clear by bringing to our attention, usually on our TV screens, what is happening to our fellow human beings in all parts of the world. In particular we are the first generation to know of cries of distress from all over the globe, and once we know we bear a responsibility for alleviating this. Things indeed move fast. We have had 400 years of colonialism, 200 of industrialism, and but a few decades of advanced communication and space technology. And in our Western setting we have had 30 years of relative prosperity, stability and peace, which has now received a check. This was the background of the MIT Conference.

Through these years of the development of ecumenical social ethics the methods employed have remained much the same. The conferences are called not to speak officially *for* the churches, but *to* them, to advise them. The aim has been to try to bring the churches up to date with what is going on, so that they can address themselves to a present and not a past situation. What use the churches make of the material is for them to decide, but at least for the first time for centuries the disciplined work of the Ecumenical Movement has enabled them to be up to date, and in a global perspective. They are encouraged to send their best lay persons in the fields in question to these study conferences; and the WCC also selects relevant experts, often men and women of the highest distinction who have never previously had the experience of the churches asking for their help. Often preparatory work is done, commented on from different intellectual and confessional angles and from different countries, and then redrafted. The conferences themselves have to be short for what they need to do, because of limitations of time and money; they have large and varied themes; they work under intense pressure; and there is hardly time to sort out the varied reactions of people finding themselves in dialogue for the first time with those from a different geographical area and from different intellectual disciplines, and thus meeting differing opinions not on paper but embodied in persons of whom they have to take account. The process is confused and wearing. Criticisms can be made of it. I have made some of the Geneva Conference in a book I edited, *Technology and Social Justice* (1971), and I don't think the MIT Conference was any better. Nothing is without flaws. Nevertheless the end result has been an extremely valuable source of material for which there is no substitute. The work produced by the MIT Conference is thoroughly in this succession and will need to be drawn upon for several years.

It is not my intention to work through this material. This is not practicable. There is far too much for one lecture, and it is already concentrated so that to reduce it further would be to make it quite indigestible. Rather I wish to consider the three terms, Just, Participatory, and Sustainable, drawing partly upon my own reflections and partly upon the ecumenical material. At first glance it might be thought that Just referred to the Third World, Participatory to the Second or Communist world, and Sustainable to our First World, but in fact the three terms apply to the three worlds. After looking at them I want to refer to three theological issues which arise in the present state of ecumenical social ethics, before adding a concluding reflection.

II *Just*

There is, of course, nothing new in the requirement that Christians should seek a just order of society. The treatment of justice in traditional Moral Theology has been extensive; the trouble is that it has been much too ready to assume that the *status quo* as it has found it at any given time has been basically just, so that the development of a separate and critical concept of social justice is a recent one. I have just been speaking of the Catholic tradition, which inherited a good deal of thinking on justice from the legacy of Greek moral philosophy, which fused with Judaeo-Christian thought in the Platonism of St Augustine and the Aristotelianism of St Thomas Aquinas. The Protestant tradition, being more biblicist, has had a different difficulty, how to deal with justice at all. The heart of Christian Ethics is the radical understanding of *agape* as taught and lived by Jesus in his ministry, which he saw as the announcing of the kingdom or rule or reign of God, a paradoxical kingdom brought near to men in his own ministry. It remains exercising its influence in the world as leaven in the lump. The ethic of the kingdom of God is unlike the commonsense ethic of 'do good turns to those who do good turns to you', according to which the world rubs along more or less; the ethic of the kingdom of God is non-reciprocal, like the love of God himself which is poured out in the creation and recreation of men and women, and never gives up if it does not get a response even while it yearns for a response. How to relate the ethic of the kingdom of God to the ethics of the ongoing kingdoms or structures of this world? This has been hard for many Christians to see, because the teaching of Jesus is not focused on this problem. It is centred in the radical and inexhaustible love of God, transcending realization in the life of any single person, still less any social structure. We can see the problem if we ask ourselves such questions as (1) What should the Good Samaritan have done if he had arrived at precisely the moment when the man going on the road from Jerusalem was set upon by thieves? (2) If the poor widow had thrown her last two coins into the treasury, who was to maintain her or how was she to live? (3) Granted that there is only one reward available in the kingdom of God, so that whether you get into it early in the day or at the eleventh hour your reward is the same, how does this insight bear on the economic order as part of God's creation? The New Testament does not answer these questions. The earlier letters of St Paul, on the other hand, show him wrestling on the basis of *agape* in a very illuminating way with a number of specific ethical questions arising in the life of the young churches, but he does so with a foreshortened horizon because of his apocalyptic expectation of an imminent *parousia* or return of Christ. Some later New Testament writing, like the Pastoral Epistles, show with the fading of these expectations Christianity beginning to settle down with a subordinationist ethic which accepts the structures of society as it finds them, and emphasizes the duties of those in subordinate positions to obey those in superior ones. Today we do not want to preach a submissive love to those with less power, but rather to empower them. In neither case are questions of justice specifically faced. If the Christians, however, turned to Jewish traditions embodied in what we now call the Old Testament, they could find quite a lot about social justice both in the Torah and the Prophets, but once more it is of a paradoxical kind. What stands out is a strong witness to Yahweh's righteousness which is particularly evinced in his concern for the poor, the weak, the oppressed; what Bishop David Sheppard of Liverpool has recently referred to as the 'divine bias for the poor'. Indeed it was in fulfilling this Old Testament tradition that Jesus showed himself particularly concerned for *all* society's rejects, and not only the economically poor. This radical element in the Christian faith is one which Christians and the churches have found hard to take seriously – they have been much more conscious of the need for law and order and the fear of anarchy should this break down – and it remains as a constant challenge to look at the *status quo* through the eyes of those least benefited by it. But the problem of relating it to the running of the ongoing structures of economics, industry and politics remains, notably where men and women find themselves living inextricably bound up in the bundle of life with those of other faiths and ideologies or none. The upshot of these difficulties has been that while traditionally Catholicism has tended to say that the Christian *must* be just and he *may* be loving as a work of supererogation, Protestantism has tended to say that he must be loving and there is no such thing as a work of supererogation, and thus to produce an individualistic ethic which has ignored social justice.

Nevertheless it is easy to see that problems of social justice are inescapable. The relationship of justice to love arises even in the intimate structure of a family. Parents, for instance, may have three children. They love all three dearly. But children are very different, and they must try to be *fair* to each. Justice as fairness is fundamental, and indeed it is the first abstract idea which comes home to us. As soon as a young child is socialized sufficiently actually to play with other children, quarrels arise, and someone rushes to Mummy and says 'It's not *fair*'.

There have been three positions on the relation of love (*agape*) to justice.

1. This opposes them to each other. Justice is seen as concerned with rights and obligations, love with needs; justice with what is deserved in rewards or punishments, love with making a gift of what no one has a right to as a matter of justice; justice with force, love with persuasion; justice as impersonal, stressing what we have in common, love with what is personal and peculiar; justice with what is cool and deliberate, love with warmth and spontaneity.

2. This is the opposite position, that justice and love are the same as soon as more than two people are involved; justice is maximizing *agape*. This is only so if *agape* is confined to what is done and not the motive by which it is done. It also fails to face the problem of not only maximizing the amount of *agape*, so to speak, but also the manner of its distribution.

3. This holds that justice and love must be related but also distinguished from one another. There can be no love without justice; love can never require less than justice, it can never make 'acts of charity' a substitute for justice. Justice restrains egoism and provides stabilities in society for the common good; love is a free gift in addition, embodying the creative righteousness of God who is concerned with the good of *each* as well as the good of *all*. On the other hand there is no justice without an element of love, because justice involves affirming other persons in their otherness and not merely because of their function. So love is the principle of justice, and justice both prepares for love and partially expresses it. The expression of love and justice involves discernment, which is an insight into situations on a base of thoughtful reflection arising out of the best knowledge of the facts which we have been able to acquire. Society can never be content with the level of justice it has achieved. Injustices are endemic. The strong oppress the weak; and privilege can hide behind justice, so that not only must justice conform to law, but law must conform to justice.[6]

This third view is, in my judgment, much the most adequate. It prevents us confining love to the realm of the personal, and it will teach Christians never to be content with a social ethic based on rational self-interest with no element of altruism (as in John Rawls' *A Theory of Justice*, 1971). At the same time, whilst it contributes the Christian understanding of *agape* as a vital element in an adequate social ethic, it does not provide any one particular model of a social order, but rather the basis for a continual critique of all social orders. There is no direct step from the Bible or any Christian doctrine to one particular type of society; neither provides a blueprint for one.

Christians have not found it difficult to agree that justice, in the case we are discussing, involves giving every man his due (*suum cuique*), but of course this is a purely formal requirement. Aristotle said it meant equal benefit for equals and so could differentiate slaves from the rest of humanity, and presumably the South African Government could justify *apartheid* on this basis. Various bases for distributive (and attributive) justice have been proposed on the basis of *suum cuique*: (1) distribution according to existing rights; (2) distribution according to merit, involving the knotty question of differentials; (3) distribution according to need, which lies behind the welfare state. Similarly there are three basic models of society which correspond to these three principles of distribution. (1) The liberal view, according to which men are thought of as independent, autonomous units who only co-operate with one another as far as their self-interest requires; (2) an hierarchical model, which could be feudal or a meritocracy; (3) a view which stresses altruistic and collaborative relationships between citizens. I do not think that Christianity can produce a fourth view peculiar to itself; rather it agrees that there are these three basic views. Christianity certainly favours the third as the best reflection of the ethics of the kingdom of God, but it recognizes that the other two have their place in the kingdoms of this world, and the third must be the leaven of the other two. Social orders will be a mixture of all three, but the Christian knows which one he particularly wishes to foster by suitable institutional expressions because it is the weakest of the three. Our sense of altruism is a reality but it is weaker than our sense of self-interest or of merit.

Recent ecumenical social thought has not done much to further these basic discussions. What it has done is to illuminate in devastating detail the injustices of the present time within nations and societies, and between them. It has done so in particular by providing a forum for the disadvantaged in the world to be heard. The mass of material is a unique source of learning what things look like to those two-thirds of the world who are not among the favoured wealthy nations. They are not necessarily right in everything they say; no individual and no group is; but they must be heard. It is not pleasant for the privileged to hear, and we are going through a period in which whatever we do we are likely to be faulted, but this is a necessary phase which must be lived through. Meanwhile we, the privileged, are made to think more thoroughly and in a wider perspective of our own problems.

This wider perspective is vital. Far more important than immediate preoccupations in the midst of a post-OPEC recession (though these must not be minimized) is how to mitigate the gross imbalance of the world's resources. Three-quarters of the people of our planet control only 20 per cent of its resources, as the result of a world-wide market system largely inherited from the era of colonialism. The overwhelming bulk of the world's wealth, trade, and skills, lies in the industrialized states where a third of the population is to be found, and little has happened in the last thirty years of rising affluence to alter this, except the politics of oil since 1973. Initiative must come from the wealthy West. In a broad sense we know what to do but we don't do it. The Willy Brandt Independent Commission on International Development Issues, *North-South: A Programme for Survival* (1980), called for a concerted programme to reduce the imbalance. It proposed a transfer of resources of 0.7 per cent of Gross National Product by 1985 and 1.0 per cent by 2000, a doubling of lending by the World Bank, a global food programme, an international energy strategy, and a greater stability in raw material prices; in short, to take seriously the United Nations' call for a New International Economic Order. It said that all countries have more mutual interests than they recognize, that because most Communist countries are left out of the World Bank or the International Monetary Fund they can stand aside and talk of capitalist plots, and that the less developed countries are under-represented in both. Some among us are calling for a steady state economy, or even one involving a planned decline in Western standards. I can do no more on this occasion than say that I do not think either practicable, and I am doubtful whether either is desirable in terms of the end it is supposed to achieve. But I am sure that action along the lines of the Brandt Commission's report is overdue, has for some time been known to be needed, and should be worked for. The wealthy take some shifting. I will mention later the type of arguments open to those who strive for international social justice.

III   *Participatory*

The stress on the need for a participatory society has grown markedly in the last fifteen years. It was latent in the concept of a 'Responsible Society' which was widely used in ecumenical social ethics from 1948 for the next twenty years, but was regarded in many countries as being too tied up with Western liberal political democracy (mistakenly, as I think).[7] Be that as it may, one of the marks of a responsible society was held to be that it is one where those who hold political or economic power are responsible for its exercise to God and the people whose welfare is affected by it. It is only a step from requiring responsibility to the people who are affected, to requiring that all those affected by decisions should be involved in the process of decision-making. It seems that without this the proper respect for each person as made in God's image and re-made in Christ is not expressed in the structures of human life. Most people for most of human history have lived in structures of power and dominance which have pushed them around. Western political democracy has begun to bring an end to this in its own sphere, and probably requires a certain level of wealth before it is possible. To extend it further into economic and industrial life in the West is painfully slow and far from agreed. Witness the muffled response to the Bullock Commission. In many parts of the world the process of participation has hardly begun. This is the context of 'conscientization' of the peoples on the margin of existence, begun in Brazil by Paulo Freire before he was thrown out.[8] Its necessity can be seen from considering the 'Green Revolution' of hybrid seeds, fertilizers, pesticides, water and mechanization which has raised agricultural productivity so markedly in the last decade in many less developed countries, but which has benefited the larger farmers rather than the villager, so that even more labourers are displaced from the land to join the under- or unemployed in the urban shanty towns. Technical change without social transformation is not enough; governmental or voluntary experiments to renew village life fail if the village community is not consulted and brought to participate in the necessary changes. In many developing countries cash crop revenue is spent on industry, or urban consumer demands or land speculation. Indeed food imports can be growing, so that all the exports of beef or soya beans are procuring is wheat and maize which could have been grown locally at less expense. The vital question is whether the small man is involved. If not the future is grim. I quote Barbara Ward's admirable *Progress for a Small Planet*:

> It is precisely in countries of violently skewed wealth and rural hopelessness that the annual population growth rate does not fall much below 3.5% per annum. The outlook is thus a dynamic and growing misery. As the land grows ever more crowded, the hillsides clear-felled, wood and crop residues burnt for fuel, and water sources fouled by an ever greater press of disease-ridden people, it is not simply this unhappy generation that must suffer and die. What is vanishing is the chance of providing even the shell of life for the generations still to come (p. 189).

The urgency of working towards participatory societies is evident, yet the problems need more exploration than they have so far received. Some of the advocates talk as if society could be run by small-scale spontaneous meetings of all affected by a decision rather than by structured institutions. Representative processes are not liked, and there is often a preference where they exist for mandated delegates rather than representatives, which destroys flexibility in negotiations. Elites are suspect as the recipients of unwarranted social prestige and privileges, and so are professional experts. Behind this there seems to lie an assumption that in a fully participatory society run by decisions at a grass roots level there will be no serious conflicts of interest and so agreement will not be difficult. Doubtless I am over-simplifying tendencies which have been around in Europe certainly since the events of 1968, and which find echoes around the world. In fact greater participation means greater complications. This is no argument against it, merely for being prepared to deal with them. There will always be conflicts of interest in society between the producers of a product and the consumers of it, between those who in particular situations primarily manage and those who primarily are managed. The experience of Yugoslavia in running a much more free socialist society than that of the USSR provides valuable evidence on this point. It is also impossible to run an advanced industrial society without the expertise of the trained professional, together with the greater potentiality of the trained mind to perceive the secondary consequences of possible courses of action, and thus provide a better basis for decision-making. Exactly what payments and privileges such professional experts receive is another question.

Further, we are faced with a need for both smaller and larger units at the same time. In the nation state we want things decentralized and localized where possible, following the principle of subsidiarity as adumbrated by Pope Pius XI in his encyclical *Quadragesimo Anno* (1931); on the other hand we find it necessary to develop bigger units (for instance to secure water or energy supplies), and to begin to create trans-national ones, of which the EEC is one. Certainly air, sea and river currents are indifferent to national boundaries. It is the same in the church. The emphasis is on small, informal groups on the one hand and the deanery on the other; the parish as a unit is less and less seen as the all-purpose unit.

Further, the more people are involved in decision-making the longer it takes. Nor does it necessarily follow that the decisions will always be wise, or made in time. There is a price to pay. Efficiency can be secured at too high a price. It was said of Mussolini that he made the trains in Italy run on time, but Fascism was surely too big a price to pay for that element of efficiency. On the other hand there will come a point where the pursuit of participation exacts too high a price. We are slowly adjusting ourselves in this country to a relatively new situation in which it is impossible to run industry without the consent of the bulk of its wage earners who in the past were not consulted at all. Various groups of workers as they participate more fully in decision-making which affects them, represent their own interest, which is by no means always the same as that of other workers, let alone the community at large. A participatory society has to create institutions for handling these conflicts of interest, and this will include institutions or means for bringing home the needed element of co-operation for the common good, as well as the element of the expression of conflicting interests. Christian social ethics is concerned with both; not only with preaching co-operation (as is often thought), but also with the handling of conflicts. The more complex and interlocked the world becomes the greater the political skills needed for this, but this is what life in two kingdoms at once sets before us.

IV *Sustainable*

Sustainable is a new term in ecumenical social ethics. Its origins are not theological; rather it reflects preoccupations in the West (not shared by the Second and Third Worlds) which can be dated precisely. In March 1972 the Club of Rome (a private body of MIT natural scientists, financed by an ecologically interested Italian industrialist) published a report which purported to show that, assuming the exponential (i.e., the constant per cent through time) annual growth in the world of population, food production, level of industrial activity, pollution and consumption of non-renewable natural resources, the end of present civilization could be predicated by the year 2100 unless drastic changes are made. A state of global equilibrium is needed, and to effect this the rate of use of natural resources should be quartered. (Two months earlier in this country the journal *The Ecologist* had produced a *Blueprint for Survival* along similar lines). The proposals did not have a mass effect, but they greatly influenced the kind of person in the Western world who reads what we call the 'quality' newspapers, and among these were many active in the Ecumenical Movement.

Since then the Club of Rome has added three more reports,[9] modifying the first, and its work has been widely and carefully scrutinized, not least by the Science Policy Research Unit of the University of Sussex, who published in 1978 an important study, *World Futures: the Great Debate* (ed. Christopher Freeman and Marie Jahoda). The Club of Rome reports gained prestige because they used computers to handle (in the second report) 100,000 equations simultaneously, which of course the human brain cannot do. But computers have to be programmed, and if the assumptions built in are inadequate so will the results be. I have to cut a long story short by saying that it is clear that a lot of the pessimism produced by the *Limits to Growth* report is not justified. In brief it did not take account of technological innovation, which also proceeds at an exponential rate. There is no reason why we should not plan to reduce the gross disparities between rich and poor countries, not by reductions in standards, but by increasing the standard of living in the poor world much more rapidly than in the rich world. The trouble lies not in any inherent impossibility in doing this but in our reluctance to do it. By the year 2000 absolute poverty could probably be eradicated in the middle-income countries, and be down to about 15 per cent of the population in low-income countries. This depends, among other things, on getting inflation under control and on the rich countries admitting the manufactured exports from the poor ones. The fact that they do not show much disposition to do so does not alter the basic options. In this discussion I am of course assuming that the world is not involved in a nuclear war, as one must if one is to engage in serious reflection on these issues. How far this is a likely assumption is another and fateful question.

What the alarm about the limits to growth has shown is that in the twenty-five years or so of steady growth in the West after the second world war, we behaved brashly as far as polluting the air, the sea and the rivers were concerned, and our monitoring devices did not keep pace with our technological innovations. We were in danger of exceeding the saturation point of the natural flushing properties of the atmosphere, the waterways and the oceans, as well as of inadvertently destroying the planet's nutrifying bacteria found in the soil and natural water systems. This is a warning which, once it is taken to heart, is not too difficult to attend to. Nor is it particularly costly. Think of the vast improvement made to British cities at little cost by the Clean Air Act of 1951. But it requires politicians and electorates who have the will, and an increasing level of international co-operation.

Nuclear energy is a question of special complexity in this discussion, and the WCC has devoted special attention to it in recent years. It is also one where experts differ, and yet where the issues come so close to every citizen that none of us can afford to be indifferent to the discussion. Our present fission nuclear reactors already foul the universe with their waste products; they are also wasteful in the use of the uranium 235 isotopes, of which supplies may only last to about 1990. Fast breeder reactors are so-called because they breed as much as they use, but they produce fissile plutonium 239, the most dangerous substance known to man, and with a radioactive half-life of 25,000 years. We have an experimental fast breeder reactor at Dounreay, and a commercial one is being built in France and another in West Germany. The further option of producing nuclear energy by fusion at incredibly high temperatures in a vacuum, which burns up all its waste and uses as fuel heavy isotope hydrogen from the sea, depends on a technology not yet invented. The EEC research centre at Culham in Oxfordshire is engaged on this. Given sufficient resources to work on the problem it may be invented – we do not know – but it is unlikely to be a commercial proposition until well into the next century. There are other options such as solar power, but they all require far more resources to develop them, whereas the bulk of resources has gone into developing nuclear power. Meanwhile the more the population of the world grows the more energy is needed; and at the same time the affluent nations use it wastefully. Without going into the details of the discussion, I report that there is not surprisingly a considerable difference of opinion among Christians on this issue, but that the WCC studies have not tended to rule out the development of nuclear energy, but to argue for great caution in developing it. The MIT Conference voted for a five-year moratorium on the development of nuclear energy while a more thorough public discussion is undertaken. It is an alarming thing to leave such dangerous polluting detritus on our planet for so many generations after us. Meanwhile there are serious studies[10] which show that if we made a major effort to use fuel less wastefully we could probably do without nuclear energy altogether, or at least until the fusion process becomes possible; and if it does not, there is time to develop the harnessing of solar energy or to develop other sources which I have not mentioned, the wind, the tides and geothermal sources.

The question of a sustainable society has not impressed the Third World, which tends to see it as one more way in which the affluent countries can keep their advantages. An Indian economist, Dr Kurien, said at the MIT Conference (paraphrasing I John), 'If you claim to be concerned about the unborn humanity that you cannot see, but show no regard for the humanity that you can see all around you, then you are a liar.' It has also raised in an acute form the theological understanding of the relation of man and nature, of science to faith, and of our responsibility for the future. It is to these three theological issues that I turn in the last section of this lecture.

V   *Theological Issues*

1. *Science and Faith*

Of the 400 official participants at the MIT Conference half were natural scientists, unprecedented for a church conference of this kind. To some extent they were no doubt self-selected, in that those actively hostile to churches or to the Christian faith would not come. Nevertheless there was a striking absence of the divisions between scientists and theologians which have characterized the recent past. The philosophy of science has become much more open (perhaps as physics has become more ethereal), and its sense of social responsibility much greater; theologians on the other hand have become more circumspect and less disposed to give *simpliste* religious answers to complex questions. At any rate at the MIT Conference there were no arguments which found scientists on one side and theologians on the other; both were found on both sides. The scientific utopianism of even a decade ago had disappeared (what is often called 'scientism'), and so had any kind of technological determinism. Perhaps a conference which met when it was not clear where Skylab would come down, and in the wake of the Harrisburg nuclear reactor accident and the grounding of DC 10's, was rather easily preserved from utopianism. The chief difference lay between those who saw science primarily in terms of understanding and those who saw it primarily in terms of power. The former get only about 5 per cent of the resources devoted to scientific research, and it is among them that the liberal values of the scientific attitude are found – universalist, communal, disinterestedness and organized scepticism. The radical critics of applied science saw it as the captive of military and political power structures, and pointed out that

95 per cent of Research and Development work is in the West and a vast amount is in defence contracts. The upshot is to make clear that whatever element of neutrality there may be in pure science, the practice of science is a social activity which cannot be divorced from the challenge of a Just, Participatory and Sustainable society which faces us all.

2. *Man and Nature*

The ecological aspects of the *Limits to Growth* debate have activated a vigorous debate on man's relation to nature, made the more pointed because of the evidence of so much brashness since 1948, which I have already mentioned. For Christians it was sharpened by a much quoted article by Professor Lynn White, a medieval historian, in the American journal *Science* for March 1967, on 'The Historical Roots of our Ecological Crisis', in which he alleged that Christianity, especially in its Western form, is the most anthropocentric religion the world has ever seen in its arrogant attitude to nature. He repeated the charge in 1973. It would take a lecture in itself to deal with the debate which has ensued, but something must be said now.[11] Much of it turns on the meaning of man's dominion in the Genesis creation myths. In Genesis 1.26–28 man is made in the image of God to rule the earth for God and stand in the place of God (but under his command) for other living creatures. In Genesis 2 man's centrality is emphasized by putting him first, a kind of king in paradise who names the rest; the creation is a trust given to man under God. In Genesis 3.17–19 man's sin affects nature, which now resists him so that creativity and destructiveness go together; his duties are not altered but they are now more onerous (Genesis 9.2–3). It seems clear that man in these myths is distinguished from the rest of creation by being made a steward or vicegerent over it, with limits on his authority set by God.

Many of those with strong ecological concerns, however, want to go much further than this, and their influence can be found in places in the sectional reports of the MIT Conference, which move uncertainly on this issue. It is one thing to say that we should open ourselves to the wonder of creation, and that we should respect plant and animal life, but another to bring humanity into a common world of justice and the right to live with animals, plants and even non-animate matter, or to say that in the eucharistic meal human beings and things are set free to serve one another (Section 2), as if they are on the same level. Elsewhere a different note is struck in a reference to man as a maker and cultivator, whose reshaping of nature in co-operation with it for human needs is a parable of God's activity. Much depends upon what is meant here by *co-operation*. Does it mean that if, for instance, I want to do something with wood I must understand the nature of the material? Or is more than that implied? One cannot tell.

A word of caution needs uttering about these tendencies. Valuable as they may be as a warning to man against blundering about in the universe in a brash way, nature is ambiguous. She is neither sacred nor demonic. She is a source of wonder to man, of necessities for him, and yet at times she is his enemy. Blurring the difference between man and sub-human life can easily lead to a quietism with respect to remediable suffering, to sloth, and to the rationalization of privilege. A monistic religion of this kind is a dominant force for conservatism, as readers of Gunnar Myrdal's *Asian Drama* will remember, enslaving man to nature. This is not the witness of the Genesis myths. But this raises a further question. What is being presupposed about the use of the Bible in wishing to derive too detailed a doctrine of man and nature from myths which (in the case of Genesis 1) seem to be a magnificent adaptation of a Babylonian creation myth which came into the Israelite tradition at the time of the exile, ridding it of any of its associations with cosmological fatalism? From the Old Testament we certainly get the witness that nature is desacralized for man's good, and from Jesus in the New Testament the witness that dominion and authority are drastically modified in the kingdom of God from the way earthly rulers are accustomed to exercise it. We are then left once more with the perennial task of living in the two kingdoms at once, which is a call to creativity under God even as we heed his warnings. We must not become prisoners of our existing structures in a kind of homeostatic ecological conservatism. The Third World has remained sceptical of this whole approach, regarding the situation which the ecologist wants to preserve as an artificial garden restricted to a privileged group. Yet this is also too simple, if only because wind and sea currents are as heedless of the divisons between the First and Third Worlds as of the divisions between nation states.

3. *Our Responsibility for the Future*

Burke in his *Reflections on the Revolution in France* said that society is a partnership between those who are living, those who are dead, and those who are unborn. What is our responsibility if a conflict arises between the needs of the present generation and those of future generations? If the unborn have claims on us they cannot make them (nor can those alive now who are too young to vote), nor can they give the informed consent which is needed of a patient in medical research in the matter, for example, of the storage of radio-active nuclear waste. It seems to me that our responsibility extends *pari passu* with our powers of forecasting. Here our powers are limited. Forecasting is in any case a conservative activity, because it is based on present trends, when in fact we are constantly surprised by technological innovations which have not been foreseen, as well as what I make bold to call the accidents of history. Discounting the future at 10 per cent per annum gives us a horizon of fifteen years. Even that has a number of uncertainties. To think twenty-five years ahead is much more sketchy. And that does not take us as far as our grandchildren, for whom we might well think we have some responsibility. Much forecasting is a matter of expertise, and techniques are improving. But experts differ. I could quote five or six concerning the year 2000, which are all broadly within the same range of discourse but differ enough to make the taking of decisions on the basis of them a matter of considerable uncertainty. Sometimes experts make serious errors, as in the first Club of Rome report. Furthermore our time scale in connection with radio-active nuclear waste is unusual and alarming. Risks must be taken in human life, but is this one that ought to be?

We must clearly accept some responsibility for the future, varying according to our reasonable ability to forecast, which will rarely extend beyond the next generation.[12] To discharge this we shall need more sophisticated tools of analysis. It cannot be left to the free market system, which does not cover the unborn; nor to current welfare economics, because the gainers and losers are in a different market. Beyond this a doctrine of providence is needed whch will trust the future to God to bring to fruition the purposes he has already begun.

VI

Looking back at the vastness of the issues which I have only touched on, the question arises, Are the problems too big to cope with? Can the human mind and spirit rise to them? Christians will not shirk them if they are secure in their faith in Jesus Christ, whilst at the same time they are alert to the inevitable uncertainties in particular policies and to the ease with which we are self-deceived in considering them. They will take the inevitable risks of decision-making without being overwhelmed. Christians will be in the forefront of a resistance movement against fatalism. The church will learn to free itself from the shackles of unjust structures, and not lose its nerve in doing so. We shall learn to work for tolerable solutions if not ideal ones; and these solutions will uncover further problems. A defect of a good deal of the material from the MIT Conference is its sweeping and total demands in a whole range of issues, and its implication that Christians, the churches and the World Council of Churches have more influence and freedom of movement than is the case. This is partly because actual decision-makers were scarce at the conference. I am thinking of industrial managers, trade union officials, politicians, social workers, the military, officials of transnational companies, and public administrators. This is not surprising, because they are the hardest people to get away from their jobs. But their relative absence does tend to leave the field to various theorists who do not carry the day-to-day task of wrestling with the intractable features of the world.

A good deal more also needs to be done on the basis and methods of Christian social ethics, and the role of the churches as such in these complex and diverse questions. Moreover much more examination is needed of how national governments can be influenced to move even in a modest way towards policies that are so clearly desirable. The Conference constantly demands that governments behave with a magnanimity that they never do, and in many cases could not do if their country is to be sufficiently cohesive to maintain its unity; at least unless its citizens are to be held down by force. For any government subject to free elections which attempted it would be swept away by an angry electorate. How can governments and electorates be moved towards what is necessary? Neither is without some element of altruism, and this must be appealed to. So must prudence in pointing out where long-term self-interest lies as distinct from short-term advantages. Fear is also a weapon; the consequences of failing to work reasonably together in our one world must be spelled out. All three tactics of persuasion are needed. There is talk in the Conference material of recognizing in events the activity of God for righteousness and peace in the world, and of participating in God's new creation of the whole world, but how exactly this is to be done requires closer examination. However, these criticisms are far outweighed by the debt we owe to the World Council of Churches for the steady work it has done over the years, encouraging us to face these immense issues of social ethics with realism and with vision and unafraid. That it has all been done in a global context is an essential element in its value. We in Britain are inclined to distance ourselves from it with a regrettable insularity. We do so at our peril.

5

The Integrity of Creation: Issues of Environmental Ethics

I

The demand that the church should let the world provide the agenda is obviously inadequate by itself. It ignores the fact that the church may well need to draw attention to issues that the world is not awake to, or chooses to overlook. Selective inattention is a familiar human trait. Nevertheless the demand is a useful challenge to the church to look beyond inward ecclesiological concerns. It is a legitimate reminder that if there are issues which clearly preoccupy the world the church in its solidarity with humanity should pay attention to them.

The question of environmental ethics is such an issue. It has been latent for some time in the affluent one-third of the world and has exploded in the last twenty years. It is now being taken up beyond it. It was therefore inevitable and right that it should be explored by the Ecumenical Movement, particularly by its sub-unit on Church and Society.

The citizen, and the citizen who is a Christian is no exception, finds it hard to see the wood for the trees in the confusing mass of issues and data that reach him every day through the media of communication. So it is a help if key issues can be identified and related to one another in broad categories, and criteria for delimiting and evaluating general policy directions for dealing with them can be indicated.[1] This has been the way in ecumenical studies in social ethics. The first broad category was that of The Responsible Society.[2] This was elaborated in the preparatory years before the foundation of the World Council of Churches in 1948, and taken up by it in its early years. It was the time of the 'cold war'. The WCC was then an overwhelmingly Western body in composition and, moreover, to a large and generous extent financed by the churches of the USA. It could not ignore the cold war, but it realized that the transcendent perspectives of the gospel of the kingdom of God did not permit it to align itself too simply with one side in that war. The concept of The Responsible Society provided a criterion which could be brought to bear on any social order and it was used in practice to express challenges to both sides in the cold war, to the capitalist economies of the West and the centralized Soviet economy of the USSR and its satellites.

In principle the concept could be used today; for instance it could be brought to bear on issues of environmental ethics. But as the WCC became a truly global body rather than a Western one, the experience of Christians from the Third World was drawn on and they did not like the concept. It had not been arrived at with their help, and in their eyes it was too Western. So a new concept was arrived at, The Just and Sustainable Society, to which the term Participatory was soon added.[3] This proved a useful concept and a spur to co-operative Christian reflection all over the world. The previous chapter in this book indicates something of the ground to be covered by the concept, and the many problems raised both by the criteria of sustainability and participation. The former bears primarily on the economic order and the latter on the political, though in the end economic issues always lead to political ones, even in the most extreme *laissez-faire* economics.

Now a third concept has come to the fore, The Integrity of Creation. It is not clear why this is so. There has been no great change of context such as led to the replacement of The Responsible Society by The Just, Participatory and Sustainable Society. Indeed it is arguable that it takes a number of years before work done at a high ecumenical level seeps down into local churches. The introduction of a new concept may thus lead to confusion and a loss of impetus. Time will tell. It is too early yet to know what may be achieved by corporate Christian reflection on The Integrity of Creation. There has been such an explosion of writing in the field of environmental ethics in the last decade or so that the effort to sort through it all will certainly be useful. The problem will be with the coherence of the criterion, The Integrity of Creation. In this chapter I begin by printing the substance of a paper I prepared a decade ago,[4] and then I ask how far it needs modification in the light of the abundance of work on the theme since then. In doing this theological questions concerning the meaning of The Integrity of Creation will be raised.

There are two basic aspects of the discussion. One is our attitude as Christians to the material world, to all in 'nature' at a sub-human level. The other is the context today in which economic, ecological and environmental decisions have to be made. In this aspect the moral theologian can do little by himself. He depends upon, and must engage in, interdisciplinary studies with natural and social scientists and philosophers, in which the assumptions and conclusions of everyone involved are open to mutual scrutiny and correction. The WCC has been a leader in promoting such work and it is becoming slowly more common under other auspices. I have drawn upon such work. It is subject to all the hazards of my own failures to understand, and hence mistakes of judgment (to which the corporate process offers some check, though it does not escape the hazards). But that is the way issues in Christian social ethics have to be tackled. There are no unambiguously clear and certain answers. As Reinhold Niebuhr said, 'There are no solutions to problems, only temporary solutions to insoluble problems.'

II

Ecology is the study of an organism in relation to its whole environment. When humans are brought in the study is called Ekistics. Human beings have been changing the face of the earth ever since they started to cultivate it. For example, the draining of the English fen lands changed them from a swamp ecology to one of rich farm lands. Left to itself Britain would return to a forest ecology in two centuries. Today, however, human activities have produced a startling growth in a literature of ecological crisis. On the one hand the standard of living in the West has been raised dramatically (despite a diminution in growth since 1973),[5] on the other the question is asked whether we have gone too fast and too far. Are we using up irreplaceable new materials, like metals and fossil fuels, carelessly? Are we polluting the world beyond its powers of renewal? Is our attitude to nature exploitative and lacking in reverence? 'Technical fixers' are at one end of the argumentative spectrum and 'doomsayers' at the other.

Current discussion can plausibly be held to have started with the publication of Rachel Carson's *The Silent Spring* in the USA in 1962 and in Britain in 1965. It attacked the misuse of chemicals in agriculture by over-application, so that pesticides accumulated in flesh, bone and soil. Many at the time thought it hysterical, but most of the chemicals she attacked are now banned.[6] A whole series of other hazards have by now come to our attention, such as lead in petrol, or the dangers of asbestos. We are well aware of the pollution of rivers, like the Rhine or the Thames; of seas like the Mediterranean;[7] of the damage caused to forests by the sulphur dioxide and nitrogen oxides from power stations producing 'acid rain'; of the problems created by nuclear waste (a study in itself).[8]

Looking back now we can see that the debate was greatly accelerated by two publications a decade later, in 1972. In January the journal *The Ecologist* published a *Blueprint For Survival* which advocated, among other things, a reduction in the population of Britain from 53 millions to 30 millions so that it could live off its own agricultural resources and thereafter maintain a stable society with zero population and economic growth.[9] In the same year the Club of Rome produced its first report, *The Limits of Growth*, which caused a sensation among the readers of quality newspapers.[10] It used computers to predict dynamic interactions between population, food production, pollution, the level of industrial activity and the consumption of non-renewable natural resources. It stressed the danger of exponential growth, that is to say an increase by a constant percentage of a whole over a constant period of time. A fixed limit is approached suddenly. An example given is that of lilies in a pond which double themselves daily; if they could cover the pond in thirty days on the twenty-ninth they would still only half cover it. So on this assumption the world, which is finite, could move quickly from a situation of apparent abundance to crisis. Various predictions were made about the exhaustion of aluminium, iron, oil and so on, and the conclusion was reached that the end of civilization would be threatened by the year 2100 unless drastic changes are made and a state of global equilibrium established, population included.

It is important to recall this now because of its considerable effect on educated public opinion, including church opinion, even though subsequent reports from the Club of Rome considerably modified the picture.[11] It was the original one which made the impact. It is a good example of the problem 'lay' opinion has in evaluating the work of experts. For it was not expert enough. In particular it lacked sufficient input from economists. It had a serious flaw. The conclusion followed from the assumptions fed into the computer. If population increases exponentially so will the consumption of natural resources and levels of pollution, other things being equal. But the technological level was assumed to be constant. So existing exponential growth was plotted against elasticities of substitution within known technology. In fact technological development leads to innovations.

In the last century Professor W. S. Jevons of Manchester University, one of the founders of the 'Manchester School' of economics, predicted that coal reserves would last only another sixty years. The resources of the earth must indeed be finite but we have little idea of what the limits are. Known reserves may be only a few decades ahead of demand because beyond that they are not worth looking for. Examples of possible areas of innovation to take seriously include the harnessing of solar power, obtaining metals from sea water, taking re-cycling of waste seriously, inventing processes with less energy requirements, inventing better sensors for mining to utilize geothermal energy, passing on one-tenth of the expertise of the ten per cent best farmers to others, and pursuing the possibility of producing energy by nuclear fusion. Commenting on the first Club of Rome report *The Economist* said that it was as if in 1872 someone had said of the population of London in 1972 that it would make life impossible because there would be no room to stable the horses and we would be asphyxiated by the amount of manure.

Far more work has been done since 1972. We cannot complain that not much is known. Even if some of the analysis has been faulty, real dangers have been pointed out. On the other hand there are opportunities, despite attendant risks, to be taken. As to dangers, ecologists have been right to stress that the explosion of knowledge after the 1939–45 war outran human monitoring devices and safeguards. There has been the danger that the natural flushing properties of the atmosphere, waterways and oceans might be near saturation point. There has been the danger of destroying the planet's nutrifying bacteria found in the soil and natural water systems, which are versatile in decomposing thousands of chemicals and so releasing carbon and nitrogen for future growth. Technology as such has no inbuilt criteria for control, nor can ecology by itself provide them. To this we shall return. Moreover ecological problems require a global focus, which politically is hard to achieve. Economics cannot decide the issues. The price mechanism of the free market, its most sophisticated device, can at its best cope only for a relatively short term ahead, perhaps up to fifteen years. Economic problems always shade into political ones. These become increasingly complex, partly because the desire of human beings to participate in decision-making grows, whilst governments need adequate power and public support to act in time and participation makes the process of decision slower. Resistance also arises from a fear of the unknown, as the rate of change more and more upsets traditional ways. Then there are problems of the extent of human adaptability. Most of us find it hard to take in new ideas after the age of twenty-five, and yet the knowledge explosion is such that in some sciences it doubles in ten years.

However let us turn to consider opportunities. If we do make good use of our greater powers of control over matter and energy, and in processing and retrieving information, we have the possibility of producing a much fairer society with much greater possibilities of human fulfilment in a more affluent world, in which the primary poverty which has haunted the two-thirds world from time immemorial has been eliminated. Ethical criteria are clearly needed to guide technological change with all the social and political consequences that go with it. These criteria if at all possible should be acceptable to people of different faiths and ideologies. A special responsibility in this matter rests upon those in the Judaeo-Christian tradition, for it is in a society profoundly influenced by a combination of that tradition with classical humanism that modern scientific and technical development was pioneered, with the global effects we are now facing. So we proceed to examine what resources can be derived from the biblical and theological resources which we have inherited in the West.

III

Changes in the contemporary context have the effect of sending

Christians back to their Bible with new questions in mind as they read the text in new ways. There is nothing necessarily sinister in this. Living as a Christian in one's own context must mean a continual reflection on what one has inherited from Christian reflection in the past on the content of the Christian faith and life, in the light of the challenges of the present. The same source materials, the Bible and theological positions all claiming to be derived from the Bible or consonant with it, are being continually reappraised in the present by Christians within the fellowship of the worshipping church. So there is nothing surprising in the fact that the ecological and environmental alarms of the last twenty years or so have had the same effect. Some confusion does indeed arise. That is because there is confusion in all the main confessional traditions on how far, or the precise way in which, the Bible can be used to establish ethical criteria (or perhaps even detailed policies) with respect to current problems. These confusions are not new, and questions of environmental ethics are just one more example of it. Ecumenical work has helped to clarify confusions, but it has not resolved differences within churches and between them. Reassessing the biblical treatment of God, man and nature has not escaped the difficulties.

A reassessment was made all the sharper by an attack by a medieval historian from the USA which put biblical scholars and Christian theologians on the defensive. In a widely quoted article in 1967 Professor Lynn White attacked the Judaeo-Christian attitude to nature,[12] maintaining that Christianity, particularly in its Western form, is the most anthropocentric religion the world has seen, in its arrogant attitude to nature. For example, while Byzantine illustrations of Genesis 1.28 show Adam and the animals in repose in the Garden of Eden, Western ones show a minatory Adam and animals huddled together against him. White urges a recall to the Franciscan attitude to sister earth, to the Beatitudes, to Zen Buddhism (according to which a man climbing a mountain does not conquer but makes a friend of it), and to Taoism (whose effect is seen in Chinese landscapes where humans fit in modestly). There has also been a recall to the unity of man and nature in African traditional societies, to a kind of cosmic union in which nature, humans and God are merged and men and women do not see themselves as distinctively apart.[13]

We should give intrinsic value to sub-human nature, even to rocks.

Too much attention has been paid to White. He exaggerates the influence of Christianity but, more important, there is more in the Christian tradition that he allows of a sensitive attitude to nature.[14] But the statement of an extreme view, whilst it may unnecessarily polarize discussion, can often sharpen reflection. In this case it has led to a fresh look at the biblical material, especially the Genesis creation myths or sagas. Of course it may be asked how far a Christian attitude to God, man and nature must depend on the creation sagas of Genesis, but they are at any rate key elements among the biblical material, which itself is a prime source of a Christian doctrine of creation, though the Bible itself has no overall conception of nature, of an ordered organic unity.

In the earlier of the two creation sagas (from Genesis 2.4b) man's centrality is emphasized by putting him first. He shares a material origin with birds and beasts but his distinctiveness is recognized because he names them (which means he exercises a lordship over them), and because they are not adequate companions for him; hence the creation of woman. Under God man is a kind of king in paradise. But that he is under God is emphasized by the prohibition, a tree with its fruit. When he disobeys God and infringes the prohibition nature rebels against him, and the woman who helped to lead him astray becomes his servant. Man's duties have not altered but they have become more onerous. Creativity and destructiveness go together. The later creation saga (Genesis 1–2.4a) which seems to have been adapted from a Babylonian one at the time of the exile, has removed any cosmological fatalism from it. Nowhere in antiquity is human dominion over nature so stressed. Nature is de-sacralized; its numerous powers are demythologized. The human-shared material origin with nature is suppressed in favour of a stress on the distinctive creation of men and women. Humans are to rule the earth for God and stand in the place of God for other living creatures. But, again, they are under God's command; and under it they can subdue the earth for food and exercise dominion over fish, birds and animals. (Psalm 8 has much the same attitude.) After the sagas of the Fall in Genesis 3 and the Flood in Genesis 6–8, Yahweh's covenant in Genesis 9 is not only with Noah but with every living creature, though now beasts, birds and fish are to have fear and dread of Noah and his sons. Once more, however, their lordship is under a divine prohibition, not to eat flesh with the life (or blood).

This more sombre note with respect to nature is not the only one in the Old Testament. There is also an admiring and affectionate one, for instance in the Psalms and Job and the Wisdom literature, In the Wisdom literature moral lessons are drawn from nature for the benefit of human beings. But the significance of nature is not solely in its significance for humans. Job is led to confess the foolishness of his criticism of the human situation by a demonstration of the wonders of the sub-human creation. And the more sombre side of the creation sagas is counteracted in the apocalyptic strain, the beginnings of which are found in the Old Testament, as in Isaiah 11, which looks towards peace among animals in the messianic era. In general apocalyptic looks towards a cosmic catastrophe followed by a new order involving both humans and nature.

The New Testament does not add much to this. Jesus shows appreciation of the natural world in his teaching,[15] though Paul's attitude to oxen in I Cor. 9.9 hardly echoes this. Attention is mostly focused on what he says in Romans 8.19–23, which seems to have as a background Jewish apocalyptic conceptions of a world subjugated by evil powers which are responsible for disorders in nature and sin in human life. It looks to a glorious future in which nature as well as humankind are to be trans-figured. This thought is taken up in the vision of a new heaven and new earth in the Revelation of St John (chs. 21f.). In this new order there will be a return to the idyllic pre-Fall condition of the original creation.

In the present order the whole notion of dominion over human beings in the Christian community is drastically modified by Jesus in his words to the disciples.[16] It is an example, as in much of the Sermon on the Mount, of an impossible ethic if it is transferred directly to the administration of human beings in the political and economic order, and its bearing on nature must be even more indirect. But at least it puts a question-mark against any domineering interpretation of dominion. The Bible, how-ever, gives us no further help in working out its implications in detail.

From this biblical material I draw the conclusion that human beings have a distinctive place in nature. They are distinct but not separate; there is a unity but not an identity between humans and nature. In our terminology we can say that the DNA is the same for all, yet differences in kind can emerge. From one point of view the human brain can be regarded as 'an electro-chemical device, weighing about three pounds and running on the power of glucose at 25 volts'; from another, humans have the power of abstract reasoning, imagination and humour. It is true that there are no complete discontinuities in nature. Some sub-human creatures share more with humans than humans are apt to realize. But we need to move from God to nature via men and women and not to nature direct.

What models of the relation of God to humanity have we? There is an unbiblical one of the clockmaker winding up the clock, which is a pallid form of deism. There is that of the potter and the clay,[17] which is biblical and is a more monarchical form of deism. And there is that of father and child. In the interpretation of fatherhood which sustained Jesus the most distinctive aspect is that of unconditional love bestowed on just and unjust; a persuasive love which once it is grasped by the person loved elicits a loving response. Hence the motivation to the ethical way of life which divine love is seen of its very nature to require is expressed in Jesus' graphic phrase, 'Freely you have received, freely give.'[18] What is that response to be with respect to nature?

The best concept that can be drawn from the biblical tradition is that of responsible stewardship. This would call us to respect nature as a craftsman respects the grain of his material, but not to romanticize it. Nature is a source of delight to God and humans. It is a source of necessities for human persons, but also an enemy as, for instance, microbes and hurricanes can be. Fundamentally it points beyond itself to God. It is neither divine nor demonic. It is ambiguous. Human beings under God have a certain transcendence over it. They can improve it. They can be creative. But there are limits, which they must have the wisdom to search out and respect.

Biblical material does not suggest an undifferentiated unity of man with nature. There is a monism which leads to a rationalization of privilege, and has often made religion a dominant force for conservatism, and prevented it from inspiring the removal of unnecessary poverty and injustice in human life.[19] The

Judaeo-Christian tradition would emancipate humans from this kind of captivity to nature, as it would from capricious deities and irrational fate. Emphasis on harmony with nature easily leads to quietism and a cyclical view of life. Emphasis on stewardship, or dominion carefully interpreted, leads to creativity. But it can easily be abused. And it has been. Dominion over nature is much harder to exercise than we have thought. Nature is not infinitely malleable and needs careful study. She is not fixed, but a realm of interacting processes which need to be understood. We must beware of thinking of nature in terms of homeostatic stability, of a cosmic conservatism in ecology which would require us to preserve every species and to regard the extinction of any one as a disaster. Nor is technology necessarily alienating. It can save drudgery. It can provide new pleasures (such as water skiing). Nor does it necessarily eliminate wonder or gratitude. (Ships are affectionately referred to as 'she'.)

Yet we have responsibilities to other living creatures as well as to humans. It is true that they cannot be held responsible to us. However even in human life rights and responsibilities do not entirely go together, for we affirm that infants have rights, and so do the mentally handicapped, despite the fact that they have no, or much diminished, responsibilities. In the case of nature our responsibilities must increase according to its degree of being in relation to the personal. About this there will be difficulties of determination (as indeed there is in the case of the personal in deciding the status of the foetus in its earliest days of existence). However in ethical questions the presence of difficulties because of the twilight areas does not excuse us from recognizing differences between two ends of a spectrum and of striving for careful discrimination in making moral judgments.

IV

The area of our responsibility in space has grown with our ability through modern communications to know on a global scale what is going on. The extent of our responsibility in time because of our growing powers of decision over our circumstances and environment, and the diminishing area that we are content to leave undetermined and to regard what happens in it as an 'act of God', mean that our responsibility for future generations has become a sharper issue. Burke, in his *Reflections on the Revolution in France*, says that society is a partnership between those who are living, those who are dead and those who are yet unborn. If, however, the unborn have claims on us they cannot make them; they have even less possibility of exercising moral and political weight than have those alive but too young to vote. They cannot give the informed consent which is required from patients who may be involved in medical research in, for instance, the question of storing nuclear waste which we have already bequeathed to them. Their position is more like that of a child too young to give informed consent to a medical research project. It can be held that parents should never give such consent. But it can also be held that parents may give consent on grounds which in their judgment it would be proper for the child to consent to had it the discretion to do so. A similar position can be taken with respect to future generations. In that case our responsibility will depend upon the extent of our powers of forecasting. This responsibility is not easy to exercise, and because of the lack of political weight behind future generations we are prone to ignore them in favour of immediate considerations. We cannot rely on market forces to settle matters because they do not include the unborn, nor does current welfare economics, because the potential gainers and losers are not in the same market. A more sophisticated cost-benefit analysis is required. Even so forecasting fifteen years ahead is far from easy, and twenty-five much more problematical.[20] That takes us as far as our children. When it is a case of our grandchildren and beyond it is still more hazardous. There is some comfort in the apocalyptic foreshortening in the New Testament. This stresses faithfulness and obedience to the commands of the kingdom of God today, leaving the rest in God's hands. Nearly all the New Testament writers thought there was in fact little time left. We, of course, do not know; but plausibility is on the side of a long time series. However our limited powers of forecasting bring us close to the New Testament perspective, and show us the necessity of a doctrine of Providence to undergird men and women of faith who must make many decisions affecting the future, but not by sight.

We may pause for a moment to consider the development of nuclear energy as an instance of the difficulty of decision-making which involves the future. First there is the danger to persons in it from radio-active contacts. It is one of the safer industries as a health hazard. An accident, however, could be on a serious scale, with effects far beyond those working in it. Stringent precautions are taken, but the more minutely they are routinized the danger arises of a breakdown in carrying out routine instructions occurring through sheer boredom. Then there is the question of the permanent disposal of nuclear waste, which is far from resolved. If it can be stored perpetual surveillance will be needed, as of the dykes in Holland. Prior to permanent disposal is the problem of avoiding the hi-jacking of potential sources of plutonium for military purposes, and the authoritarian climate which preventing it may encourage. These problems may be soluble but we have embarked on creating them in far too bland a manner. Whether the development of a nuclear fusion process which could avoid them will be technically feasible we do not know. There is a strong case for putting more resources into investigating the possibility.[21]

We appear to need not an ethic of scarcity but one which illuminates the relative affluence which technological develop-ment has produced. There are demands for a pro-worldly wisdom as against a voracious consumerism. There is also an other-worldly ethic which underplays this world as compared with the other-worldly destiny of human beings, and an inner-worldly one in which concentration on disciplined hard work in an individualistic setting produces myopia with regard to the concerns we are discussing. Neither will do. A pro-worldly one will take our global responsibilities for human flourishing seri-ously. This will involve a long campaign, for we have only very imperfectly accepted it within national boundaries, let alone taking seriously a wider frame of reference. Persuasion is needed to advocate a change of direction. It will require a challenge to the relatively wealthy one-third world on how it can best use its increasing wealth (in spite of setbacks since 1973) with the two-thirds world in mind. We must assume that people are alike in their basic needs in life (unless in some respect some cogent reason to the contrary can be produced), and ask ourselves if we can in good conscience live as an affluent enclave in a global slum. This is the heart of the matter. The material future of the West is relatively hopeful (failing a nuclear war), but the moral problems of affluence will become more acute. The gospel warnings about wealth, that in the last resort it is a distraction because concern for it obscures our common humanity before God, have to be brought out of the New Testament world of relative scarcity and brought to bear on one of relative abundance. It is clear that it is against relative disparities that Jesus spoke. There is no reason to suppose that if he lived today he would advocate drudgery for its own sake, any more than in a world of anaesthetics he would have advocated pain for its own sake.

However persuasion by itself is unlikely to be enough. There is abundant evidence that the relatively rich do not listen to the relatively poor until the latter can put pressure on them. How can they be empowered to do so? It is hard to see. Oil rich states have done so (though of course they were not all notably poor). Are there any other commodities where something similar could be attempted? Copper? Bauxite? Mercury? Phosphates? Ironically, rich South Africa has threatened us with respect to chrome. There do not seem many possibilities, even if the two-thirds world achieves a much greater cohesion against the one-third world than it has so far managed. The economies of the one-third world are so strong relatively that they can find substitutes or dictate the terms of trade. Maybe a good case can be made out that failure to take the two-thirds world more seriously will produce disorder there out of desperation, and that this will spread to the one-third world which will not be able to insulate itself from it. In that case its own long-term interests would indicate more far-seeing policies now. The Brandt Reports made as much as they could of this argument. So far it has not impressed Western governments into significant action. Clearly there are years of campaigning ahead, using the arguments of altruism, fear, and long-term interests. As the prayer says, 'Save, Lord, by love, by prudence and by fear.'

V

So far this is substantially what I wrote a decade ago. How far does it need modification in the light of recent discussions of environmental ethics and of the concept of The Integrity of Creation? The phrase appears to have arisen in the Programme Guidelines Committee at the Vancouver Assembly of the WCC in 1982. There is little reference to it in the Report of the proceedings of the Assembly and it did not occur in the MIT Conference on 'Science, Technology and the Human Future'.[22] However the phrase has been taken up with enthusiasm and linked with justice and peace, so the umbrella concept which has replaced the Just, Participatory and Sustainable Society is Justice, Peace and the Integrity of Creation. What precisely are the reasons for the change have not been explained. If the impetus has come from the staff of the WCC it has been backed by the Central Committee. It may well be that the flurry of writing in the last decade has suggested that the traditional Christian doctrine of creation be re-examined as a first priority.

In fact there has been much more than a flurry of writing. There have been numerous examples of human blunders due to over-confidence, short-sighted self-interest, or sheer negligence which have had serious human consequences, and damaged the environment, or were lucky near misses, or have created alarming hazards for the future. I need do no more than mention names like Seveso, Flixborough, Three Mile Island and Bhopal. Evidence is accumulating of serious pollution in the USSR (which so far has done more harm by it to itself than to its neighbours). 'Green' political parties, under various names, have come into existence, the most well known being that in West Germany. Humanity, at least in the West, is getting more alert to ecological issues.

Another aspect of this greater awareness is the spate of philosophical writings on the status of animals and their 'rights'. This is part of a marked shift of attitude among moral philo-sophers, most of whom a generation ago eschewed any responsibility for moral advice and confined themselves to analysing the logic of moral terms. Now they are active in taking up issues of practical ethics. Perhaps the almost complete absence of previous work on the moral status of animals has encouraged attention to it with the zest of a sense of intellectual pioneering.

Still another strain, and one to which the WCC has given much attention, is the growing realization of the unintended effects of the growth of science and technology. It is too simple to regard it essentially as a neutral phenomenon, to be evaluated ethically according to the way it is used. There is an element of truth in its alleged neutrality in that its assumptions transcend the social settings in which they have been worked out. But its procedures need ethical scrutiny, and these social structures influence its practice so that it easily becomes caught up with militaristic-nationalistic forces, and short-sighted commercial ones which have adverse effects on the environment and, indeed, on human self-understanding; humans and not only animals can be improperly treated.[23]

Warnings reach us from several quarters. A World Alternative to Growth Conference was held in Texas in 1977; the Club of Rome was involved in this. Herman Kahn, who was generally regarded as a technological optimist and certainly no doomsayer, included in a book published in the same year warnings against a cavalier attitude to nature.[24] Peter Singer has coined the unlovely term 'speciesism' to upbraid humans for concentrating on their own species and not bothering about the status of animals.[25] Several writers have come to the conclusion that with respect to our responsibilities for future generations we ought to leave the planet in no worse state than we inherited it.

This is the background against which increased Christian concern for the environment is set. There has been a startling change in theological preoccupation. For much of this century it has been concerned with exploring the understanding of the personal as our best clue to the understanding of the mystery of God. God is thought of as at least personal and as supremely expressed as self-giving love in Jesus Christ. In this approach God is related to the sub-personal in terms of the degree of personal being it exemplifies.[26] This accords with the traditional Christian emphasis that the rest of creation achieves its goal by being at the service of mankind (who must not abuse it), and in doing so manifests the goodness of God. However James Gustafson after decades of distinguished work in Christian Ethics has in his recent two-volume work arrived at a very austere doctrine of God in relation to human beings.[27] There is no privileged place for humans in creation: they are subordinate to the cosmos. The universe is not ordered to human ends. We need a courageous resignation to, and co-operation with, the cosmos on which humanity depends, or, in Gustafson's phrase, 'the powers that bear down upon us and sustain us'. The powers that create human life also destroy it. Nature and God will not be defied; death comes to all, whether we consent or not. This seems to be a revival of pre-Christian Stoic ethics which called men to conform to and conserve nature. The Stoics believed there was a shared logos underlying the order of nature and the rationality of human experience, and therefore they adopted a piety towards nature according to which we should harmonize our human actions with the order of nature. But how to tell when we have correctly interpreted nature? That cannot be settled by ecology. It is a matter of a faith or a philosophy, and here the Judaeo-Christian faith is potentially much more fruitful than Stoicism.

The most useful discussion of this for Christians is by Robin Attfield.[28] One of his aims is to show, against those who demand a new environmental ethic, that the Judaeo-Christian traditional doctrine of stewardship has adequate resources to deal with these issues. He discusses the sub-human realm in some detail, and asks whether our approach to it is too human-centred. How far do our moral responsibilities include animals, trees and plants? What of rivers and rocks? And eco-systems, and the entire biosphere? What weight should we give to them? He is disposed to allow more to these than does the other most useful book, that of John Passmore, who is quite clear that humans and nature do not form one community.[29]

Where in these discussions do those of the WCC on the Integrity of Creation fit? They are only at the earliest stages, and are looking towards a substantial and well-prepared international consultation on the theme in 1990. But there are references in some of the provisional documents which indicate problems ahead. I mention some examples.

1. References to an 'ecological balance' and to a 'global society, which will be ultimately sustainable in view of ecological limits and technology'. This suggests a static view. Of course there could be human actions which had such untoward ecological effects as to harm or even go far to destroy humanity. However short of this there is scope for much flexibility and dynamism, and it is here that decisions have to be made. Similarly the world 'ultimately' conceals the problem. Since the universe is finite there must be some limits, as I mentioned when referring to the Club of Rome's first report, but our powers of forecasting are so limited that we have very little idea what these limits are. There is much too static and fixed an idea of nature hidden in these words.

2. The right of each species to flourish. To have rights is to have some moral standing. It is quite true that to limit moral standing to rational autonomous beings (as in the Kantian tradition of moral philosophy) is too restrictive and might properly be termed 'speciesism'. It should certainly be extended to sentient creatures who can suffer or enjoy, be benefited or harmed, as Bentham saw. Some want to extend moral standing to all living things, plants for instance; and some would include the non-living, like rocks. These last two are highly disputable. The level of moral standing would appear to depend upon the extent to which sentient beings have or do not have the conceptual ability to conceive of themselves as distinct entities, with a past and a future. That is why human beings must in some way be an exemplar, as the WCC documents say in places, though they do not co-ordinate this with the other statements we are considering. However humans themselves, as I should contend, do not have *absolute* rights devoid of any contingent circumstances, or clashes with the rights of other humans.[30] How much less do sub-human species? There is no right of each species to flourish. But if, for example, the question is asked, 'Have whales a right to life?', the answer might well be, 'Not absolutely, but more than we used to think!' On the other hand we are told that 'every day one species of animals or plants disappears for ever', and it is implied that this is necessarily deplorable. It is not self-evident that it is.

3. The need for a new work ethic to replace the famous Protestant work ethic. This raises a new problem, too large to enter into here, except for one point. Certainly many features of the Protestant work ethic are obsolete, but at bottom it is concerned with the efficient use (or stewardship) of relatively scarce economic resources compared with the possible alternative uses of them. This is a perennial problem in any society. It is a different issue from that of the integrity of creation, and I suspect has crept in because of unavowed and mistaken assumptions lurking in the background which go back to the original Club of Rome report.

4. The need for 'non-negotiable biblical affirmations'. Much depends on what is expected by this. There may be hidden here

assumptions from the days of the Biblical Theology movement
which strove to weave the different biblical strands and texts into
a unified statement on, for example, 'the biblical doctrine of
work'. In this case it is Nature. The Bible in fact provides varying
raw materials on which to reflect, and out of which Christian
doctrines have come. As already mentioned, changing social and
cultural conditions are the occasion of continued reflection on the
doctrines we have inherited. This is right. Evidence of human
environmental blunders make us look for resources within the
Christian tradition with which to deal with them and lessen the
danger of future ones.

What is now being stressed is that the non-human creation has
more than instrumental value. God enjoys its variety. But it is
another matter to go on to talk of 'adapting man to nature'.
Careful delimitations are required. There is obviously some truth
in it, but it must not obscure the flexibility and creativeness of
humans. There is too easily lurking in such a phrase a sentiment
like 'If God had intended us to fly he would have given us wings.'
Underlying much of the recent Christian discussion of these
issues is the meaning of the apocalyptic biblical language of a
'new heaven and a new earth', and of other apocalyptic passages,
like that from St Paul in Romans 8.16ff., already mentioned.
Some are interpreting biblical texts to mean that the whole world
(cosmos) including nature is to share in the redeeming work of
Christ. John 3.16 is quoted, 'God so loved the world that he gave
his only begotten Son . . .', but the second part of the verse 'that
whosoever believes in him should not perish but have eternal life'
is not quoted. St Paul says that the material world shares in the
same destiny that God's goodness desires for humanity. He looks
to a recreation of the material order and says that the whole
creation is travailing now in birth to bring it about. And it is all
basically the work of God's Spirit. A Faith and Order report says
that resurrection is promised to all creation, for creation
embodies 'God's own finalities'.[31]
What is being said here? Does the Bible give us an alternative
source of knowledge about the future of the universe to that
which we get from the natural sciences? From these we are led to
think of a very long time series in the course of which conditions
of life in the universe will cease to obtain, probably because

through the degradation of energy it will get very cold. Are we to suppose from the Bible that on the contrary there will be an abrupt end to the present time series and an entirely new heaven and earth will be created in which the present creation will be resurrected in a transformed state. Is this what is meant by the phrase 'Christ will come again'? If, however, we are to treat this language as mythical on the grounds that the beginning and end of time are not scientific but mythical concepts, and this is how we view the Genesis creation myths (or sagas, to repeat the term I used earlier), what is the myth of the end, and of the new heaven and new earth saying in terms of our attitude to nature? Historic Christianity clearly involves the belief that humans are intended for fellowship with God and with one another in God beyond the world of time and space whither the exalted Christ has 'gone before'. Is nature to share in this? Here apocalyptic is straining language to the breaking point. A statement like 'the new heaven and the new earth do not destroy but complete the act of creation' is ambiguous where we need clarity.

The trouble lies with apocalyptic language itself, which makes it a dubious basis on which to build a theological and ethical construction for today. It was part of the mental furniture of late Judaism and early Christianity which is of little use to us now.[32] Eschatology, on the other hand, has permanent significance. Apocalyptic is concerned with the 'last things' chronologically (of which we are ignorant) whilst eschatology is concerned with the 'last things' in terms of significance. That is why the coming of the kingdom or rule of God in the ministry of Jesus is regarded by Christians as the inauguration of the 'last things' in significance. There will never be days of more significance in human history, however long it lasts; they give us the clue to the entire panorama of human life and destiny. The church which arose as a result of that ministry is the pilgrim people of God, the conscious agent of the kingdom of God, calling all in every generation to respond to the challenge of the kingdom and to recognize signs of its presence wherever it can be discerned in the multiplicity and variety of human life. Chronologically last events, the concern of Apocalyptic, are of little significance. We do not know and do not need to know about them. Each generation is called to follow, to make decisions as far as it can reasonably foresee, but there is no immanent process in history which guarantees where it is going.

We have a terrestrial hope that humans can improve the qualities and circumstances of human life, but we have no guarantee that improvements once achieved will be maintained by future generations. They may be given a better start by their predecessors but they will have to win their own moral battles. We also have a celestial hope founded on what God has done and is doing as Jesus Christ has led us to understand it.

In a recent study of apocalyptic Christopher Rowland[33] maintains that it is as much concerned with an attempt to understand human existence in the present as with future prediction. It is preoccupied with the unveiling of divine secrets. Its witness in a grim situation that things are not out of control but are in God's hands is permanently valid. This is indeed the case. But it is not peculiar to apocalyptic. And its visions of the fulfilment of the divine purpose whether in history or beyond it (or both) remain open to the difficulties I have mentioned (especially in note 32). It is taken up in some WCC documents because of the influence of Eastern Orthodox theologians, who draw on the work of the early Fathers of the patristic period as supremely relevant today. But behind the thought of many of them is the belief that sin and the Fall were cosmic, and therefore redemption must be cosmic too. This pushes the mystery still further back, where there can be no empirical check, and is in danger of taking theology further and further from human experience.[34]

If it is hard to give meaning to a celestial hope for the sub-human creation, that does not mean that it has no moral status. Human beings are called to exercise responsible stewardship of it. This is what Christian reflection drawing upon biblical materials suggests. We have had enough recent examples of human brashness in blundering about the universe without due care. Stewardship is harder to exercise than we had thought. But it remains the key concept. Only humans can exercise it. It is a mistake to subsume them with the rest of creation. I do not see any reason to alter the essentials of what I wrote a decade ago, which is the substance of the first four sections of this chapter. We need to learn from distortions of the use of stewardship in the past so that we can exercise it more wisely in the present. Natural processes are not infinitely malleable; they need a more careful approach.

WCC documents are at the beginning of spelling out the

significance of the Integrity of Creation. Indeed the Faith and Order report suggests it would be better replaced by the biblical term 'new creation', which brings us back to all the difficulties I have just been discussing. We are told that the integrity of nature is not an all or nothing static concept, but that it has a dynamic sense of wholeness and fulfilment embedded in it. Much is hidden here. If it means that creation is good, as the Genesis saga maintains, we must agree. If it means that we must rejoice in it, as Jesus did with his illustrations of salt, yeast, fruit, seed, wine, oil and water, to name a few of them, we must agree. On the other hand its dark side shares in the mystery of humankind. If it means that it has the same resurrection destiny as humans we must demur. If it means that there is some fixed connection between all the different elements such that any humanly engineered change is ruled out, we must demur once more. If its dynamic character is stressed we have to ask how far this is thought of as built into it, as in the process of evolution, or how far it is properly administered in terms of human purposes.

Time will tell whether the selection of this theme is wise. There are many pitfalls. Meanwhile more work needs to be done on the Just, Participatory and Sustainable Society, particularly with reference to participation. Justice remains in the new formula, so does Sustainable if a caring attitude to nature really does cover what the term Integrity is concerned with; and without care to see that it does it may not. However the WCC Commission on Churches' Participation in Development has pointed out that Participation is not always understood as an integral part of Justice, and this concept could easily be lost. It is important that this unfinished work, difficult as it is and not conducive to easy hopes, should not be set aside and left at its present stage.[35]

Appendix:
God in Creation: a note on Moltmann's Gifford Lectures

Jürgen Moltmann's Gifford Lectures 1984–5 were published shortly after this chapter was written. They are a good example of the way contemporary currents of opinion drive theologians to look at traditional biblical material and doctrines with new questions, and to arrive at new treatments of them. The sub-title, 'An Ecological Doctrine of Creation', and his early remarks make it clear that, although he does not go into detail, a conception of an ecological crisis lies behind the lectures. One element is the effect of a nuclear war, which as an ethical issue is better dealt with in terms of international political relations than in terms of an ethic of nature; and it is this latter that is Moltmann's main concern. He thinks that we are being brought up against limits in nature, and are at the beginning of a life and death struggle for creation on this earth. That may be the case, but it is far from certain that it is necessarily so. Taking for granted an extreme position in this respect is paralleled by an extreme solution of the crisis when he says that 'the only alternative to annihilation is a non-violent, peaceful, world-wide community in solidarity' or, in another similar statement, a network for reciprocal relationships in co-operative communities. Here the influence of Marxist utopianism, as mediated by Ernst Bloch, on Moltmann is clear and unfortunate. Between these two extremes the ethical decisions we have in practice to make in the world of today are elided. On them he has practically nothing to say. Indeed the penultimate paragraph of the lectures reaches the banal conclusion that on Sundays, the ecological day of rest, we should leave our cars at home so that nature, too, can celebrate its sabbath without pollution of the environment.

On the theoretical level there is a vast array of detailed discussion in this very erudite (and very ecumenical) book. Moltmann rightly thinks that 'notions' (his word) in the Bible are not necessarily purely culture-bound but possess an inherent critical potential which can challenge 'the onesidedness of our civilization'. In particular the Creation sagas need interpreting in the light of the messianic note in the New Testament. However this leads him not only to make eschatology central to his exegesis, as indeed a Christian must do, but apocalyptic too. In passing he mentions that humanity may disappear from this planet, but his concentration on the future is on two things; (1) The creation by God of a new heaven and a new earth where there will be an indwelling of the triune God, and both heaven and earth will enter into unhindered and boundless fruitful communication with one another. (2) The kingdom of glory, or God's eternal sabbath, in which the whole creation will find bliss, and where God will dwell entirely and wholly and forever in his creation, and will allow all things he has created to participate in the fullness of his eternal life. Moltmann wants us to let our powers of imagination and fantasy have scope. He himself has certainly done so. But it is hard to see what we are to make of it in terms of living our lives as Christians today. He uses it in fact as a backdrop to the linking of humanity with nature and to a relative denigration of history. Here he moves uncertainly. We are told that history must be brought into harmony with the rhythms of nature. This is the main emphasis. But on the same page it is also said that nature must be moulded into an environment where it can become a home for humans. This is not followed up; and the two statements are not reconciled. In the same vein as the first of them Moltmann says that humans do not confront nature because they are initially to be seen as made in the image of the world rather than the image of God (in Latin *imago mundi* as against *imago dei*). This is a highly dangerous half-truth. He is nervous about any thought of progress in history, and says that 'progress in one group is always at the cost of others', a statement which seems clearly to be false. Why does he take this line? He holds that the messianic future towards which Christians are living is a project, lived for in anticipation, which goes beyond the future we can think of on the basis of our present experience (in Latin the difference between *adventus* and *futurum*). It is not surprising that Moltmann has little to say which bears directly on our present ethical decisions because he has destroyed the basis on which the decisions have to be made. It is indeed true that we have to be ready to discern the entirely new and unexpected, but that is no help in making decisions. These have to be made in the light of our best diagnosis of the present situation and its possibilities.

Moltmann does arrive at one important general insight, that the person does not take priority over the community, a necessary corrective to so much individualistic theology, especially in modern Protestantism, but he does not develop it. In general an over-simplified diagnosis of our ecological situation has sent him off on an exaggerated biblical and doctrinal quest. Stewardship plays no part in the biblical exegesis. And in doctrine there is a one-sided stress on a 'social' Trinity (a doctrine which many Anglicans have favoured in modern times). All except purely formal doctrines of the Trinity run into danger; Moltmann never mentions any involved in his.

These Gifford lectures do throw light on some of the phrases and sentences in the WCC documents as they begin to work on the theme of the Integrity of Creation, but they do nothing to resolve the difficulties in them. Indeed they compound them. They are of course only part of Moltmann's developed theology, of which there are many sides which I have not mentioned here. Most of us have been grateful to him on many occasions; this seems to me a less successful one. Moreover I think the weakness of his theology of hope as a basis for ethical decision-making is endemic to it.

6

Church and Society:
do we need another William Temple?

Efforts to assess the ongoing significance of William Temple for Church and Society do not die down. I made one in 1969,[1] another in 1976,[2] a third in 1981,[3] and this is a fourth attempt. The year 1984 marked the fortieth anniversary of his death and this produced an assessment by David Nicholls in the journal *Crucible*[4] which has provoked my further reflections. Temple also plays a large part in E. R. Norman's substantial survey, *Church and Society in England, 1770–1970*.[5]

His death at the comparatively early age of sixty-three was widely regarded as a disaster. Soon his name came to be commemorated. There is a William Temple Church in Manchester; there is a William Temple Association which is a small body of graduates concerned to make an effective Christian lay contribution to society, and to be lay theologians in order to make it; and there is the William Temple Foundation. This was formerly William Temple College, the nearest equivalent which we have had in this country to a 'lay academy' on the lines established after the war by the Lutheran Church in West Germany.[6] Now it is a social action research unit housed in the Business School of Manchester University, with a network of resource persons all over the country.

Temple has been described as the most variously distinguished Archbishop of Canterbury since Anselm. He was certainly the first to become both a national and world leader. In this country he was better known and listened to by the general public than any previous Archbishop of York or Canterbury in modern times. Now his name has faded from the general public, whilst in the church it is residually known but without any clear idea for what he is honoured.

Among those who know most about him, his outstanding qualities are generally acknowledged. But is he still relevant today? Are we in need of his contribution? Some years ago I came to the conclusion that just because he faced so strongly the issues of his own time we no longer need to turn to his books as an indispensable source. Indeed I find the philosophical idiom of the first two of his three main theological books, *Mens Creatrix* (1917) and *Christus Veritas* (1924) so alien as to be almost unreadable; and his uncritical approach to the Fourth Gospel a hindrance to appropriating the many fine thoughts in his *Readings in St John's Gospel* (1939 and 1940).[7] Rather it is his basic stance, and the method he developed and arrived at in Christian social ethics, which are permanently important. This has become evident since we have had something of a relapse in these respects since his death.

In a tribute shortly after Temple's death Reinhold Niebuhr wrote that he 'was able to relate the ultimate insights of religion about the human situation to the immediate necessities of political justice and the proximate possibilities of a just social order more vitally and creatively than any other modern Christian leader'.[8] We might exempt Niebuhr himself from the last six words; in other respects I think it is a broadly fair verdict. If Temple had had the time in the last years of his life better to integrate and revise the various strands in his thought it would be an unequivocally fair verdict. Alas, however, his last years were lived under the enormous pressures of a world war.

David Nicholl's article does not support this verdict. The tone of Temple's writings is said to be 'a somewhat uncritical "left-of-centre" statism'. In relation to the political events of his day he 'usually adopted a moderate position which was generally calculated to reinforce the *status quo*'. In *Christianity and Social Order* this 'generally conservative position' is clearly embodied:[9] 'By insisting that Christians, as such, should be concerned with principles rather than with policies he ensured that nothing they said, as such, would be likely to have much immediate effect.' The idea of a general interest or common good which it should be the object of public policy to realize he never doubted, and it went together with the assumption that 'there are no basic conflicts of interest in society and that with a bit of good sense and Christian charity, adjustments can be made which will satisfy all parties'.[10]

Nicholls maintains that such thoughts merely echo the liberal capitalism of many Western countries where 'class conflict has been contained by paternalistic legislation, mitigating the harsher consequences of the capitalist system, combined with a subtle manipulation of political and cultural institutions'. This last remark is an echo of the thought of Marcuse, who was one of the main prophets of the student activists of 1969–71. This is not the occasion to discuss Marcuse, but as far as Temple is concerned the grain of truth in Nicholl's article is outweighed by the error.

Take the point about the common good. Temple certainly held to the concept. It goes back far beyond the Oxford idealist philosophy in which he was reared to at least the weighty political philosophy of Thomas Aquinas. But whereas there had tended to be an assumption in the Thomist approach that, rightly understood, all legitimate claims in society can be met and there is no fundamental conflict of interests, Temple was well aware that there are such conflicts. It was the way he held together both the concept of the common good and the conflicts of interests in society that prompted Niebuhr's praise of him.[11] On the question of the role of principles and how the gap between them and detailed policies can be bridged I shall have an analysis to make shortly. Before that I think some words on the continuities and changes in Temple's social theology are needed.

Temple moved in basic position from a relatively utopian to a relatively realistic outlook. In 1908 he could refer to socialism as the economic realization of the Christian gospel,[12] and in 1912 write of England as a potential province of the kingdom of God. This is both theologically and politically inadequate. Theologically it fails to take account of the fact that Christians live in two kingdoms (or cities), the kingdom of God and the kingdom (or structures) of the world. The kingdom of God is always in search of political and social expression, and always challenging with its radical implications existing political and social structures. Politically it fails to distinguish between the ideologies which accompany political parties and their particular programmes (as John XXIII did so delicately in the Encyclical *Pacem in Terris* in the course of making room for a less negative attitude of Roman Catholicism to Marxism). The ideology behind monetarism, for instance, is that of 'possessive individualism', which needs to be brought under theological criticism, as do all ideologies, for they often serve as quasi-religions. Criticism of particular monetarist policies is not the same thing, in that it involves at some point technical analysis and assessments in which Christians as such have no special competence. There is however a middle area where ideology and policy are difficult to separate, to which I shall return; this both provides opportunities and occasions difficulties. But the fact that there is a grey area in between does not negate the fact that there is a difference between ideology and policy.

In the 1930s Temple moved to a more realistic position. The economic crash of 1929 produced mass unemployment. Connected with it was the rise of totalitarianism in Europe. And the influence of Reinhold Niebuhr on Temple increased throughout that decade. Related to this was the very thorough international study work organized by Dr J. H. Oldham[13] for the ecumenical 'Life and Work' Conference at Oxford in 1937 on 'Church, Community and State', into which Temple was drawn, together with many of the leading theologians of the day. In his Gifford Lectures, *Nature, Man and God* (1934), Temple tried to steal the Marxists' clothes by using the term 'dialectical', and by his often quoted remark that Christianity is 'the most avowedly materialistic of all the great religions' (because of its doctrine of Incarnation).[14] But he never came seriously to grips with Marxism. However he did begin to develop a theology of power in relating love to justice, especially in working out the bearing of the apparent powerlessness of Jesus on the structures of power in society. This came out in his treatment of the nature and authority of the state, and within that to his view of pacifism, which among other things he held to be without a significant doctrine of the state.[15] By 1934 he saw that conflicts of interests are perennial in society. They occur, for instance, in industry between those who in the end manage and those who in the end are managed (except in a workers' co-operative small enough not to need any devolution). He saw that various groups in society are represented by those who are trustees for their interests and cannot behave as if they were isolated individuals. Hence the 'law of love' bears indirectly on group relationships, where the aim must be that groups show enough transcendence over their immediate interests to allow for the interests of other groups and arrive at some approximate justice between them. This is the vocabulary of the common good. It led Temple to see that there is a need for structures in society which harness the motive of self-interest to the common good, and to his remark that 'the art of government in fact is the art of so ordering life that self-interest prompts what justice demands'.[16] It cannot be left to the 'invisible hand' of Adam Smith's *laissez-faire* society. He re-marked that it is no use having a Christian view of society which requires devoted Christians to make it work.

Where did Temple stand in relation to the various Christian Socialist groups in England in the traumatic decade of the 1930s? Most of them looked back for inspiration to F. D. Maurice, and most of them advanced a rather simplistic three-pronged attack on capitalism. They condemned it: (1) because they thought competition itself to be unchristian; (2) because they were suspicious of profit and said production should be for use and not profit; (3) because they advocated the public and not the private ownership of the means of production. These criticisms do not face the basic economic problem of the allocation of relatively scarce resources which all societies have to solve. Competition, and profit as a directive (not necessarily as an incentive), in other words a free market, is probably the best human device for dealing with this problem, provided it is not elevated into some kind of basic 'law of nature' or overall philosophy of how human beings should relate to one another, and provided that it is set to work within social structures which exemplify a basic fairness in meeting basic human needs. Temple shared many of these traditional socialist Christian attitudes and never did get basic economic concepts sorted out; that is the reason for some unwise utterances on monetary matters in his last two years of life, for instance in a lecture to the Bank Officers' Guild. He thought economic 'laws' are based on experience, and did not realize that the free market is an ideal model, an heuristic device; it is an abstraction which runs into difficulties when brought to bear on the realities of human experiences in economic life. This is the reason for the divergencies of practical recommendations among economists. The one basic fact of human experience is the relative scarcity of resources available to human beings compared with the possible alternative uses of them and between which a choice has to be made.[17]

As we have seen, however, a new realism came into Temple's

thinking alongside his previous attitudes. This meant that he did not fit into any of the existing Christian Socialist groups. The Catholic Crusade, led by Conrad Noel, on the basis of 'the fatherhood of God, the brotherhood of man and the sacramental principle' (an interesting example of liberal Protestant influence on Anglican Catholic theology), took Communist ideals for realities in Stalinist Russia, as did Hewlett Johnson, the 'red' Dean of Canterbury. The Order of the Church Militant split from the Catholic Crusade because it favoured Trotsky rather than Stalin. The Socialist Christian League had some splendid leaders (of whom Donald Soper is still with us), and was less clerical, but it shared the over-simple critique of capitalism. The Christian Left, which lived in the ambience of the Left Book Club, had no relation to F. D. Maurice, but took a broadly Marxist analysis and held that socialism was standing for and would achieve what the church should really be about. The Christendom Group had abandoned socialism as being as unsatisfactory as capitalism, and was engaged in promulgating a 'Christian' social order of a highly theoretical kind which, when it ever came down to earth, revealed some nostalgia for a pre-industrial society, and a total ignorance of economics. Behind this position lay a view of Natural Law which had developed in Roman Catholic Moral Theology from the period of the Counter-Reformation, and which nearly all the Roman Catholic text books of Moral Theology over the past generation have abandoned, though it is still found in the Curia. There was an informal network of those who agreed with Reinhold Niebuhr that it was necessary to move to the Left in politics, not least because it looked in 1932 as if capitalism was breaking down, and to the Right in theology; that is to say from the mixture of liberal Protestant and Anglican incarnationalist theology of an evolutionary progressive kind which dominated the COPEC Conference of 1924,[18] to a more Augustinian way of thinking which was alert to the subtle corruptions which feed on human achievements and are much more dangerous than various gross sins, and also to the intransigencies of group behaviour with which governments have to work.[19] Temple in the 1930s seemed nearest to this last position. It is the one that underlay much of the preparation for the Oxford Conference of 1937, previously mentioned, and was expressed in the critique of capitalist economies in the report of the third section of that Conference.[20]

However Temple did not entirely fit in here. He never shed elements from the key influences which had formed him as a young man – Thomas Arnold, Robert Browning, F. D. Maurice, Edward Caird, Charles Gore and, of course, Plato! In his last years he began to use the vocabulary of Natural Law. We can see that it could be congenial to him because traditionally it was rooted in a theistic metaphysic, though it need not be. He was not uncritical of it. He thought it was too fixed in conception and did not allow enough for novelty; nor did it allow enough for the conditioned character of moral reasoning, nor for the power of sin, so that an absolute character is given to contingent moral judgments, and the ambiguities of history with its conflicts of power are smoothed over.

The Malvern Converence of 1941, which he sponsored and chaired, was organized by a combination of those in the Christendom tradition and those in the traditional Christian socialist tradition.[21] They did not agree with one another, and all Temple's well known skills as a Chairman and synthesizer could not rescue it from incoherence. Neither of the two groups paid attention to any ecumenical thought on these matters going on in Britain or outside it; there is no reference at all to the preparatory essays for the Oxford Conference or to the Conference itself.

As we have said, pressures of war prevented Temple from integrating the strains in his social theology, or from thoroughly working out his method in Christian social ethics, which we are about to consider. His Penguin book, *Christianity and Social Order* (1941) is still important. Three successive stages of Temple's social theology are found together in it, the older Christian Social Union and COPEC style of thinking, the later Niebuhrian realism, and the later still Natural Law mode of thought. Opinions are divided as to which, or whether any one, is dominant. Doubtless we are all tempted to latch on to what we most approve. In my judgment the Niebuhrian strand is the strongest. Common to them all is a basic criticism of the individualism of capitalist ideology.

The continuity which underlies these changes of emphasis in Temple's social theology is his stress both on the centrality of the worth of each person and on that of the social structures within which full personhood is realized. Person and community go together. This may seem obvious. But it is in fact far removed from nineteenth-century individualism which has so powerfully influenced Christian thinking. It is an indication of how far there has been a regression since Temple that the Call to the Nation of the Archbishops of Canterbury and York in 1975 was based on two questions; (1) what kind of society do we want? (ii) what kind of people are needed to create such a society? It omitted a third question, what kind of social structures are needed to form the kind of people we need? Temple would never have made that mistake.

In his method in social ethics Temple began with the traditional root doctrines of the Christian faith, especially the doctrine of the Incarnation. These were not understood by him in a rigid way as if expressed in forms of words devoid of intellectual background and cultural context, but flexibly by one who was self-conscious about the intellectual and cultural situation in which he lived, and increasingly aware of the particular influences of his young manhood, notably Oxford idealist philosophy. Later he began to see these doctrines in a more eschatological dimension, as anyone who ponders on life in the two kingdoms is likely to do. In this respect he is superior to some of the religious utopians we meet today, who think of only one kingdom and regard any thought of two as a sinister dualism, leading to quietism and passivity in the face of injustices. It is true that the doctrine of the two kingdoms can be misinterpreted in this way, but all the classical Christian doctrines have been interpreted in too static a fashion, and have too easily given divine sanction to the existing social order. However this has not been characteristic of those in the Ecumenical Movement who have thought through the problems of life in the two kingdoms, and Temple's thinking drew upon them as he grew older.

From basic Christian doctrines Temple moved to what he called 'primary principles' which derive necessarily from Christian faith. These, as mentioned, express the basic importance of each person and of the structures of relationship in and through which each person should grow to his full stature in community with others. Temple was prone to stress the community of family and nation, but to stress the nation is a mistake. The state is certainly a basic structure, but the nation is a much vaguer concept, and it is important in a century which has seen so much virulent nationalism and the assumption that every group that thinks of itself as a nation should have a separate state, that the notion of nation should be critically examined. Temple never did this. Nation can be better understood under the broader and very real category of culture. Also Temple was prone to omit the structure of economic life in his demarcation, though of course he often wrote about it. All this is to say that his thought on structures when he wrote of 'primary principles' was under-developed. The structures of family, economics, politics and culture were not clearly examined and differentiated.

Temple's next step was to move from primary to 'derivative' principles. In the end he listed these as freedom, social fellowship and service. In his earlier and more utopian period, for instance at the time of the coal crisis leading to the General Strike of 1925, he wrote of the principle of sacrifice. But he was confused between corporate self-sacrifice on behalf of a claim (eg. miners' solidarity in a strike) and corporate self-sacrifice in refusing to make one. Later, under the influence of Niebuhr, he dropped sacrifice from his derivative principles and wrote instead of the necessity of so arranging things that personal and group (including national) self-interest would promote social and international justice. But he never ceased to call for endurance in the cause of justice.[22] Strangely enough, in writing of fellowship and the respect for each person he did not develop thoughts on equality, in spite of his friendship with R. H. Tawney. If each person is to be enabled to play as responsible a part as possible in the network of human relationships which make us human, one would think that this is hindered by great disparities of wealth and by any lack of the basic provisions in life which one's society assumes as a norm in social intercourse. In many ways the Liberty, Equality and Fraternity of the French Revolution, although derived from the Enlightenment (and concealing the Christian influences in their background) can be regarded as 'derivative principles' from the gospel.

These derivative principles have an eschatologically radical note. They are likely to lead us to a negative judgment on the *status quo*, because we are not likely to be satisfied with any existing attempt to embody them. This distances Temple from the largely static and conservative tendency in traditional Christian social thinking, with its strong emphasis on law and order. Giles Ecclestone, a former Secretary of the Board for Social Responsibility of the General Synod of the Church of England has written of the basic tradition of 'critical solidarity' of the church with the government of the day.[23] Narrowly interpreted, Temple would fit in with this because he believed order to be the basic necessity of social life. But in a wider sense there has been much more emphasis in the church on the solidarity than on the criticism since the Reformation, and Temple does not fit in with that.

There is some difference in emphasis between Temple and Niebuhr on the relation of love and justice. Social justice is the realm of claim and counter-claim, of *suum cuique* or rendering to every person his due. How does one decide what is due? It is a weakness of Temple that he never discusses the three main criteria, rights, deserts or needs, though it is clear that his main stress is in fact on needs. To Niebuhr justice and love are in tension because love to him is essentially self-sacrificial, and to him there are elements of self-interest in the sense of mutuality between persons and groups even though it allows enough transcendence of interests to make possible a pursuit of justice and the common good. Temple stresses more the element of love in the sense of mutuality. Maybe the truth is more with Temple on this point. Niebuhr overstresses the heedlessness of sacrificial love. If it is really concerned for the good of the other the question is what course of action is best likely to promote this. It is the good of the other, not the sacrifice of the self, which is the key question. Interests can coincide: they do not always conflict. Mutuality and self-sacrifice are not necessarily in contradiction. Both add a transcendent element to justice, which cannot replace love nor exhaust it. There can be a smooth continuity between them; and there can be fearful dilemmas between them.

We have mentioned primary and derivative principles. But neither the church nor the Christian can stop there. How can we move from them to something more detailed and specific? Temple thought that it might be possible to reach some agreement at a middle level between them. It is easy to agree on the principles; but they can appear merely bland. The rub comes when they are brought to bear on particular issues. Detailed policies involve appraisals of evidence and estimates of the likely effects of different possible lines of action, so that it is unlikely, except in remarkably clear-cut cases, that Christians will come to the same conclusions even if they are committed to the same principles. However they might agree on defining significant issues, and on the general direction in which society should move, without agreeing on which detailed policy is most likely to move matters in the desired direction. This middle ground Temple called that of 'middle axioms'. It was a term which first occurred in the proceedings of the COPEC Conference of 1924,[24] and was taken up by Dr J. H. Oldham and others in the preparatory work for the Oxford Conference of 1937, and again after the war. It is not a happy term (any more than Natural Law is), for it suggests a logically deductive exercise which is far from what is intended. In order to arrive at a middle axiom it is necessary to bring the theologically grounded principles along-side an empirical enquiry into a contemporary issue. This involves drawing upon all relevant available experience of the problem in question, and is best done by group work. Ideological disagreement on interpreting 'facts' and evaluating tendencies may be so great that no agreed middle axiom is possible. But if some consensus does emerge it is a help in creating an informed Christian opinion, which may then feed its influence into the body politic. To take an instance, there was a considerable consensus among Christians after 1945 about the aims of the Welfare State which helped to establish it. That has now been eroded and the question has to be worked at afresh. This is the way the Ecumenical Movement has for the most part worked in the field of social ethics, though it has not clearly spelled it out; and since the Pastoral Constitution of Vatican II, *Gaudium et Spes*, a similar way of working has begun to develop in the Roman Catholic Church. The work of the Roman Catholic bishops of the USA in the areas of nuclear warfare and economic life are notable examples.[25]

If ideological and other differences of interpretation prove an insuperable barrier to agreement at a middle level, it is at least useful to list the serious questions which Christians who take different views put to each other. In order to achieve anything in the political realm it is necessary to be committed to groups and to policies. If one is led to listen to the criticism of Christians who have different commitments it sharpens one's awareness and diminishes the element of fanaticism to which the political realm is prone. And if this probing leads to further insights which society is tempted to ignore or has not realized, that is a further Christian contribution to the body politic.[26]

If a sufficient agreement is reached at this middle level (it need not be unanimous, something that rarely happens), it is a very appropriate level for church pronouncements. Practical action, however, must be specific. The churches themselves have of course to be specific in the handling of people and resources in their own internal life, and need watching that their actions do not belie their sentiments. But Temple was always clear that the primary Christian influence must be brought to bear by lay Christians in their families, at work and as citizens. In the last two of these areas the lay Christian is most likely to find himself alongside fellow human beings in structures which cannot depend for their working on convinced Christians. We find in them those of many faiths and none, and we must use our influence to express God's concern for human good in the way they work. Temple realized this, but was not consistent in his expression of the place of 'natural' morality in Christian thought. At times, especially when writing about education, he was liable to pose the antithesis 'either religious and Christian or sceptical and atheist', which fails to allow for a 'natural' morality of the common good, whether held by Christians, adherents of other religious faiths or the secular humanist faith.

Temple was still moving with one part of himself within the parameters of Christendom thinking, at least until 1939. Had he lived longer he would have had to come to terms with the plural society of today. Of course there have been other changes of great significance since his death, amid the many continuities. There has been a vast rise in living standards in one-third of the world, but Beveridge's five giants of Want, Idleness, Disease, Ignorance and Squalor are still much in evidence there, whilst in two-thirds of the world they remain endemic. Inflation worries us as well as unemployment. The invention and development of nuclear weapons has raised in a more central form the question of how the peoples of the world are to live together in some tolerable harmony and not destroy themselves; and within this perspective the role of other world religions and the attitude of Christians to them is raised as a matter of urgency. In the churches the role of the laity is slowly coming to the fore, both liturgically in worship and in life and witness. Within this the feminist movement has begun to make a serious impact for the first time since the Suffragette movement.[27] Temple died before the churches had launched on industrial mission. New theological movements have come. Indeed 'death of God' theology has come and gone. There has been Bonhoeffer's 'man come of age', political and liberation theologies, and the Theology of Hope, which in different ways have stressed the 'established disorder' and put question marks against the *status quo*. Environmental issues have also come to the fore. So have questions of bio-ethics since the cracking of the genetical code by Crick and Watson. And the morality of the treatment of animals has been highlighted.

These are perhaps the main changes since Temple's day, but of course they could well be elaborated and extended. If Temple's general approach to Christian social ethics is sound, as I think it is, he would have the tools to deal with them. The basic criticisms advanced do not seem to me well founded. Criticisms of detail, and of lack of consistency or finished expression, are another matter. These must be accepted. Apart from David Nicholl's article the chief criticism comes from those who in one way or another want to move from Bible-based doctrines to the experiences and detailed decisions in the world today without the intermediary steps worked out by Temple. I do not think this is possible. In practice those who do this seem inescapably arbitrary about what they draw from the Bible, or they take over some secular analysis of the world without a sufficient theological critique of it. Either they ignore the social sciences or they accept some among varied expert evidence uncritically. Temple's procedure is better, even though he did not follow it consistently and it needs developing.

E. R. Norman has said that Temple was fortunate in dying just as some of his ideas were to be recognized as obsolete.[28] This is not a percipient verdict. It is too vague to be illuminating. Which ideas and who began to think so? On the contrary, the element of late nineteenth-century Oxford idealism in his thought had been recognized as obsolete for a long time, and Temple had acknowledged it in an article in *Theology* in November 1939. The essential corporateness of human life is better expressed in a doctrine of the Orders of Creation. In important ways concerning Church and Society he was just coming in to his own when he died. In his lifetime he had to spend much time in patiently explaining why the church must 'interfere' in this area (to use a pejorative term often employed). He had to do so in *Christianity and Social Order*. This came to be widely granted. It is only in the last few years that we have had a recrudencence of this blinkered objection and have had to argue against it afresh. His method of tackling questions of social ethics was promising. His basic stance was admirable. We need to develop in our time more thoroughly and consistently what he was trying to do in his.

*Christian Ethics
and the Economic Order*

7

The End of the Protestant Work Ethic?

The nature and role of the Protestant Work Ethic has been a prominent feature of religious and social thought ever since Max Weber's study of it was first published in Germany in 1904.[1] I intend to do no more than mention the salient points concerning its origin and development before considering where we stand with respect to it to-day, at a time when many are saying that rapid technological changes mean that we shall never see full employment again.

I

The Protestant Work Ethic was born at the heart of that complex theological, social and economic movement which we call the Reformation. Both Luther and Calvin made fundamental contributions to it. To understand what they were it is necessary to go back to the New Testament.

The Christian church had not found it easy to live with the really radical elements in the ethical teaching of Jesus, much of it found in the Sermon on the Mount. It still does not.[2] The process of redaction of the gospels was complex; the end product of it in the case of St Matthew's Gospel is a collection of the ethical teachings of Jesus collected in chapters 5 to 7. There are several different strands in it. In the case of one, which includes the Golden Rule,[3] there is no great difficulty in understanding its cogency, even though we are all of us conscious that in practice we incline to weigh ethical issues in scales weighted towards our own advantage, and not to follow the universalizability which is implicit in that Rule. But some strands in Jesus' teaching are much more radical. They enjoin absolute obedience to highly paradoxical commands, absolute trust, and absolute sincerity.

In the case of absolute obedience, for example, there is to be no resentment against injuries, but forgiveness without limit, which is what seventy times seven or 490 times amounts to.[4] Disciples are to follow this teaching on the sole grounds that this is how God behaves towards them. There is no suggestion that it will be a successful policy in securing repentance from those who have wronged us.[5] Exactly the same applies to the injunction to love our enemies. It is of course possible that we may win them over by doing so, but nothing is said about whether we will or we will not. The only reason for loving them is that this is how God loves us, the unjust as well as the just.[6] As to absolute trust there is the beautiful passage against anxiety as a sign that we do not really trust God,[7] together with the warning that wealth is a particular source of anxiety, and that we should not seek security through possessions.[8] As to absolute sincerity there is the passage on alms-giving and on prayer and fasting,[9] together with warnings against the subtle self-love of good people. Jesus called them hypocrites. The parable of the Pharisee and the tax gatherer epitomizes this point.[10]

All this radical teaching is not according to a commonsense ethic of doing good turns to those who do good turns to you. On the whole the world acknowledges this ethic and to a considerable extent follows it. It is fortunate that it does so, otherwise it would be hard for human societies to flourish. But this element in Jesus' teaching cuts right through an ethic of reciprocity. It *hopes*, of course, for a response in return, but it does not *depend* on getting one. It does not give up if it does not get one. Why should Christians follow such a paradoxical ethic? Simply, according to Jesus, because this is how God in his graciousness acts towards us; towards humanity as a whole. That is why it is the ethic of the kingdom of God.

But how does it relate to the commonsense world in which we live? It does seem gloriously right. That is how life ought to be lived. Yet it seems 'out of this world'. It was because of this that Reinhold Niebuhr wrote of it as an 'impossible possibility'.[11] He meant by that phrase to capture the paradox that it is both the way life ought to be lived and yet it is impossible completely to fulfil it. We cannot do so even in our immediate personal relationships, still less in collective ones. In Jesus' own case it led him to the Cross. It remains a transcendent challenge. The result of entering more fully into what Jesus meant by love will be to see further reaches of it, and greater challenges than we had hitherto imagined.

The church found this strand in Jesus' teaching hard to understand and to live with. Could it mean what it appeared to mean? Various methods of exegesis developed, all with the effect of modifying its radicalness as far as the everyday life of the everyday believer was concerned.[12] One of these became highly developed by the Middle Ages. This was the doctrine of the 'double standard'. Jesus' ethic was split into two; the precepts (*praecepta evangelica*) which applied to all Christians and the counsels of perfection (*consilia evangelica*) which applied only to a minority specially called to follow them. These are the counsels of poverty, chastity and obedience. Chastity meant celibacy, because it presupposed that marriage, though laudable, was a state inferior to the celibate. Those who followed the counsels were termed Religious with a capital R, and were mostly found in monasteries and nunneries. This differentiation was retained in Catholic circles until recently, but in the Roman Catholic Church it is unusual since the Second Vatican Council to find the call to the Religious life, which remains a very necessary one in the life of the church, presented on these grounds. The effect of this division was neatly to siphon off the radical element in Jesus' ethical teaching into a channel designed for a small minority of believers. It was like an Honours and Pass course in Christian living.

It was this which Luther broke wide open. He denied the doctrine of the double standard and, as has often been pointed out, drove the asceticism of the monastery into the market place. He made a great deal of St Paul's doctrine of the calling (German *Beruf*), especially in I Corinthians. There St Paul uses the word in two senses. A Christian is primarily called to be a follower of Christ,[13] as Paul himself was called to be an apostle;[14] but he also uses the term of the Christian's daily work.[15] From this Luther drew momentous conclusions. Daily work is the place where the asceticism of Christian obedience is to be practised. There is no higher calling than that. If one is a cobbler, one is a Christ to one's neighbour if one cobbles his shoes well. The home is also a key place of Christian obedience. These contexts of obedience, however, are also our Cross. God puts us in these basic structures, such as work, in order to *make* us serve one another. Left to our own devices we should pursue our own selfish ends, and the basic human co-operation needed for social order would not be possible. We are not to be preoccupied with anxious introspection about our own sanctification. That is a by-product of getting on with our daily work diligently under God, and thus serving our neighbour.[16]

The state is another divine order. In the state it is necessary for some to take on public office. The office is a role which we must fulfil in its own terms, again as a way of serving our neighbour. The radical Christian ethic does not apply directly to life in the orders, it applies within the church. There are two divine realms; one of God's right hand – of love, mercy and forgiveness – and the other of his left hand – of judgment, wrath and punishment. This doctrine of the two realms, which has New Testament roots, and a foreshadowing in the course of previous Christian history, notably St Augustine's two cities, has creative possibilities. But it was in fact used negatively and defensively in Lutheran ethics until very recently.[17]

In Luther himself the doctrine of the calling was interpreted in a static way. He lived at a time when the forces of merchant capitalism were spreading beyond the Italian city-states and dissolving the late medieval feudal order. The process was speeded by the influx of bullion from the New World, as a result of the Portuguese and Spanish conquests. The upshot was a large-scale inflation. Inflations are powerful dissolvents of established social orders. No one understood what was happening. Certainly Luther did not. Everyone blamed others. Luther's own social attitude was medieval. He had a fear of social change. It was far on in the history of the world. The best one could hope for was that God would preserve the present order from disintegration until the End. There was no hope of improving it. Change could only be for the worse. Everyone should fulfil his vocation in the state of life in which he finds himself.[18] One's social duty is obedience. If rulers are evil one must suffer.

Calvin has a much more dynamic outlook, perhaps because of his milieu, the city-state of Geneva. Many have thought that with a theology of Double Predestination Calvinism ought consistently to have had a passive outlook. But not at all. This is how it worked out. The sovereignty of God is the foundation of Calvin's theology. The aim of each individual and of society is to glorify God. In the words of the Shorter Catechism, man's chief end is 'to glorify God and enjoy him for ever'. God has arranged the world to suit this aim. To glorify God in the world involves disciplined work in it. Any diversion from this is idolatry. There is a certain suspicion of amusements as distractions unless they make one more fit for work. There was an attack on holy days as holidays. However, if one's salvation or damnation is predestined, is there any way by which one may have an assurance as to where one stands? A source of assurance is the ability to perform good works. By an intra-worldly asceticism, by labouring in the world without worldliness to the greater glory of God, one can make one's calling and election sure. It involves discipline, self-examination, sobriety and obedience to God's laws. Unlike Luther, who saw only two uses of the law, pedagogical (to convict of sin) and political (to restrain human sinfulness in living in the Orders of Creation), Calvin taught a third use of the law, didactic. He held that it was the duty of the two divine agencies, church and state, to establish a discipline in the lives of believers, as church folk on the one hand and citizens on the other. Together they should ensure that God's laws are followed.[19] A Christendom situation was presumed. Hence the rigour of con-trol attempted in Geneva, much fiercer than any in the Middle Ages.

One economic effect of a doctrine of responsible stewardship which went with this, of hard work together with austerity and a frown on luxury spending, was an emphasis on thrift. Thrift meant saving. Saving led to accumulation, and then to investment; exactly what the burgeoning merchant capitalism required. The converse, poverty, was thought of as usually due to personal failings; when it was not it was a duty of charity on the part of others to relieve it.

Weber's thesis is that there was an 'elective affinity' between the overall motivation in Calvinism with respect to daily work, including the disciplined and austere pursuit of gain, and the attitude appropriate to the growth of capitalism. Contemporaries noted how much more prosperous were Protestant countries, except Scotland, than Roman Catholic ones. The economic centre of Europe moved from the Italian city-states to Antwerp and then, with the Industrial Revolution, to Britain. Weber's aim was to show the part played by the Calvinist ethic in this. He never suggested that it 'caused' the rise of capitalism, still less that he was giving a 'spiritual' explanation of it as against a Marxist 'material-ist' one. He argued merely that Calvinism contributed an outlook from which elements highly congenial to capitalism could be drawn by Christians in that tradition, and that they were drawn, and were influential. In fact Weber's thesis if anything streng-thened a stress on the importance of economic factors. For there was a difference between Calvin and the Calvinism of a century or more later. Calvin had more awareness than Luther of what was happening in society, and he had the courage to break away from medieval presuppositions which led both to the banning of interest on loans and to sophistries in getting round the ban. He cautiously agreed to interest at the rate of 5 per cent per year, and later to 6⅔ per cent. But he was not a friend of capitalism as such, and it could not have flourished for long under the restrictions imposed in Geneva. However, much of Weber's evidence came from the century after Calvin, for instance from Richard Baxter, and even from Benjamin Franklin in the century after that. Elements in Calvinism congenial to capitalism had been utilized, and those not congenial were not stressed. Capitalism used Calvinists, who on the whole were willing victims.[20]

The upshot of the traditional Protestant Work Ethic is that work is 'natural' to man. But it is more than a natural necessity. It is to the Christian a sign of election, a discipline against temptation and an opportunity for charity. Clearly if we have moved into an era where full employment is no longer a possibility, the Protestant Work Ethic has become otiose. Before discussing the present situation we turn briefly to consider what has happened to it in Britain since the end of the seventeenth century.

II

The eighteenth century saw the beginning of the transformation of Britain by first the agricultural and then the technological and industrial changes which, in comparison with the previous rate of change in society, have aptly been called Revolutions. The prevailing mercantilist, nationalist economic ideas were eroded. More spacious intellectual and economic horizons opened. Christian theology played a part. Clergy were prominent in developing the discipline of political economy. The universalist element in the Christian faith led to the teaching that it was impossible to believe that God could have created a universe in which one country could prosper only at the expense of others. This was an argument against mercantilism.[21] A more deistic attitude underlay the theory of the free market as Adam Smith developed it, with its philosophy of possessive individualism and the notion of an 'invisible hand' which would ensure that decisions in the market made independently by millions of people aiming to maximize their own interests resulted in a common good which none of them had had in mind. The Christian faith also preached private benevolence to deal with the casualties of an economic system envisaged as a vast, impersonal machine. It was the century of innumerable Charity Sermons. It also added a new element in Christian teaching in John Wesley's Sermon 44 on 'The Use of Money'. The theme of the sermon is, Get all you can, Save all you can, Give all you can. It shews in an astonishing way how much the Protestant Work Ethic had superseded centuries of Christian teaching from the early Fathers to the end of the seventeenth century. It is impossible to imagine a leading churchman in a previous age telling his hearers to 'Get all you can'; still less 'Save all you can'. Here is the pre-eminent capitalist virtue of saving, provided it is invested in some way and not kept hidden in a sock, erected into a basic Christian duty. 'Give all you can' is also a new theme. In previous ages (leaving aside communities separated in various ways from the world who had possessions in common), when society exhibited a relatively fixed hierarchy, the usual Christian teaching on giving had been that one was entitled to whatever was necessary to keep one in the status in society in which one found oneself; beyond that any superfluity was due to the poor as a matter of justice and not of charity. Wesley's doctrine appears far more radical. 'Give all you can' has no qualification. He himself acted on it, and gave away most of his resources. Most of those who heard him paid attention to the first two of his injunctions more than to the third. There is no social ethic in Wesley, though of course there is a private one. Wesley ruled out any getting or saving which is not honestly come by. But the social results are left entirely to personal decision. There is no sense of the corporate structures within which the getting and saving takes place, or of corporate responsibility in distributing wealth. Most of us would agree that if it were left to our sole discretion how much of our income we would surrender for corporate purposes we would never assess ourselves at a rate of tax as high as corporate life requires.

The nineteenth century produced an explosion of production, of population and of thought. Most Christian social thought continued on eighteenth-century lines, with the exception of a new beginning in Social Theology in the Christian Socialist Movement of 1848–54, and social thinking in the last years of the century.[22] With the beginning of Joint Stock legislation the mobilization of savings became much easier, and it was needed to provide the large amounts of capital that the expanding capitalist system required. Thrift remained a key virtue in Protestant thinking. This persisted well into the twentieth century. The parish in Sheffield to which I went as a Deacon had been a prominent working-class parish in an evangelical tradition.[23] Between the wars one of its regular activities was a Monday evening Savings Club. The influence of the church was such that its members used their money more wisely and accumulated more resources than most of their neighbours. So they bettered themselves, and moved out of the parish into more salubrious parts of Sheffield. On a Sunday evening in the summer many would come back to church (before the days of mass TV); but in effect their ties were inevitably and fairly rapidly loosening. The church had seriously eroded its own congregation!

At a more exalted level Quakers exhibited the Protestant and capitalist work ethic at its best. They were models of integrity, diligence and public spirit. Some Quaker firms became household names for this. They also had a strong sense of responsibility for their employees, which was well-intentioned, even if at times subtly paternalistic.

Advocates of the Protestant Work Ethic found themselves in an ambiguous position with regard to the 'idle rich'. Strictly speaking they could hardly approve of them. Yet their savings made an important contribution to the capitalist system. So, if their consumption was not too conspicuous, they were tolerated; and in the last resort even that could be swallowed on the ground that it provided work for others. On the 'idle poor' they were severe. The nineteenth century spent a lot of time discriminating between the deserving and the undeserving poor. The undeserving should be given relief in conditions of such severity and ignominy as to induce them to get out of it as quickly as they could. Hence the policy of 'less eligibility' and the stigma of the Workhouse. It was still powerful when I was a child. The horror of undermining personal responsibility was expressed in the practice of the Charity Organization Society, which worked out careful procedures of self-help to apply when dealing with cases of social distress. There was hardly any allowance made for cyclical factors in economic development, which affected the employment and working conditions of wage earners over which they had no responsibility. In fact the economy developed in roughly a ten-year cycle of booms and slumps. Nor was there much awareness of the effect of environmental factors on human well-being, at least until cholera became a serious threat. That affected rich as well as poor, because it spread, and this was the main impetus behind the development of public health services, and the beginning of the undermining of the pure theory of *laissez faire*. Workers were expected to guard against normal hazards, such as old age, and provide for them. Exceptional hazards, such as blindness, they were not expected to guard against. Private charity should deal with these if all else failed.

One of the best examples of a Christian way of dealing with social misfortunes was worked out by Thomas Chalmers at the Tron Church in Glasgow in the 1820s.[24] The parish was organized into sections for congregational, pastoral supervision. In the case of misfortune, which would be at once known, efforts were made to alleviate the situation by mobilizing resources, first of all self-help if at all possible; failing that, the help of relatives; failing that, neighbour help. If all else failed an appeal was made to the charity of the better off.

The distinction between the deserving and the undeserving poor was blown apart by the Minority Report of the Royal Commission on the Poor Law of 1909. One of the great state documents of this century, it was written by Sidney and Beatrice Webb. No one remembers the Majority Report. The Minority Report lay behind the reforms instituted by the pre-1914 Liberal government, and finally came into its own under the post-1945 Labour government. This produced the outline of the Welfare State, which has had some striking successes. But its benefits were not established at a sufficient level to achieve what the Beveridge Report had intended,[25] so that instead of a small

number who were expected to need uncovenanted help through
what was then called National Assistance (now Supplementary
Benefit), ever larger numbers have had to be dealt with in this
way. Moreover the idea of the Welfare State presupposed a state
which would accept the responsibility for securing full employment. While there would be some unemployment as people
changed jobs, as changes in the economy made it necessary,
there would be no long-term unemployment. For a long time this
was the case. An unemployment rate of 3 per cent is thought in
practice to amount to full employment. For a time the rate was
reduced to 1½ per cent, at which level almost anyone capable of
holding down a job at all has got one. Now unemployment has
soared, especially since the OPEC oil price rise of 1973.[26] Social
service expenditure has been skewed by this. The present
government denies that any government can fulfil the responsibility previously accepted. It argues that if one tries to it will only
make a mess of it, partly by producing an inflation. So the concept
of the Welfare State is being argued out all over again.[27] As part of
this, daily work is inevitably a central part of the discussion.

Remnants of the Protestant Work Ethic, with its horror of being
beholden to anyone else, remain among the elderly. Many are
reluctant to claim benefits to which they are entitled. Some have a
horror of debt. They were brought up to save, and to wait until
they had the money before buying anything, even a house when
there were so many to rent; now there are very few. The world of
Hire Purchase and of the Credit Card is alien to them. Low take-
up of benefits is more of a problem than the attempt to secure
them by fraud. The public is slow to realize this. Periodically
there are outbursts against scroungers, and extra Civil Servants
are employed to track them down. Yet investigations of social
security have never revealed more than 3 per cent fraudulently
claimed, and the actual amounts involved are much less than that
involved in tax evasion, which does not attract much comment.
So a secular form of the Protestant Work Ethic remains fairly
widespread, its religious roots scarcely extant, according to
which those in work or living on invested income incline to
condemn those not in work as lazy. However the prolonged and
growing unemployment figures have done something to undermine this attitude. Now there is serious talk of there never being a
return to full employment. Does this mean the end of the

Protestant Work Ethic? I turn to the question of the future of work in the next section, before considering in the last one whether there is any further role for that ethic.

III

The possibility of there not being a return to full employment arises from what many fear will be the result of rapid technological changes now taking place. It may be so, but it is wise to take a long perspective, and also to consider alternative ways of ordering our economy than the one advocated by those at present in possession of political power.

Looking back we know that the technological changes which launched the first Industrial Revolution caused an immense social upheaval. Luddite opposition to the new machines destroyed them in cottages and in the newly built mills, by arson.[28] Yet the longer-term result was a large increase both in population and in standards of living, albeit by a rough and ready process which brought great hardship to individuals and groups on the way. Our understanding of the defects of the *laissez-faire* philosophy ought to allow us to avoid similar hardships as we adjust to a new technological revolution.

It is not easy to foresee the effects of technological innovation, though if we make a serious effort we might hope for a better record than our predecessors in the last century, with their nonchalant attitude to it. When the steam engine was invented no one foresaw its application to the railway train. It was not until the invention of the internal combustion engine that public opinion swung decisively in favour of machines. People working with horses had to adapt to dealing with motor engines. Other vast changes of occupation took place. In 1911 there were 1,500,000 women and 45,000 men in indoor domestic service. Most of the former have become office workers, and are now being threatened by mechanization. In Western economies the number working in agriculture has fallen dramatically, and food production has as dramatically increased. In Britain agricultural workers now number less than 3 per cent of the population.

Whilst the overall growth of the economy was enormous it proceeded unevenly, as we have mentioned, in roughly ten-year cycles of booms and slumps. A good deal of this would in any event have been hard to control, because Britain is heavily dependent on international trade. In this century it has become more dependent, as have other Western economies, on the immensely strong economy of the USA, so strong that it could be relatively independent of international trade if pushed. How can other countries avoid being carried along by it willy-nilly? At present its high interest rates, due to huge budget deficits caused by increased military expenditure and unwillingness to raise taxes, are a serious hardship to others. They can only avoid it by creating a larger economic unit, something that the countries in the EEC find it hard to have the vision to do. A lot of mercantilism is still around. Rival short-term interests crowd out common long-term ones.

The pattern of boom and slump in Britain has been different this century. There was the stagnation and depression of the 1920s and early 1930s, only relieved by rearmament. After the second world war there was a prolonged period of growth,[29] followed by the check after 1973, accompanied by inflation because of the inadequate way the oil price rise was handled. Perhaps the worst is over. The British economy grew by 2½ per cent in 1984. But it is this revival which is causing anxiety, for it is accompanied by a persistently high rate of unemployment, which shows no sign of any significant fall. Many middle-aged people who are out of work think they will never work again; many school leavers doubt if they will ever work at all. Among these the coloured, and the disabled, are at a particular disadvantage.

I used to say in the 1950–70 period that we would never again have three million unemployed in this country, as we had in 1933; that no government would allow it to happen because people would not stand for it and there would be social disorder. I was wrong. It has been accepted comparatively meekly. Why? Perhaps on the one hand because the majority of the working population, who are in jobs, are doing quite well, enjoying their comparative affluence, and forgetting the low paid and the unemployed; and on the other hand because the social services to-day at least keep the unemployed and poor from starving and being clothed in rags. One no longer sees children running about with no shoes and socks and grey with hunger as one did in the 1930s, a condition which shocked the public when war broke out and evacuation made it widely known. That led to a move for reform and the welfare legislation of the Attlee government after 1945.

Clearly the present level of unemployment is not due to a cyclical movement of boom and slump. It is long-term and structural. There are three main reasons for this.

1. The speed of technological change. In 1913 parsons outnumbered scientists by ten to one. Now scientists have more than reversed the proportion. Much of their inventive activity and technological development is concerned with military inventions, alas, but these in the end spill over into civilian life. Old manufacturing industries are declining and moving to the Third World: shipbuilding first to Japan and then to South Korea, Taiwan and Brazil; textiles to Hong Kong and then to Mexico and Thailand. They may perhaps reach Bangladesh, one of the poorest countries (for it is by the manufacture of textiles that poor countries begin to lift themselves from abject poverty). The older industries of the West are uncompetitive. And the newer growth industries require much less labour, and that labour more skilled.

How new these industries are is shewn by the fact that the transistor, with all its possibilities of miniaturization, dates from 1947, microprocessors from 1972 and microcomputers from 1978. Annual cost reductions have been dramatic, about 25 per cent per year. Information technology will have far-reaching influence through satellite-based telecommunication.[30] In the computer world the blockage is in software or programming, which is a highly skilled labour intensive activity.[31] A fully automated factory is getting closer, but robots tend to be blind, deaf and dumb and have a poor sense of touch. Better sensor techniques are needed.[32]

Current trends suggest that the development of micro-electric technology means the phasing out of unskilled manual and routine mental jobs in all three spheres of product manufacture, services and the home. These jobs are dead-end ones, mindlessly repetitive and boring. There is no inherent reason to regret their exit. But they have had immense social significance. Half the school leavers have earned their living in such jobs all their working life. They could move easily from one job to another according to what was available. They reached their maximum relative earning power in early manhood or womanhood, and remained in that relative position until retirement. Unless drastic changes are made in our priorities it is their future which is grim. It is inhuman to say to them, in effect, You have nothing to contribute to society which we think worth paying for; but we will pay you to be idle at a rate which will feed and clothe you at a very modest level, if you use your money with exceptional care; and we hope you will find ways of making a contribution to the community by some kind of voluntary work.

2. There are rigidities in our society which hamper adjustments to change and a readiness to accept innovations. The relative affluence produced by economic growth until 1973 is new to most people. Many are still conscious of the relative poverty of the 1930s, if not from their own memories, then from what they have learned from their parents. They like the present relative affluence, and cling to their present jobs to maintain it. Professional bodies in their Trade Union aspect are just as insistent on this as any weekly wage earners. Part of their professionalism is to create a built-in protective system which makes dismissal or redundancy almost impossible, or indeed any change which does not enhance their economic weight. It is not surprising that the weekly wage earner, who in most cases has no such security, reacts in the same way. These attitudes are reinforced by the present level of unemployment. The dislocation of change is feared. Most wage and salary earners want three things which are incompatible in a free society; full employment, free collective bargaining, and a stable price level. The last is the least powerfully desired of the three, because most people notice the level of their nominal income much more than their real income, and pursue the raising of the former without much thought of what it might do to the latter by way of inflation. In practice it has become almost impossible to reduce nominal wages as a spur to move out of a declining occupation. Any free society will have to arrive at some mixture of these three desiderata; it cannot have the fullness of all three. One element will be some kind of wage and salary policy, difficult as it is to implement. Advocates of free collective bargaining jib at this at their peril. If they want a centrally planned, command economy they may get full employment, but they will not get free collective bargaining, and they will find the concentration of economic and political power

bearing down on them in ways they will not like. One of our tasks is to search for institutions which ease the burden of adjustment to new technological and economic realities in the way our present social provisions do not. Another we shall discuss very shortly.

3. A third reason for the rise in unemployment is simply that there are more people seeking jobs. This is mostly due to the rise in the number of women seeking work, a new phenomenon in this century. Most of the additional jobs created in recent years have been taken by women; many of them are part-time. This increase in the number of folk seeking work is expected to cease from about now.

What remedies are there for this situation? The policy of the new Right is roughly to cut public expenditure and taxes, put more money into the pockets of the people, particularly the better off, so that they will spend and invest and create new jobs. That of the Left is roughly to stimulate the economy by increased public expenditure on the grounds that unemployment is worse than inflation. We need to go beyond these simplicities. But we must first of all rid our minds of two fallacies which are widespread. The first is that a job transferred to a less developed country is a job lost for ever. This presupposes that world trade is a fixed entity, so that if one country has more of it others have less. In fact such a transfer would be likely to mean extra income for the less developed countries and a growth in world trade. This is what the two Brandt reports have argued.[33] The snag is that although no job is permanently lost in the old world it is lost to the person who loses it. The job has changed. A new one will need a different skill and perhaps be in a different town. As has been said, our social policies are inadequate to cushion people over such changes, and are not firm enough in dealing with the location of industry. We cannot sterilize a past situation, but to ignore past and present personal and physical infrastructure is in the long term wasteful and socially cruel.

The other fallacy is that labour-saving technology permanently kills jobs. So far it has in due course led to new ones, but it takes time, and once again we come to the problem of how social policy can help towards the necessary adjustments. Labour has moved from agriculture to industry, and from industry to service. Only

25 per cent of the work force in Britain is now working in industry. Among services we include maintenance and repair jobs, personal services of very varied kinds, education greatly expanded beyond the school leaving age, commercial services, entertainment and tourism. In all the talk of de-industrialization it must be remembered that the smaller proportion working in industry will, by new technology, have a much higher productivity. It is this that pays for the services. So how the proceeds of the productivity are distributed is a key question. It is the routine jobs, however, that are being phased out. So the other key question is how those displaced from these or who are deprived of access to them are to be treated.

This is not the place to dwell in detail on remedies. Churches now have official organs like Boards for Social Responsibility, and unofficial ones like Church Action on Poverty, to monitor continuously the changing situation. It is likely, however, that short, medium and long term policies may point in different directions. In the short term various government schemes to provide jobs and training have a role. And with the infrastructure of the country visibly running down, in roads and housing and public building maintenance, the labour-intensive construction industry has been foolishly allowed to contract. As it employs a lot of unskilled labour it should be galvanized into expansion by public expenditure. Surely it is better to employ people to add to the country's resources than to pay them to be idle. *Charter for Jobs* has shown that the risk of inflation in this case is minimal. In the medium term there are various plans to reduce the labour force by instituting a shorter working week, earlier retirement, the removal of those under 18 from the labour market by extended education of a mixed practical and theoretical nature, and by job sharing. All of these have a point. But they are not far-reaching enough to deal with the decline of routine jobs. It is the long term which will require different social goals from the one most of us now assume.[34]

I think it will be necessary to pay every adult citizen a basic social wage independent of work. On this basis every citizen could choose the particular mix of work and leisure that he or she prefers, within the broad structure of industrial regulation. I would class this proposal as a 'middle axiom'. That is to say it is half-way between a general principle and a detailed policy. It derives *both* from a general insight drawn from Christian faith, *and* from an empirical diagnosis of the present trends with respect to work, leading to a recommendation as to the *direction* in which it is desirable for social policy to go.[35] The general principle is that in view of the essential equality of every person in the sight of God, there is a need to express this in the way basic provisions of life are secured in the social structures which are the matrix of personal growth. I would hope that as Christians consider more fully questions of work, and lack of it, they would agree on this middle ground as the direction to take in implementing the principle in our present context. There has always to be some step between a Christian insight and a detailed practical conclusion. No direct leap is possible between a biblical text or a doctrinal formulation and a detailed policy conclusion. There has to be this middle stage of broad empirical judgment. If there is widespread disagreement among Christians about this middle level of judgment, no middle axiom is possible. Then Christians who hold different diagnoses must in that case ask one another pertinent questions as they listen to those who arrive at a different one from their own, in an effort to arrive at a common understanding. On the other hand if a broad consensus does emerge among those who have carefully considered the matter, a middle axiom may emerge. It then has a presumption in its favour, and is a help, in forming an opinion, to the undecided in the Christian public. There is of course no claim that it is certainly right, nor any suggestion that the minority which disagrees is not entitled to do so, provided it produces a reasoned argument for its position. In fact there will nearly always be some minority. Only in rare cases will there be practical unanimity in diagnosis, because of uncertainties in obtaining and assessing the necessary evidence. Therefore how the 'middle axiom' concerning a basic social wage should be implemented is a matter of detailed policy, about which there will be different proposals. A choice must be made, but different ones could well be chosen by Christians equally committed to the general aim.[36] If I mention any detailed policies it will be with this proviso, as Temple did in the appendix to his *Christianity and Social Order*, separated from the main text.[37]

It has been suggested that the basic social wage might be 140 per cent of the long-term Supplementary Benefit rate, but there are other possibilities. If the objection is made, What about scroungers? the reply would be that undoubtedly a small percentage would contribute nothing to the common good, but no social policy is totally free from drawbacks, and that we would have to tolerate them as we have tolerated the idle rich. The evidence suggests it would be a small percentage. The climate of opinion in the milieu in which one lives will be the decisive factor, as it is in fact in the case of crime.

However we need to go further. We should be prepared to use, and pay for out of the profits of manufacture and commerce, the personal services of the relatively unskilled whose jobs are disappearing. Very few are unemployable. All have personal qualities which need to be drawn on and developed through use. There is great scope here. I give two examples. Domestic work came into disfavour as demeaning, and putting the domestic worker too much at the mercy of the whims of the employer. But, properly organized, there is much need of it; Home Helps are an example. Or again, anyone connected with the world of mental handicap knows that if the handicapped are to achieve whatever they have it in them to achieve they need continuous personal attention. Skilled medical and nursing care needs to be available, but what is continuously needed is personal concern, sympathy and patient perserverance. One to one attention requires a very high staffing ratio. Not everyone is suited to provide this, but many with limited technical skills have the personal qualities which are needed. It is the necessary amount of personal attention which the mentally handicapped do not get. Mental hospitals are notoriously short staffed; and the attempt to close most of them and re-locate their patients in smaller groups in the community will require more staff if it is to work, not less. There are no signs of this being appreciated, and it appears to be a disguised cost-cutting exercise. Public policy is not prepared to pay for adequate staffing. Six hundred thousand more people could well be used to care for the mentally handicapped. How they are treated depends upon our priorities in wealth distribution.

All personal service jobs are labour intensive; and it is difficult to raise labour productivity in the way technological investment can do in industry. In view of the poor quality of many of our social services there is no need for idle hands. But we must be prepared to pay for improvements. That means more communal and less individual consumption, and a redistribution of resources within the community by taxation policies in relation to income and wealth.[38] It means a move towards greater equality and away from the individualistic philosophy which has characterized public policy since 1979. Economic growth is still required, but we shall not eliminate the worst of poverty and unemployment purely by economic growth. If we are to move towards paying for the personal services of the relatively unskil- l ᴖ ᴵ displaced by technological change we need a society with a different mood and different goals. How we achieve this within the constraints of our international dependence on others and our responsibilities to the Third World, raises complex questions which require detailed and continuous analysis. Church and secular organizations can work at this. But if most of us could agree on the general direction at which we should aim, at the middle level, it would be a major advance. Our present policies are taking us in the wrong direction, and every year wasted makes the situation worse and the necessary adjustment more difficult.

IV

Where does this leave the Protestant Work Ethic? Obviously the boundary between work and leisure becomes more blurred if a basic citizen wage is instituted, and if there is a shorter working week and life. Work cannot have the same commanding place that it had in the Protestant Work Ethic. Education will be seen as a lifetime enterprise. Enjoyment will be seen not merely as an interval of relaxation necessary to enable us to work better. Creativity in personal choices will be stressed. Celebrations will be encouraged. Contemplation will be an element in Catholic spirituality which needs cultivating to complement the active stress of the Protestant ethic. Workaholics will have to be weaned from the boredom which afflicts them when not working. Both work and leisure will need better liturgical expression.

Nevertheless work will remain as a prime requirement in human life, and it will still be needed as a key element in a person's social significance. Those who have good reasons for taking the basic citizen wage and doing no more will be like the conscientious objector who makes a point which has substance but which can be valid only as a minority reminder to the majority, in this case that there are values in life which far transcend work. The scrounger will have to be left to public opinion. The work which is needed should be properly paid and organized, with proper participation in its running by all involved in it, and it needs to be well done and not scamped. The merit of the Protestant Work Ethic is its stress on efficiency. Waste is an offence to it. Efficiency is the economist's virtue. He is constantly exercised by the relative scarcity of our resources as compared with the many uses we might make of them, and he thinks it a pity if we do not do as much with them as we might when we keep costs artificially high, and cling to obsolescence. Of course there are other virtues besides efficiency.[39] To pursue that to the exclusion of all others quickly leads to inhumanity. Nevertheless vested interests often cause us to pay too little attention to it, or to fudge the issue. The Protestant Work Ethic has a perennial relevance in its stress on diligence in the job on hand and avoidance of waste as a way of glorifying God. But it needs to be communalized in terms of the way society orders its affairs, and not thought of in purely individualistic terms; and it needs to be balanced by an ethic of celebration. That we must make the best we can, other things being equal, of our relatively scarce resources is the strong point of those who emphasize the creation of wealth.[40] How it is created, what is to count as wealth, and how it is distributed are the underlying issues of social, economic and industrial politics. The mistake was to exalt the Protestant Work Ethic to a solitary eminence. It has become discredited, and we are left with a secularized and rather unpleasant residue. It needs to recover more of its gospel basis.

8

The New Right:
a Theological Critique

I take the term New Right to refer to the resurgence of a self-confident advocacy of a free market economy and the capitalist system, associated with what is popularly known as Reaganomics in the USA and Thatcherism in Britain. Historically it is a return to what could well be called Gladstonian liberalism.

The New Right is associated with certain political and economic theories and with an overall philosophy of persons in society, or ideology. It represents a recoil from politics in favour of a more impersonal way of running the economy. At least that is the theory. But in politics, theory and practice coincide only roughly and, for instance the USA (where in theory *laissez faire* and free trade is most vociferously promulgated) is a highly protectionist country in practice. And the Thatcher government does not hesitate to intervene in the economy explicitly or implicitly if it suits it. This leads one to look somewhat critically at the professed devotion to theories which are so often flouted, and it raises the ideological question in another and less neutral sense of the term. One is tempted to ask such questions as: How far is this professed belief which can so often be ignored a deception? If it is, is it a conscious deception or not? In whose interests is it being advanced? In a post-Marxist world this last question is always one to be asked.

All this means that the ideology of the New Right is in need of assessment by moral and political philosophers and by theologians. However it is worth pausing for a moment to note that in so far as it uses what are claimed as theories derived from economics, the most developed of the social sciences, philosophers and theologians have only a minor part to play in assessing them. There is an autonomy of the sciences which has to be respected. There is a certain level of technical expertise which is required to discuss them for which there is no substitute. But experts are notoriously people who are indispensable, but difficult to co-ordinate with their colleagues and with the general public. They differ among themselves as much as they agree, and some discrimination has to be used between them; and it is also necessary to ask if they are speaking beyond their expertise. In the case of economics this is particularly acute. Basic economic theory is becoming either increasingly mathematical and precise, but at the price of a high degree of abstraction; or by the use of computers it applies mathematical formulae to piles of statistics in order to find relationships between economic variables, but whether any relationships established in this way have actual significance, or how far they have, is another question.

Yet in fact economics has largely developed throughout its history in response to the challenge of changes in the real world, and it still does. The quadrupling of oil prices in 1973–4, with the re-cycling of the huge surpluses of OPEC oil exporters, and the combination of inflation with unemployment, have been the focus of attention in the last decade. It is therefore particularly hard to separate the scientific from the ideological in economics. It always has been. From the days of Adam Smith onwards economists tended to preach *laissez faire* with an evangelistic fervour; they had a moral conviction that the market mechanism was desirable wherever possible. At the same time as they were freeing the subject from the utilitarian philosophical concepts in which it was enmeshed, in order to establish it as a science based on a few presuppositions which it is hard to deny, e.g. that human beings have more wants than their relatively scarce resources can satisfy, so that scarce means have to be allocated between alternative uses. The value criterion which the economist as such subscribes to is that of efficiency in making the maximum use of these relatively scarce resources. However he must admit that the public may want to put other values higher; for instance economic efficiency could be purchased at a high price in inhumanity. In that case the role of the economist is to make clear the economic cost in the possibilities foregone by reason of the relative inefficiency, so that the public knows what it is doing. This is an important service, for many groups have an interest in fudging the issues, and we are all tempted to think we can eat our cake and have it.

In the steps to the actual economic situation from the abstractions of economic theory, many assumptions have to be brought in as to how people will react, individually and in groups, which are inherently disputable. The economist is in a difficult position because the situation is changing all the time he is studying it; no part of the phenomena can be kept stable while he examines the rest. History – past precedents – can be some guide, but behaviour changes and, in particular, the effects on others of the economists' own predictions cannot be precisely determined. So it is not suprising that there are divergent opinions among economists on contemporary issues of policy. Assessing them becomes a matter of judging both their economic plausibility and the moral preferences hidden in them. The philosopher or theologian may possibly be more skilled than others at detecting ideological assumptions hidden in the various opinions, so that their economic plausibility alone is what has to be estimated, but it does not necessarily follow that he will. It depends what sort of philosopher or theologian he is. If he is able to, he will demythologize some economic theories, to borrow a term from modern New Testament studies. For instance the effort to free economics from extraneous philosophies should have made clear that the free market has been ideologically overcalled. Its economic laws have been regarded, and by some still are regarded, as laws of God in the sense that the laws of physics have been. In 1870 the Drummond Professor of Political Economy in the University of Oxford, G. K. Rickards, published a book *Popular Lectures on Political Economy*, which was devoted to making this point, and it was published by SPCK! On the contrary the free market is a human construct, to be judged in accordance with human purposes, such as responding to consumer preferences, achieving innovation, and avoiding waste. It is useful in these ways over a certain range if put within a firm political framework; and it requires a strong moral undergirding if it is to work. As F. H. Knight said in 1939, in an article in *Economica*, without an adequate ethics economics has little to say on public policy.

My difficulty with the economic theories of the New Right is both on the grounds of their economic plausibility and their ideological stance. The economic theories coming from the Reagan and Thatcher administrations are not new. I have not detected any argument not being used forty or fifty years ago. In my view they were shown to be implausible then. They are no more plausible now. Our disastrous experience since 1979 should discredit them completely. Yet on the whole the government clings to them, allowing for the vagaries I have mentioned. Why? I can only put it down to ideological reasons. There was an interesting comment in *The Economist* of 19 January 1985. It occurred in a review of a book on the Think Tank introduced by Mr Heath in 1970, and scrapped by Mrs Thatcher in 1983[1] (the body called the Central Policy Review Staff). The reviewer remarked that meritocrats don't make good governors, that one can't de-politicize politics and that what ministers need is not rational policy analysis but politically charged advice. Our democracy is run by 'those with the drive to implement a set of prejudices – subject only to the constant probing of their colleagues and the electorate'.

The ideological reasons lie in the composition of the Conservative Party. To whom does it appeal? From where does it get its money? Who benefits from its policies? Obviously it appeals primarily to the relatively prosperous in British society at all levels. It is these who do not object to the significant redistribution in favour of the relatively rich since 1979, and who appear to subscribe to the paradoxical doctrine that the rich need their wealth increased to induce them to work effectively whilst the poor need their wages reduced in order to make them do so. This is, of course, a very rough psychological and sociological analysis. It is enough to indicate why we expect a large Tory majority in Bournemouth and a large Labour one in Barnsley no matter who is leading the parties, and no matter what would be a 'rational' analysis of the party programmes. It illustrates the point in the review I have just quoted. But it will not do entirely, because it does not account for the considerable number of quite poor working-class people who vote Tory. This is because of two divergent elements in Conservatism.

It is no particular criticism of the Tory party to draw attention to two very diverse strands within it. In our electoral system any party which hopes to gain power by attracting a mass vote must represent a spectrum of groups and interests. The sectional interests in the Labour Party are notorious. The two main strands in Toryism are the hierarchical and patriarchal on the one hand, and that of the New Right on the other. The latter has succeeded in fastening the label 'wet' on the former. The last time I heard Mr

Heath speak (at a private meeting) it was hard to see what he had in common with Mrs Thatcher. It is this patriarchal Toryism, with its sense of *noblesse oblige* and of a traditional right to govern which attracts some of the less well off working-class vote, especially the woman voter. A good expression of it is Roger Scruton's 1980 Pelican book on *The Meaning of Conservatism*, and he is a good example to quote because of his regular articles in *The Times*. To him the principle of liberalism with its notion of freedom is the principle *enemy* of Conservatism. The Conservative attitude is not about the free market economy or individual freedom, or minimum government, but about the right to rule, about civic community and order, and the authority of the government. It is concerned with legitimacy (not notions of a social contract), with patriotism, custom and tradition. Its instinct is to make a future in the image of the past. Liberalism on the contrary is the creed of an elite and an impossible substitute for the pieties of ordinary existence, a sense of a common moral order and social cohesion. Conservatism involves private property as necessary for self-realization (not necessarily for private consumption), but it does not necessarily involve capitalism, or wealth creation. Property needs distributing through all classes of society, though there is no absolute right to it; and duties go with it. Social and political unity is more important than the creation of wealth, and the citizen must not feel that he is at the mercy of uncontrollable forces that could plunge him into destitution. The state must be paternalistic, but it should be cautious in engaging in activities where the power of sections of citizens might thwart it (*sic*). Conservatism is not antiquarianism: it supports the welfare state (as far as ordinary humanity requires), and public before private considerations, society before the individual, and privilege before rights.

It would be an interesting exercise to appraise these various elements in Scruton's portrait of Conservatism, but that is not our present concern. The point of quoting it is to show how different it is from the ideological position of the New Right which we are about to examine, though sharing with it, as I hope to show later, one common approach to politics, and that a pessimistic one. Scruton says that the most dangerous opponent of Conservatism is the reformer with his spirit of improvement.

If I am to examine the ideology or prejudices of the New Right, I must state my own. I seek to draw from the Christian faith certain broad considerations (an American social theologian has called them 'presumptions')[2] in the light of which all political philosophies are to be appraised. (I am using various terms here because common usage is not precise in these matters.) That is to say that my theological appraisal is a Christian one, though it may well overlap to a considerable extent with presumptions drawn from other faiths, especially some types of humanism. These presumptions are constantly being put forward and explained, and I do not propose to do more than mention them briefly. The core of Christian belief is that in the ministry of Jesus Christ, his activities and his teaching, the kingdom of God drew near to men and women, and its power remains embodied in the new community of those who own allegiance to the kingdom, a leaven in the lump, a foretaste of how humanity should live together. The term 'kingdom' is the biblical way of expressing the way God rules in the world, a way expressed in teaching by the parables of the kingdom and in action by Jesus' death. It is a very paradoxical rule: to reign from a cross and through it to triumph over sin and evil. But it is a way of ruling which discloses God's inmost nature. It presents a radical challenge to the various structures in the world- family, economic and political life – in which human beings live, and is always seeking expression in them. It is also a challenge to the churches who proclaim it. It will not allow us, now or in the future, to settle down satisfied with things as they are. It is from this basis that certain criteria or presumptions arise which bear upon the structures of life and the ideologies which support them.

1. A belief that fundamentally all human beings are of equal signficance in the sight of God, and that this equality is more significant than any empirical differences between them, and needs expressing in the social structures within which they live. I think this is a very powerful Christian insight, and a study of why it has not had a more powerful expression in the history of the church is a study of the pathology of the church. But it is not an insight peculiar to Christians. It was vividly expressed, for instance, by the humanist Walter Lippmann, 'There you are, sir, and there is your neighbour. You are better born than he, you are richer, or you are stronger, you are handsomer, nay you are better, wiser, kinder, more likeable; you have given more to your

fellow men and taken less than he. By any and every test of intelligence, or virtue or usefulness, you are demonstrably a better man than he, and yet – absurd as it sounds – these differences do not matter, for the best part of him is untouchable and incomparable and unique and universal. Either you feel this or you do not . . .'[3] R. H. Tawney has been the most powerful exponent in Britain in this century of this conviction and its implications for social ethics.[4] In the many confusions of contemporary socialist thought the element of this stress on equality remains of permanent importance, not as a politics of envy or levelling down, but as the basis of a proper way for human beings to relate to one another in the social order. I need hardly say that a literal, wooden equality is not in mind, nor that other criteria besides equality have also to be brought to bear on the social order, but these are not our present concerns. (The universalism of this, as against any form of racism, is clear.)

2. Following from this there is in the gospel what is being called to-day a 'preferential option for the poor'. This is a shorthand expression, for while it does refer to the literally poor, Jesus also seems especially concerned with all those who were in some way marginalized, whom the majority tended to write off. The effect should be to make us particularly concerned with those who are getting the rough end of things in society. Very often for that reason they find it hard to get a hearing. We do not understand our own society until we listen to them. Sometimes they are hardly considered; sometimes indeed they are thought of and efforts made to deal with their problems, but they are not listened to. It is paternalistic aid 'from above'. This was the case in the vast philanthropic efforts of Victorian Britain.

3. The Christian understanding of men and women does not idealize them. It is well aware of the corruptions and sins in human life, and this is expressed in the conviction that Christ died for all, for all fall short of what they ought to be, and what God must wish them to be, and all need a way of forgiveness and renewal opened to them. The social expression of this understanding would indicate that the dignity of human beings requires that they participate in decisions which affect them as worker, and as citizen, along with other workers and citizens;

and also that all the necessary sources of power, in the state and in voluntary bodies, including the church, should be subject to some possibility of check to safeguard the person against the possibility of its abuse. For no one is good enough to be entrusted with power over others without the possibility of check. Power (for instance that of the proprietor of a newspaper) needs scrutiny; and in social life countervailing power is needed.

4. These three presumptions have to be applied to the state, whether the nation-state or whatever basic political authority under which human beings live. There has been a tendency in Christian thinking to regard the state too negatively, as primarily a divine ordinance for restraining disorder and compelling people to live in sufficient harmony to make corporate life possible; but it also has a positive task, to encourage social institutions, structures, and conventions which facilitate rather than hinder the kind of social life to which the first three criteria point. Human beings need to live in a community of giving and receiving and to be freed from the effort to achieve a mistaken independence, 'not beholden to anyone'.

How can these criteria be brought to bear upon the ideology of the New Right? I am in a certain difficulty at this point because I have recently discussed this matter in a chapter of my Scott Holland Lectures.[5] I do not see any need to modify what I said there, but it is unsatisfactory merely to repeat it. So I propose to go for the most part by a different route to the same conclusions.

The New Right is characterized by an appeal to individual responsibility, and the desire as far as possible to get government off the backs of the people, in view of what it regards as the incompetence of public bodies. There is a good deal in this which is congenial to Christian opinion. Individual responsibility must be stressed by Christians because it follows from their doctrine of conscience. This holds that the ability to make moral decisions is essential to one's understanding of a distinctively human life, that humans have a duty to make them, and to follow what they conscientiously think to be right, and shun what they think to be wrong. No one can live someone else's life for them. We must take responsibility for our own, including the responsibility to educate ourselves morally so that our conscientious judgments will be sensitive to the issues involved. It is true that this can easily spill over into the exaggeration that individuals are the only responsible entities in society, and to that I shall turn shortly, but the fact that it needs balancing by other considerations does not destroy the point.

The removal of economic restrictions in the thought of the New Right has also had a favourable Christian response. In the early days of industrial capitalism several Christians who contributed to the growth of economic theory took *laissez-faire* seriously in international trade, as opposed to the protectionist mercantile system. They argued that God has not provided any state with all the commodities it needs, therefore international trade is necessary; and the universalist outlook of Christianity makes it impossible to believe that God could have created a world in which one country can prosper and grow rich only at the expense of another. Some of them also argued that the rationality in choice required of the ideal economic man who calculates the consequences of his choice also reflects an affinity with the Christian understanding of the use of reason in moral judgments. Some also argued that international trade is an instrument of God for proselytizing the world!

However when the New Right adopts an ideology of what is often called 'possessive individualism' the Christian raises queries. I have dealt with this in my Maurice Lectures,[6] and will not merely repeat myself here. The main point has also been made by some who are humanists, and who are in favour of the free market. I refer once more to Frank Knight, one of the most acute economists of this century. In the articles I quoted (and elsewhere) Knight explores the implications of the economic and ethical individualism embodied in liberalism. It can be defended on grounds of efficiency, or of not overloading the state with what it is incompetent to do; but behind it there is the idea that freedom is an end in itself, that it is *right* that the relations between individuals are based on mutual free consent and not coercion by other individuals or society; the individual may not be a perfect judge but he is a better judge than any other judging for him. However, he goes on to say that though this doctrine was thought out in economic terms it cannot be isolated from political ones, because every form of human association gives rise to power relations and conflicts of interests. Here those who own productive capacity only in the form of their own labour power are in a weak position. Economic man treats other human beings as if they were slot machines. Freedom of accumulation leads to an increase in economic plus political power. Here the main weakness of liberalism is exposed. It takes the individual as given, though in fact individuality begins and is formed by relationships in the social processes, traditions and institutions into which he or she is born; the family, and the form of economic life and political authority. All three are basic to society and to the formation of the person, who as he or she grows in maturity is increasingly able, but never completely, to transcend them. This is what the Christian teaching on the Orders of Creation points to. Knight says firmly that the safeguarding and improvement of these structures must be the first concern of any intelligent social policy. The tendency of liberalism to be indifferent to problems of human equality, and to distributive and commutative justice is a grave defect. Another non-Christian humanist, Iris Murdoch, has argued that the completely autonomous man is a dangerous delusion, and that respect for persons involves their *inter*-dependence in giving and receiving, in response and responsibility, personally and corporately.[7] It requires a much stronger basis than the freedom of each to pursue his own interests: it requires a commitment to the common good.

The classical liberal outlook is being explicitly revived, and implicitly it is powerful. Robert Nozick[8] argues, on the basis of respect for persons and human dignity, for a minimal state to preserve law and order and the inviolability of persons and property, on the grounds that any interference with property infringes the right of some individuals, without their consent, for the benefit of others. On the contrary persons have basic needs which require fulfilment if they are to pursue any goal; needs relating to physical survival, and at a level which gives them the space to make autonomous decisions. They need basic welfare rights as well as basic rights of liberty.

Both the Hierarchical Right and the New Right are disposed to call on the doctrine of Original Sin to support their position. It is a doctrine with a name which easily leads to misunderstanding. Those on the Right if they use it do so in aid of a doctrine of the Politics of Imperfection, whilst those on the Left are liable to reply with a doctrine of the Politics of Hope. It is necessary in my view to rescue each from its supporters, as I hope to show. But it is too easy to use it without qualification to support and confound one side or the other. Ayn Rand, for instance, who has become popular among advocates of the New Right, repudiated the doctrine in her novel *Atlas Shrugged* in the interest of an optimistic version of the New Right, who usually tend to use it to denigrate the political optimism of the Left. She denies it in the interests of the freedom and responsibility of the self as it pursues rational self-interest, relying on the money verdict of the market as the criterion of value, and eschewing any snivelling, whining or cadging by individuals. Christian theology is probably responsible for the confusion, not only because of the name of the doctrine, but because of its tendency in the course of church history to be used not to account for the abuses in human life but perversely to devalue what is best in human beings.

Be that as it may, it is time to look at six emphases of the New Right which point to a Politics of Imperfection.[9] The roots of it are found chiefly in the reaction of Burke to the challenge of radical change presented by the French Revolution, though behind him there is Hobbes. The six emphases are these: (1) A stress on human sin; from this the inference is drawn that people cannot be trusted to be responsible, and hence a strong stress on law and order. The hierarchical element on the Right draws from it a stress on traditional élites who have a natural ability for governing; and the New Right stresses the irresponsible log-rolling in politics, and advocates impersonal economic mechanisms which take decisions away from political choices. (2) A stress on human ignorance; human abilities to forecast the future and mould policy in the light of it have been grossly exaggerated. Innovations, which are vital to economic growth, and their consequences for policy-making cannot be foreseen. (3) A stress on human irrationality: people only see what is in front of their noses and are tempted to lash out blindly. A study of the role of 'the mob' in politics is salutary. There is all the more need therefore for a coercive framework. (4) A stress on the value of impersonal mechanisms rather than the dubious art of politics: people can be trusted to be rational as consumers to a far greater extent than they can be in politics. Some lament the demise of the automatic mechanism of the Gold Standard which removed decisions about national currencies from governments. (5) A stress on the fact that many problems are insoluble: the belief that they are soluble leads to disappointment, an unreasoning back-lash, and the danger of becoming ungovernable. (6) A stress on the fact that societies are kept going by the traditions of the past: and if they disintegrate there is anarchy. These six emphases all point towards minimum government; beyond that governments are sure to make a mess. In 1980 Nigel Lawson wrote a pamphlet for the Conservative Centre for Policy Studies, *The New Conservatives*, in the course of which he said that Conservatism is the creed of Original Sin and the politics of imperfection (while Socialism is the creed of the perfectibility of man).

These points are valid against a utopianism to which the Left is undoubtedly prone. Peter Townsend, for example, whose investigations of poverty in Britain are of great value, affirms his 'faith in people, in the fundamental goodness of man', and that 'these are generally recognized as Christian virtues and yet they are the essence of Socialism'.[10] However, utopianism is not confined to the Left; paradoxically it can also underlie supporters of the New Right. Norman Macrae, the Assistant Editor of the *Economist*, is one such, but he does not fall back on Original Sin in his book *The 2024 Report*.[11] Jo Grimond in a perceptive comment on it said: 'The Macrae theology rests on the belief that human beings are essentially good and sensible and their goodness and rationality will be fortified by education. I hope he is right. In my lifetime there has not been much evidence to support him. Original Sin seems as strong as original virtue.'[12]

In that last sentence Grimond strikes almost the right balance. A stress on original sin is certainly important against a simple optimism which is liable to suppose that it is only the structures of life which are flawed; reform them and human goodness, thwarted by corrupt structures, will shine forth. Or this optimism may assume that human beings are indefinitely malleable; or that participation in decision-making by 'the People' will be wise, in time, and agreed without dissentient minorities. The truth embodied in the doctrine of Original Sin is that the subtle sins flourish on virtues, not vices. We cannot and must not exclude the possibilities of gains in human history, but we cannot assume they will be permanent; and the greater the gain the greater the possible fall. Nazism is the supreme instance of this: a previously unimaginable collapse of German moral perceptions.

But Original Sin is not the main emphasis of the Christian

gospel, which is *good* news. It is the news of God's essential graciousness, a graciousness not rare but continuous and overflowing. This is the theological basis of a Politics of Hope. If Original Righteousness is as much characteristic of human beings as is Original Sin, the virtues of faith, hope and love, which Christians particularly stress, are 'natural' to human persons, and the adumbrations of them found in human life are built upon and deepened by the Christian faith.

This is not the occasion to discuss the possibilities and dangers of the Politics of Hope. The point is that the first five stresses of the Politics of Imperfection can be accepted, but they do not point to the economic and political conclusions drawn by the New Right. There are indeterminate possibilities open to mankind, but there is no immanent drive towards perfection in history, and no utopia to be expected at the end of it. Moreover there is force in the contention that human beings are now 'come of age', not in the sense of being securely morally mature, but in the sense of no longer being suitably subject to the tutoring of traditional political élites, nor to the workings of impersonal mechanisms in matters vital to their fundamental well-being over which they have no say. One does not need to be starry-eyed about politics to appreciate the folly of its denigration.

However, the sixth stress of the Politics of Imperfection on the traditions of the past cannot be accepted. Not only does the understanding of the kingdom of God in the Christian faith present a radical challenge to the *status quo*, but there is also a real danger that traditions which are inflexible and block social change at a time of rapid technological innovation will produce a social explosion.

Insights of both a conservative and radical kind come from the Christian gospel. God is both a preserver and a challenger. It leads to a perception of the ambiguities both in the *status quo* and in the policies of change; and to the realization that moving things on in the social order will reveal fresh problems. But the realization of ambiguities must not cut the nerve of action. The Politics of Imperfection must have a dynamism for change within it or it becomes an ideology, in the bad sense of the term, of those doing well out of things as they are. That is what, in my judgment, the theories justifying the New Right have become. And that is why they need theological scrutiny.

9

Brian Griffiths on Capitalism and the Creation of Wealth

Professor Brian Griffiths is a Christian and an economist whose thinking it is important to follow. This is because he is in an influential position as Dean of the Business School in the City University and a non-executive director of the Bank of England,[1] and because he is continually correlating his Christian faith and his work as an economist. Moreover his thought is on the move in both respects. Formerly a Plymouth Brother, he is now an Anglican and, whilst remaining in the evangelical tradition with its strong individualist emphasis, which goes very well with certain liberal approaches to the economic order, he is making serious attempts to meet critics of his views in this area. There is a distinct movement, as well as continuity, from his London lectures,[2] through his chapter in the symposium *The Kindness that Kills*,[3] to *The Creation of Wealth*[4] which is the subject of this appraisal. For this he has had the help of a Research Assistant, which has doubtless helped him to refer to a wider range of sources. This book, which has been written at the request of the Christian Association of Business Executives, has especially the entrepreneur in mind.

It starts by referring to the increasing Christian criticisms of capitalism. This is surprising, for I would have said these criticisms had been more muted in the last few years, partly because many traditional Christian socialist criticisms have run into the sand, partly because the self-confident ideological slant of the Thatcher-Reagan era has been music to the ears of many Christians who never accepted the Christian criticisms of capitalism but lacked a coherent Christian defence of it. It seems more likely that it is Griffiths who has become more aware of the criticisms but, be that as it may, he sets out to deal with them one by one.

First of all, however, it is well to be clear about his positive thesis, which is a modest one. He favours a social market economy (a term more familiar in West Germany than in Britain), together with a sense of community responsibility expressed in an anti-poverty programme as, for instance, he finds in the Pentateuch. He does not believe that there is a 'Christian' economic order; certainly not that capitalism is a 'Christian' one, or the only economic system compatible with Christianity. Rather his contention is that wealth creation within a market economy, compounded with a concern for justice, is compatible with the Christian faith and a better starting-point than most economic systems. He does not in fact discuss others (except in one aside). As an economist he is in favour of zero inflation and a balanced budget as the priorities for today, but he does not argue with economists of other views. I myself would not agree with these priorities, but this is not the place to discuss issues which are tied up with questions of the nature and status of economic prescriptions.

In appraising Griffiths' arguments in detail I have not found the book so well arranged as at first appeared, but I hope I have represented it fairly. As an aid to clarity I have arranged my appraisal under five main headings, each with subsidiary points.

I Christian critiques of Capitalism as discussed by Griffiths

(i) The evils of competition. Griffiths agrees that the philosophy of possessive individualism is profoundly unchristian, thereby accepting the basic contention of F. D. Maurice and the subsequent Christian socialist tradition, though he does not refer to it. He says that possessive individualism cannot be reconciled with a sense of human solidarity deep in the Christian tradition, still less with the further implications for society of using the phrase 'the body of Christ' for the church. Nevertheless competition is a genuine human phenomenon resulting from the relative scarcity of human resources and has a necessary place in human society.

(ii) Profits. Griffiths makes another important point that there is no logical connection between profit and the profit motive, i.e. between profit as a directive of economic activity and as an incentive to it. This also could have been expanded, especially as he says ownership cannot easily be separated from incentives. This ignores the very extensive separation of management from ownership in modern enterprises to which Berle and Means first drew attention more than half a century ago.[5] Griffiths argues that profits are not restricted to the market (e.g. sermon fees!), and in so far as they are an occasion of selfishness and aggression these are just as common outside the market as in it, for instance in families. Self-interest needs unpacking: it is characteristic both of the highest and the lowest kinds of human behaviour, as Bernard of Clairvaux showed when in his treatise on love he built up to love of self for God's sake.

(iii) Growth and prosperity as morally dubious. Griffiths stresses Jesus' warnings on the dangers of riches, but argues that wealth is not inherently wrong nor poverty inherently virtuous. He argues for economic efficiency as the most effective way of reducing poverty, and points out that wealth is created more effectively by the better use of existing resources than by securing greater resources (Hong Kong is a good example of this). Many points are raised here, especially about the relation of economic efficiency to other values, and about the distribution of the wealth created, which need more discussion.

(iv) Inequality. Griffiths does not deal with considerations which point in an egalitarian direction and which appeal to many Christians (R. H. Tawney is not mentioned), but asserts that in a fallen world inequality of wealth and income is an essential *aspect* (my italics) of Christian justice. But what of other aspects of the problem of distribution? Merit? Need? Griffiths recognizes that a caring attitude leads to income redistribution, but more needs to be said on this whole area than is covered by what he says on distributive justice, to which I refer under the next heading.

II *Griffiths' wider understanding of the economic order*

He denies that a liberal economy has a natural tendency to equilibrium. This is a major modification of the grounds on which many defences of capitalism have been based. He stresses distributive justice (in contrast to, for example, Hayek or Friedman), and states that there should be no permanent poverty, no exploitation and no gross injustice. He thinks a social market economy has the best chance of realizing what he wants, not least because economic freedom is an important condition for political freedom. It is here that he refers in passing to 'red-blooded socialism' as an alternative, and says that it leads to the Gulag Archipelago. He makes his task too easy. Who is advocating that? Everyone knows of the inefficiencies of the Russian economy. Can anything be learned from, for example, Sweden? Hungary? Yugoslavia? Most of our problems are found here and Griffiths does not give much help with them. However he says that human attitudes and skills are as much capital as are machines; and so are a good human environment, and art collections. This makes it clear that labour cannot properly be treated solely as an inert factor of production like land and capital, and that there are important human criteria which cannot be satisfied purely by the haggling of the market. These modifications of *laissez-faire* theory need expanding.

III *Individualistic assumptions made by Griffiths*

Griffiths is the product of what is not unfairly characterized as an individualistic type of Protestant Christianity, and this is reflected on occasion in what he assumes in incidental remarks as well as in some explicit reflections.

(i) Public enterprises are relatively inefficient, and the growth of government is the main cause of the crisis in wealth creation. In fact some public enterprises are efficient and some are not (assuming an agreed criterion of efficiency), and they are of varying types of management and ownership. Similarly with private enterprises. Is the hugely subsidized Western agriculture efficient or not? Or industries protected by tariffs and quotas? An assumption against public enterprise is not warranted.

(ii) Redistribution through the coercive power of the welfare state breeds dependence, a new class (a term used loosely here) dependent on the state for basic goods. And why not? Can the whole of Beveridge's five giants of Ignorance, Idleness, Want, Squalor and Disease be dismissed so easily? Why should not basic goods be the patrimony of citizens as such? Why is it demeaning? Is it not a bearing of one another's burdens by the community in respect of goods which are so basic that if they are lacking it cannot be left to the hazards of private benevolence to supply them?

(iii) A global welfare state would require a global coercive government. It may well be difficult to see how we could achieve one, but why take such a negative view of government? And why limit the coercion to matters such as law and order and the maintenance of contracts? Why can the state not have wider and more positive aims?

(iv) The kingdom of God reigns over the lives of individuals. The important truth here is that no one can live someone else's life for them. Each person is challenged to respond to the kingdom of God; but in the very moment of doing so becomes a citizen of it, and in a community which is a foretaste of God's intention for all humanity.

(v) Man's problems are spiritual, not political; legal redistribution of wealth is useless without a simultaneous change of values. Why simultaneous? This reveals a basic fallacy, that human persons can be essentially thought of in isolation from the structures that mould them from birth, even pregnancy; structures of sexual, economic and political life. Structures and persons both need continual change, for both fall short of what they might be, but the changes need not be simultaneous. To say otherwise is to repeat the unsatisfactory Call to the Nation in 1975 by the Archbishops of Canterbury and York, when they raised the questions, What sort of society do we want? and What sort of people do we need to be to achieve it? but left out the third question, What sort of structures do we need to foster the right kind of people? To some extent Griffiths allows for this when he says that the basis of community for the Christian is a created order in which the individual needs others to develop himself, but then he goes on to say:

(vi) Social phenomena must be understood through individual action, for to start with the individual and not the collective implies a much surer doctrine of man. But the created order as we experience it has a priority in time even though we grow in the capacity to transcend it. Nevertheless Griffiths is not at ease with individualism, and he has a passage in which he contrasts a mainly British type according to which order is the unintended result of the individual actions of fallible beings, with a mainly French one where it is intended by conscious design. The first is approved and the second is regarded as too rational. I am baffled by this, for the British one is also a highly rational theory of the market, and presupposes economically rational behaviour by each consumer.

IV   *Griffiths' basic Christian diagnosis*

The kingdom of God is basic, and behind it is the doctrine of the created world which takes time seriously and is not fatalistic; it requires of us a responsible use of our resources, and this leads to wealth creation and a challenge to avoid its hazards. Private property (subject to some constraints) is the norm for ownership in the Old Testament, and absolute ownership is expressed in the New Testament by the Parable of the Vineyard; indeed property rights are sanctified by the Eighth Commandment and the Parable of the Talents. So we arrive at the free market and private property for each family. This is an extremely jejune use of the Bible. For example, the Parable of the Vineyard has nothing to do with property rights. It is about the kingdom of God and shows that rewards in it are paradoxical by everyday standards; if you get in at the eleventh hour the reward is the same as if you had worked all day. This must be so, for there is only one reward in the kingdom. So Jesus prods and teases us into thinking about what kind of kingdom it is and what kind is its sole reward.

Griffiths, however, does stress responsibility not only for creation but for others; one of his most insistent points is that libertarians make no such demand, whilst Christians must care for those who cannot care for themselves. This leads to

V   *Griffiths' theological analysis of the current situation*

He maintains that there has been a decline in moral standards in the last two decades, economically, socially and politically. Such comparisons are not easy to make, and Griffiths here reads very like the rhodomontade which has been the stock-in-trade of the evangelical preacher since the eighteenth century. He thinks that Christianity has been replaced by a rationalist humanism, derived from the Enlightenment, and that we are reaping the economic consequences of this. The rejection of theism leads to a meaningless world. Thus he deliberately separates himself from the secular ideology of the market economy of such thinkers as

Hayek, Nozick or Friedman. Here there is both error and truth. The error is to take such a negative view of humanism. It is a many-faceted phenomenon, some of it crude, some of it noble. The same is the case with Christianity, for some types of Christian theology and church strategy have led to terrible deeds. The Enlightenment saw this and was an important corrective of a defective Christianity. For example, it taught Christians that toleration is a virtue and not to be dismissed as a lack of concern for truth, in reaction to a Christianity which had torn Europe apart for a hundred years in religious wars. Over a fair range of issues concerning human beings the better types of humanism and Christianity overlap in attitudes. This is what the 'natural law' tradition – in moral theory, not in the modern scientific sense – is concerned with, and Griffiths neglects it.

The truth that Griffiths perceives is that the free market and the liberal economic position are not 'natural' phenomena akin to something studied by the natural sciences, but a device designed by humans for human purposes, and to be judged by whether the purposes have been adequately defined and whether they have been adequately served by it. In fact it has been accompanied by an ideology which has given it a spurious overall significance. Griffiths wants to substitute a Christian for a secular one. Here he is unrealistic and mistaken. It is impossible in a plural society to bolster the social market economy with a Christian ideology; nor, if what I have said about humanism is correct, is it necessary in terms of Western attitudes. And those of Islam and the Eastern religions have also to be taken account of. It is also inappropriate. The institutions of the free market should be considered at a lower level, what R. H. Tawney in another connection called that of a 'serviceable drudge'. We can then use it where it is useful for our purposes and reject it where it is not.

At this level there is nothing inherently Christian or unchristian about it. Griffiths in his basic position seems to see this, but here and in other places I have mentioned there appear to be diverse strands in the book indicative of someone whose thought is on the move. He is right in thinking there is nothing unchristian in the creation of wealth. Wealth and poverty are relative terms in themselves and in relation to one another. The New Testament warnings about riches are about disparities of wealth, and the fact that the relatively wealthy can easily cocoon themselves from human and divine realities. We cannot read out of them that economic growth which removes drudgery from human beings is to be shunned; to think so is to be like those Christians who opposed anaesthetics on the grounds that suffering is good for the soul. But the question of the distribution of wealth is, as already mentioned, of profound importance. To use material resources properly is to be spiritual; to misuse them is to be carnal. Moreover, in our technically interconnected world this applies not only within states but between them.

Griffiths says that economic life must be thought of in personal terms, and that monetarism is a false ideology if it derives from a mechanistic view of economic society. This is exactly how it seems to be used. Used in another way it becomes largely a technical question about its success or otherwise in achieving certain human purposes. But once these humans are thought of not as isolated monads but as social beings, the question arises as to how far it does justice to their humanity to put their fate in basic matters affecting their well-being (the area of the Five Giants) at the mercy of impersonal forces over which they have no say. In fact neither entrepreneurs nor workers are willing to accept this, and so we are back at a political discussion. Economic issues invariably lead to politics; the pure theory of the free market as a social policy is a mirage.

Griffiths does not discuss the problems raised by the workings of the version of the free market we have actually experienced. They are formidable: the increasing inequalities of wealth and income it creates if left to itself, so that the effective demand of the wealthy for cake outweighs that of the poor for bread; the booms and slumps by which it develops which leave people's jobs at the mercy of remote, impersonal forces; the collective needs which the market cannot reflect (much more than defence – it was the fear of cholera in the nineteenth century which led to the demand for public sanitation and called in question much *laissez-faire* theory); the externalities, or social costs, which are not represented in market prices (e.g. much pollution); the short-term horizons of the market which hardly cover middle-range forecasting, let alone future generations; the social limits to private consumption, to which Fred Hirsch drew attention.[6] If the merits of the free market are to be utilized it must be set in a political-economic framework which provides for what it cannot do. It is here that the difficult decisions have to be made, decisions which socialist and capitalist economies both have to face.

To summarize: Griffiths' book reads like an interim discussion of these themes. He is aware of most of them, but he is preoccupied with vindicating the creation of wealth and the role of the market economy in doing so. The vindication is necessary because, taking Britain as an example, we have achieved a society in which the standard of living has risen strikingly since the end of the second world war, and in which most people for the first time have tasted relative affluence as compared with the past, like it, and want to hold on to it, but do not appreciate the flexibility necessary to maintain it in a world in which Britain is perforce tied up economically with other countries who do not owe us a living. But we do not have the social structures which help flexibility by cushioning the effects of necessary economic change so that they do not bear too hardly on some individuals and communities while others benefit (e.g. north of the Bristol-Norwich line compared with south of it). So we fight defensive losing battles. The philosophy of individualism is no help to us in this situation. Griffiths is right in what concerns him, but these wider issues need to be given equal concern.

I may be wrong, but I have the impression that whilst Griffiths and his research assistant are reading in a much wider context, he does not himself get much involved in dialogue with other Christians outside evangelical theological and monetarist circles. I wish he would. He has much more to give, and he is potentially as important for the church as was Denys Munby before a mugging in Istanbul brought about his untimely death.[7]

*Christian Ethics
and the Political Order*

10

Political Theology: An Appraisal

I

Political Theology is a term which in its current popular sense came into use about 1968, and in continental Europe rather than Britain. It was marked there particularly by the books of the Roman Catholic theologian J. B. Metz, a disciple of Karl Rahner, and the German Lutheran theologian Dorothea Sölle, though the works of both have had only a limited readership in Britain.[1] Alistair Kee has edited two anthologies which show something of the scope of writing in this area, and also the paucity of British contributions.[2] Liberation Theology, as we shall see in the next chapter, largely arose out of dissatisfaction with Political Theology as not being radical enough, but there have been no significant British contributions to this. In these respects British theology has been in a backwater. We have neither initiated nor developed a native tradition exemplified, for instance, by William Temple who died in 1944. He was the heir to a tradition of a radical social-political theology going back to the reactions to the new urban, industrial society in the nineteenth century by F. D. Maurice and his intellectual successors.

Political Theology is of course a term that can be used within any religious tradition. Islam provides plenty of contemporary examples. This chapter, however, is confined to the Christian religion. By theology is meant a systematic reflection on Christian faith and life, its worship and doctrine and ethics, and not an almost entirely technical study like the textual criticism of the Bible.

A moment's reflection brings to mind that there has always been some relation between theology and politics. Jesus' theology brought him into conflict with the religious-political *modus*

vivendi that the Jewish religious leaders had established with the
Roman occupying authorities, and with these authorities themselves. The Roman empire was buttressed by a civic and political
religion. After bitter struggles the Jews had been allowed
exemption from this, but the empire could not understand the
Christian deviation from the Jewish faith. So Christians were
liable to persecution as atheists because they were not political
enough. In such circumstances the desire to be apolitical is
understandable and, apart from the question of participation in
the state religion, the church in the early centuries tried to be
apolitical. It was inconsistent, and in the end it proved impossible. The position of the church changed radically after the
'conversion' of the Emperor Constantine in 312. Having had no
responsibility for public affairs the church found herself abruptly
in charge of a ramshackle empire and, within less than a century,
made some disastrous mistakes, the effects of which are still with
us.[3] Already about the time of the Council of Nicaea in 325 the
church historian Eusebius is found maintaining that there is one
God, one Saviour, one emperor, one church and one kingdom.
This complete tie between church and state persisted in Byzan-
tium until the fall of Constantinople to the Turks in 1453. In
England the Henrician Reformation settlement was a forlorn
attempt to establish a Byzantine situation which was not possible. It never succeeded in preventing a significant minority
dissenting from it, but its outward signs still remain. They can be
misleading in blinding the Church of England to its real position
in the country and to some of the influences which powerfully
affect the stances it takes; the outward ceremonial trappings
remain, but in many parishes the reality has in effect completely
disappeared. The political remains can be ludicrous, as recently
when a tiny group of MPs succeeded in overthrowing in
Parliament a bill sponsored by the General Synod of the Church
of England abolishing the requirement that the dean and canons
of a cathedral must meet to elect as bishop someone whose name
has been sent them by the Crown, under threat of *praemunire* if
they fail to do so.[4]

Nevertheless, although Christian theology appeared to be tied
to the political establishment after Constantine, the seeds of a
transcendent critique of it was not entirely lost. The weakness of
the political structure in the Western empire was the occasion of

St Augustine's great work *The City of God*, which he wrote as a defence against the charge that it was the establishment of Christianity as the state religion which was undermining the empire. Augustine argues his defence, particularly against the classical philosopher Varro, to good effect. The sequel was ironic. The church found herself in fact the successor to political authority, and her own pretensions in this respect led to the rivalry between her and the new political authority which fought to establish itself. The result was a struggle between the Papacy and the Holy Roman Emperor which preoccupied much medieval political theology. Nor did the break up of the church end that kind of struggle. Calvin's Geneva saw perhaps the most effective church-state control ever established, though it could not be maintained. However the built-in element of dual control proved to be the seed-bed of a Calvinist contribution to the theory and practice of modern political democracy during the Commonwealth period in Britain and in the American constitution in the next century. Behind the civic religion in the USA lies the latent thought that America is God's kingdom.[5] The Lutheran Reformation took a very different and much less dynamic route. Its clearest expression was the 'throne and altar' tradition in Germany, with its sharp separation between the two kingdoms, that of God's right hand in the church and his left hand in the state, which was in effect removed from the kind of Christian judgment which Augustine had exercised with respect to the Roman empire.

There have been other variants of the Christendom tradition. The point of giving this broad picture is that, whatever modifications an extensive discussion would introduce, Christianity has been overwhelmingly and explicitly allied with the established political authorities since Constantine. This is the political theology that succeeded an attempt to be apolitical. Its effects go deep. Today if the church makes a criticism of the political authorities it is time and time again accused of being political, whilst if it suports them this is assumed to be non-political or apolitical. War is the extreme example. If one breaks out it is expected that the church will rally to the national cause. In European history since the rise of nation-states it always has. There are, needless to say, substantial theological reasons for giving support in general to state authority. St Augustine knew that well enough in his attitude to the Roman empire. The point is that the transcendent critique in St Augustine has rarely been evidenced in the mainstream Christendom situation of Western Christianity or Eastern Orthodoxy, elements in Calvinism excepted. This was poignantly expressed by some Protestant Christians in Eastern Europe who found themselves after the 1939–45 war living under Marxist political authorities. They said in effect that for sixteen centuries Christians had lived with state power on their side. What did they do with it? They accepted established social, economic and political structures uncritically, contenting themselves with 'ambulance work', and siding with the rich and powerful. Now God has taken away that protection and they must find a way of creative witness under state authorities which are basically hostile, and where they have no longer any access to the sources of power.

This is the most dramatic illustration of the breakdown of the Christendom situation found everywhere in Europe. A partial exception is the Irish Republic, but even there it is weakening quite rapidly. Its breakdown was hastened by the discredit brought upon traditional Political Theology of the Right by the behaviour of the churches in Nazi Germany. The Roman Catholic Church quickly made a Concordat with the Hitler regime which safeguarded church rights and property at the tacit price of not criticizing the government. In the Lutheran Church a small proportion formed the Confessing Church which carried on a notable struggle against manipulation of the church by the state (though it ignored wider issues such as the treatment of the Jews), a small proportion followed the explicitly Nazified 'German Christians', and the majority followed the government line in a less crude fashion. Leading theologians, Althaus, Elert, Hirsch, Kittel, Künneth, supported National Socialism; the orders of race and nation were added to those of the family, economic life and the state as divine ordinances 'by means of which God creates and preserves our earthly life'. Thanks were given to God for giving the Führer to Germany as a 'pious and faithful chief of state' in the country's hour of need, and for granting 'good government' in the form of the National Socialist state.[6]

It is at the point of the breakdown of Christendom that the latest version of Political Theology begins. Metz, for instance, argues that its breakdown has led to a 'privatization' of religion, to an individualistic otherworldly cult of personal salvation. A perfect liturgical expression of this is the 'early Service' on a Sunday morning as it was widespread a generation ago in the Church of England. The middle-of-the-road Anglicans (and they are the majority, for it must be remembered that the self-consciously 'High Church' and 'Low Church' have together never represented half the parishes) were taught when confirmed to communicate once a month, usually at eight o'clock in the morning, before breakfast. There they would find a fairly small company of the devout, as compared with the much greater number at the mid-morning and (before television) evening services. The congregation would place themselves well apart from each other, and well towards the back of the church to be far away from the celebrant, who would have his back to them at the east end with the Chancel and choir between him and the nave. They would kneel with eyes closed through most of the service or, if not, cast down to look at the Prayer Book. A more privatized form of public worship it would be hard to imagine. As the main focus of worship for the most committed members of the congregation it has rapidly disappeared under the influence of the Liturgical Movement, with the ceremonial and liturgical revisions which the theology of that movement has inspired, and which has had a profound ecumenical influence in worship and social theology. It is noteworthy that opposition to such changes has come mainly from precisely those bourgeois parishes who have the remnants of social status and are particularly prone to a politically and religiously individualist outlook.

Metz criticizes the Christendom type of Political Theology for its explicit right-wing bias (especially its lack of any eschatological critique of established structures), and he criticizes the privatized theology of the post-Christendom situation as being ostensibly apolitical whilst in fact tacitly supporting the *status quo*, and having an implicit right-wing bias.

The 1978 BBC Reith Lectures by E. R. Norman, *Christianity and the World Order*, were a good example of both these attitudes, which lay side by side in them without any apparent realization of the fact. They attracted a good deal of attention at the time. It was not because Norman was the first Reith Lecturer with an explicitly Christian theme; in the present state of Britain that would not of itself have aroused interest. It was because a large number of regular churchgoers and culturally-minded occasional attenders heard at last someone in a prominent position articulating what they had always believed, and from which many informed church leaders and theologians had been distancing themselves, largely under the influence of the Ecumenical Movement, for the last fifty years. It is indeed an indication of a latent Christian tradition still in the country that there was such an intense discussion and such a raid on copies of *The Listener* in which the lectures were printed. That particular discussion has died down but the issues remain and it is worth recalling it.

Ostensibly Norman's attack was on what he termed the 'politicization' of Christianity, a term frequently heard since then. Using his own language the charge is that the Christian faith is defined in terms of current political values such as tolerance, flexibility, compassion and equality. They are not necessarily untrue, but they are peripheral to Christianity. Advocates of them think they are being 'prophetic' when they are in fact merely expressing a political preference. The Christian faith is lost in secular idealism. In fact it becomes no different from humanism, whose main characteristics is hedonism. In particular the Christian doctrine of man has been lost. So far Norman appears to be attacking a political theology of the liberal Left on the basis of a privatized view of the Christian faith. For he holds that this is characterized by a stress on 'the ethereal qualities of immortality', the worthlessness of all earthly expectations and human values, the evocation of the unearthly, and the fact that the kingdom of God is not of this world, and that there is a personal but no social morality in the gospels. Politics is about balancing interests and providing basic order. Christians may act as individuals to lessen suffering and injustice, but not label their accompanying ideals as Christian. There is no hope for a better social order, nor should one idealize the past.

We should pause to note here that Norman has a sub-theme, to sustain which he is prepared to use a quasi-Marxist argument. The politicization of Christianity is due to disaffected elements within the Western intelligentsia. Religion is in fact kept going by élites (an assertion which fits in well with a Christendom situation but cannot be generally true), but is now being undermined by liberal intellectuals. They imagine that they are being non-political, but Marxism exposes the naiveté of this; the content put into these liberal values (so simply identified with Christianity) varies according to class and ideology. The different understandings of Human Rights are an illustration of this. The Orthodox Church in Russia sees this quite clearly, and that is why it is content to concentrate on the main job of the Christian Church, which is to worship God. In their confusion 'Western' liberals are actually prone to an amateurish enthusiasm for Marxism without realizing that no dialogue is possible between Christians and Marxists. Short of this they, and particularly the clergy, have allied themselves with a contemporary, cultural, compulsive moralism.

It is not easy to give a clear account of the Reith Lectures, for they are often elusive, but something needs to be said about the improbabilities of this sub-theme. The situation is rather that many Christians in many parts of the world who have tended to think of themselves as apolitical have found themselves driven bit by bit into opposition to the *status quo*, often with reluctance, and sometimes with fear, because they have come to see that their integrity as Christians is at stake. To take an illustration from outside the Christendom situation, many missionaries and 'lay' Christians who went to India with an outlook very like that of Norman found themselves driven to oppose the caste structure as such. Many feel the same today with regard to racial structures.

However there is a more basic confusion in Norman. The dominant impression is that of a privatized theology, whose verbal expressions (such as 'ethereal') betray its inadequacy; but on occasion he operates on the basis of a former Christendom political theology which is not so markedly emphasized. His remark about not idealizing the past is outweighed by others. He maintains that the politicization which he attacks has been partly forced on the church because the state has encroached upon the traditional preserves of the church. He looks with favour on a past situation when the church in reflecting current ideas was reflecting religious and not secular ones. The clergy were influential, and were able to sacralize politics from within instead of operating from without as now when they are politicizing Christianity. Then the Christian knowledge of politics served the institutional interests of the church. Today no one listens to the church because it is no longer regarded as the guarantor of stability. It is worth noting that this is the view of the role of religion which functional sociologists of religion take. To them religion and law come under the same category. However it is impossible to do justice to the Judaeo-Christian tradition in this way because it has a prophetic, eschatological, radical stance at the heart of it, stemming primarily from the kingdom of God as heralded and inaugurated in the ministry of Jesus, but with roots in the Old Testament. There is of course much evidence in Christian history to support the functional sociologists' view of religion. Considering the basis of the faith in the life and teaching of Jesus it is noteworthy how the radical gospel notes have been tamed in practice. But they have not been extinguished, and they have been the source of significant renewals in church life, not least in our own time. Norman combines the worst features of both the Christendom and the privatized theological attitudes. His privatized unpoliticized theology hankers after the old Christendom political theology.

We have now considered the background to the recent use of the term Political Theology. It is time to turn to consider three main aspects of the current use, and six implications that follow from them.

II

1. Political Theology is occasionally used in a sense so general as to cover any discussion of the role of the church, or even the Christian, in society. More common among those who use the term is the sense of a theology of politics, as one might have a theology of industry, or sport, or the university, each of them considered as an aspect of the milieu in which humanity lives. Alistair Kee in the first of his selections implies this. But in its more recent use it refers not to a part of theology but to the assertion that thinking theologically is inherently a political activity because it inevitably takes place in a political milieu. Politics is a sea in which the Christian and the church cannot but swim. There is no possibility of being non-political. The question is whether the politics is handled appropriately or not by the individual Christian and by the church corporately. The same is true of the other two basic orders of creation, some kind of family

and economic structure, but the political order is fundamental to social living. Metz says that it is not a question of Christian or church involvement in social action but 'a question of theological epistemology'. Dorothee Sölle calls Political Theology a 'theological hermeneutic'. In other words it is a question of how knowledge in theology is acquired and used. There are some standard illustrations of this. The doctrine of the Atonement is one. Christians have always believed that Christ died for the forgiveness of our sins, but there has never been an interpretation of how this is to be understood which has been generally accepted in the church. Different ones have been powerfully influenced by the social milieu in the midst of which they were thought out. That of St Anselm, for instance, which held pride of place for several centuries, is barely intelligible without some understanding of feudalism. In a more general way the Collect for the Festival of St Michael and All Angels in the Book of Common Prayer, 'O Everlasting God, who hast ordained and constituted the services of Angels and men in a wonderful order', only resonates against the medieval hierarchical understanding of society. Even preaching in personal terms takes place in a context of social-political understanding, perhaps usually assumed rather than consciously accepted, of the reciprocal relations of the person and society. Sin can be understood in an entirely personal way by those who say the gospel is addressed to individuals and stop there or, less often, at the other extreme as entirely the effect of corrupt institutions and a purely social matter. Between these two there is a range of possible emphases. In Britain we have had several centuries of an individualistic culture which predisposes us to assume the former view. Why this is so involves a fascinating study of the interrelation of religious and secular ideas in the collapse of feudalism and the rise of merchant and then industrial capitalism, leading to the realities of modern, urbanized, secularized industrial and post-industrial society, a new phenomenon in human history, and one in which Britain was the pioneer.

2. The immediate intellectual background of this way of thinking has been the development of the sociology of knowledge. The rise of the natural sciences, pure and applied, has been a major constituent of modern industrial society; and after them the social sciences, including sociology. This in turn

led in due course to systematic study of the social milieu of
thinking itself. Behind it lies the influence of Marxism with its
attack on allegedly neutral thought, and its relating of thought to
the class structures, class interests and class conflicts in society.
The question concerning any theory or analysis or programme,
'In whose interests is this being advocated?' is always relevant.
One does not need to be a Marxist to see that once this question
has been systematically raised it cannot be suppressed, and
theology cannot be exempted from it. So we find the Latin
American ecumenical theologian J. M. Bonino asking 'Who does
theology? and for whom?', and saying that the answer to both
questions is 'a limited section of a social class (the academic
community mostly located in the middle and higher-middle
class) does theology basically for the same community', and
stressing the urgency of theology finding a way to overcome class
captivity.[7]

We have become much more self-conscious about thought
itself and the power of economic, social and political factors to
affect it. I have just used an indeterminate word 'affect'. The more
rigorist Marxist would use the term 'determining' factors. This
raises some logical difficulties, not least the way the 'scientific'
Marxist avoids applying the term to his own thought. But if we
substitute for it the term 'conditioning' the case is very different.
Conditioning factors are subtle and far-reaching, and among
them economic-political ones are particularly powerful. But to be
conditioned is not to be determined. In principle one can be more
and more aware of conditioning factors and thus partially
transcend them, even though one can never completely transcend them. An uncontroversial illustration will show this. If I call
something Victorian it will convey something to my hearers. It
will not be meaningless. Yet if one examines the Victorian era one
quickly finds that it was full of deep disagreements and conflicts
aesthetically, intellectually and socially. Nevertheless looking
back on it from the next century we can see things which beneath
their differences the Victorians held in common, though they did
not realize it, and which differ in important respects from us. It is
these we are acknowledging when we call something Victorian.
Similarly in a hundred years from now those looking back on us
will see things we have in common in the midst of the creativities
and conflicts of this century of which we may have some

awareness, but are far from completely aware. We cannot jump out of our skins and be completely neutral observers and reasoners. There is no absolute perspective. This applies to every aspect of intellectual and cultural life, theology included, beyond formal propositions. No person, group or class can escape conditioning. (It is important to note that university faculty members are not exempt; sometimes they think they are, and are sometimes thought by others to be, above the relativities of popular attitudes in their pursuit of 'pure' knowledge. By profession many may be alert to conditioning factors in knowledge, but the wisest know that they too are conditioned by factors of which they are incompletely aware).[8] There is no super-human, super-temporal position of 'static impartiality'. Critical thought is a corrective process towards this, but it remains 'an impossible possibility' to use Reinhold Niebuhr's phrase with respect to the ethics of Jesus. In other words thought is always in need of correction; *semper reformanda* in Luther's phrase.

Sociology is inherently a radical discipline because it asks questions about what has hitherto been taken for granted. Even to ask such a question, even if the answer tends to be reassuring, is to sow a radical seed. The sociology of knowledge asks questions with which theologians have hardly begun to come to terms. Classical Christian theologies have been thought out down the centuries with no awareness of it, and have often been held in an aggressive way against others for lack of such awareness. Part of the discomfort caused to entrenched church practices and ways of thought by the Ecumenical Movement is that it is beginning to raise such questions.

Among conditioning factors the ones to which Political Theology calls attention are the most fundamental. We are all in debt to Marxism in this respect. We cannot be Marxists but neither can we be pre-Marxists. Another way of talking about them is to bring in the term 'ideology' to refer to conditioning factors preventing 'pure' thought. There can be partial and total ideologies. To some extent the term is a more precise way of denoting something of which we were not hitherto so systematically aware. Take theology as an example. It has been pointed out that theologies produced in the differing milieu of monastic communities, seminaries training for the priesthood, and Faculties of Theology in Universities have characteristically distinctive features. They are subject to partial ideologies. The illustration previously given of Victorianism was a total ideology. In the case of these the Marxist contention is that class is the chief total ideology and the basis of it lies in the 'relations of production' at any given time. On this there is of course an immense literature and many refinements of Marxist theory. It is sufficient for our present purposes to stress that class and economic factors are a very powerful source of ideologies. A moment's reflection shows that this is merely to express in a more systematic way what we often tend to assume. When there is a general election we assume that Barnsley will have a large Labour majority and Bournemouth a large Conservative one. The voters live in the same country, are voting for parties which offer the same leaders and the same programme to the whole country. Why do we assume that the majority of voters in Barnsley will make different judgments from those of Bournemouth? They have the same access to 'facts' and the same powers of reasoning. It is because they disagree as to what are the significant facts, and weigh them differently, because they experience them differently on account of their different interests. The dominant factors in the difference are economic, leading to different political judgments. Moreover these factors are sufficiently powerful to lead to the churchgoers going along with the general distribution of opinion in each place.

3. The third emphasis of recent Political Theology is that faith and practice must go together. The immediate background of this contention is again Marxist. Marx's eleventh thesis on Feuerbach is often quoted. 'The philosophers have only *interpreted* the world in various ways; the point is, to *change* it.' In Marxist terms this refers to the unity of theory and practice. But it is not a new thought. It has been a familiar Christian theme, epitomized in one of the Fourth Gospel meditations where Jesus is made to say ' . . . if any man's will is to do his will he shall know whether the teaching is from God . . .'[9] In other words, Christian faith is not understood by the intellectual acceptance of the words of a doctrinal formulation but by taking the risk of faith in action. It will be necessary to consider this point more fully in discussing Liberation Theology in the next chapter. For the present we should note that Political Theologians who write in this way are liable to speak of the need to formulate innovative models as a

basis for action to change, or indeed transform, the world and they often call these models ideologies. This is a different use of the term from the one I have been discussing so far. Bonino, for instance, writes of ideology in this sense as a 'mobilizing force'. The 'New Deal' in Roosevelt's USA or the 'Welfare State' in the Attlee administration of 1945 in Britain would be ideologies in this sense.

A different distinction has also been made between total ideologies as to whether they are used to express the interests of privileged groups, when they are called ideologies, or of un-privileged groups, when they are called utopias. This distinction goes back to Mannheim's classic study, in the course of which he moves into stressing the importance of reality-transcending utopias without which 'man would lose his will to shape history and therewith his ability to understand it'.[10] We shall have to be concerned with the role of utopias when we consider Liberation Theology. Stress on them is indeed characteristic of the Theology of Hope, which is a key aspect of contemporary Political Theology, but we can leave that aside for the moment. For the present it is sufficient to draw attention to the different senses in which ideology is used; if they are not distinguished confusion quickly occurs.

III

I turn now to six implications of political theology.

1. Any antithesis between changing persons and changing structures as the aim of Christian witness and evangelism is false. Both need changing. Individuals need to be freed from the bondage to sin, to use traditional language; but unjust and inhuman structures need changing too because structures mould persons long before the person knows what is happening or is able to make his or her own judgment on them. The basic structures of life are those of the family, the economic order and the political order, together with the all-pervasive culture into which one is born. The empirical forms of all of them varies greatly in different centuries and in different countries, but the fact of them is perennial, and they are what political theologians are referring to when they refer to the impossibility of being

apolitical. The cultural order is less sharply defined because it is so pervasive. One reflects the cultural even in clothes and hair styles as well as in basic artifacts. The more sharply defined structure of family life, economic system or state authority one is born into profoundly affects one's personhood from birth onwards, and to the extent that they are unjust they hinder the growth of the person together with other human beings into the full maturity in Christ, which St Paul correctly understands to be God's will for each one of us. To take an obvious example, every black child born in South Africa today is grievously wounded from birth by the economic and political system of *apartheid*, including its effects on the family. This is not a new point in Christian theology. It has been expressed by many theologians in this century, especially within the Ecumenical Movement. William Temple is an outstanding example. The Political Theologians are not alone in stressing it. They do not say that changing structures *ensures* the creation of new men and women, but that it vastly increases the possibility of doing so. To put it crudely good structures influence bad people to do right things, bad structures make it harder or even on occasions impossible, for good people to avoid doing 'wrong' things. The gospel of the kingdom of God, rooted in the witness of the synoptic gospels to the ministry of Jesus, embodies an eschatological dissatisfaction with things as they are which prompts the urge to improve them. Whether this is a gradual process, which is usual, or on occasion a revolutionary one (by which I mean drastic and quick but not necessarily violent) is in this context a secondary question. By contrast, as we have seen, it is astonishing how a faith inspired by the radical challenge of Jesus' parables and gnomic sayings should have so domesticated them in the course of Christian history and been so uncritical of whatever structures existed at the time.

2. Political Theology does not depend upon seeing Jesus as himself an immediately political figure. Twenty years ago there was much discussion whether Jesus was a nationalist zealot or, in contemporary terms, a freedom fighter. This has died down.[11] It is clear that he was not. We can see why not. If he was to embody in himself God's purposes for human life and teach and live an ethic of the kingdom of God so radical that it is always seeking to be realized in human living but is never completely realized,

Jesus could not be subsumed in the time-bound political situation of first-century Palestine with its contextual human causes and conflicts. Jesus' kingdom ethic is continually raising an eschatological question-mark against provisional human achievements, but without devaluing them. Jesus could not be contained by any of the causes for which the different groups he encountered contended. All of them found something disconcerting in him, and between them they brought about his crucifixion. In any event we are not called to imitate Christ in a wooden way but to be conformed to his spirit in our twentieth-century situation. The Political Theologians need only say with respect to the role of the Christian and the church in society that its reconstruction was not technically possible in Jesus' day but that the development of the means of production since has altered the situation and now it is. They also stress that Jesus showed a partiality to the poor, and this has led to the use of phrases like 'bias to the poor' or 'a preferential option for the poor'.[12] Hence in forming a judgment on existing social structures and institutions we should begin by paying attention to the evidence of those who are least privileged and most pushed around. This means actually listening to them. This is a somewhat over-simplified picture of Jesus, who was not only concerned for the literally poor but for *all* society's rejects, lepers, tax gatherers – and women who then, as in most societies throughout history, were dominated by men. But the basic point remains. That is why a citizen of the kingdom of God is likely to begin his or her political response to the gospel by making a negative judgment on at least some aspects of the *status quo* and seeking to improve them. Granted this starting point, recent Political Theologians have no problem with the fact that equally conscientious Christians may propose different practical remedies and belong to different political groups or parties. Their quarrel is with Christians who never start there because of a spurious apolitical theology, or a false one of the old Christendom variety.

3. The role of the Bible in Political Theology. As might be expected it stresses the corporate nature of the biblical message in both Testaments. Amid the great variety of circumstances in the period covered by the Old Testament and the different types of literature found in it, that which constitutes a unity in it for both

Jesus and Christians is that it arose out of the life of a community which regarded itself as a covenant-people, a people of God, and which selected it as sacred scripture, as an authoritative source for worship, doctrinal reflection and witness in life. The New Testament likewise emerged from a community which regarded itself as a reconstituted people of God, a new covenant community. It is false to say that the gospel is addressed to individuals and stop there. It certainly is addressed to individuals in that if one is old enough to be held responsible for one's actions (and not severely mentally handicapped) no one else can properly live one's life for one. But in presenting the challenge of the kingdom of God Jesus created the core of a new community, and to follow him is to be *ipso facto* a member of it. St Paul has captured this exactly in a favourite phrase of his, 'in Christ'. He uses it 164 times (not including the Pastoral Epistles), and it is clear that he means by it being a member of this new community.[13] Its membership is in intention universal and not bounded by the Jewish community, and transcending the social and political divisions which human beings create against one another. How it is to relate to the various kingdoms of the world (including its social and economic structures) in which its members find themselves cheek by jowl with those of other faiths, or philosophical substitutes like secular humanism or Marxism, is the basic question of Christian social ethics.

In addition to stressing the corporate nature of the biblical witness Political Theologians also point to the way in which detailed ethical stances in the Bible are related to the current intellectual and social situation. To confine ourselves to the New Testament, in the earliest decades of the church's life its members seem to have expected an imminent return of Christ and the end of the present world, thus fulfilling a type of apocalyptic expectation which was current in sections of Judaism at the time and which Jesus notably did not fulfil in his ministry (so that John the Baptist never became a disciple). St Paul in his earlier letters clearly expects this. His answers to six questions on marriage matters put to him by a deputation from the Corinthian church largely depend on this assumption.[14] In his later letters he no longer thinks it will happen before his death, but he still thinks it will not be far ahead. By the time we come to the Fourth Gospel this expectation has entirely disappeared, though it lingered on, as the attempt of II Peter, a second-century document, to answer it makes clear.[15] This mistaken belief of St Paul does not in fact make his detailed ethical teaching as irrelevant to us, as might be supposed, because of his robust instructions to find the way of Christian obedience today, in the present, confident that it will not be in vain.[16] Indeed some feel that the threat of nuclear war foreshortens our horizons and in its own way brings us near to St Paul in this respect. There is, however, another conditioning factor in St Paul's teaching which cannot be matched today. In the last resort he assumes that marriage is a distraction from the single service of God and celibacy is not. From where did he get this? It is very uncharacteristic of Judaism. Not from any teaching of Jesus that was circulating orally at the time and has survived in our gospels. Perhaps from the Hellenistic Judaism of Tarsus where he was brought up, which had absorbed a suspicion of human sexuality from aspects of Greek thought at the time.

Once the imminent return of Christ ceased to be expected, a new conditioning factor came into play. The Christian church had no political power nor position in the Roman empire, and it is anachronistic to expect it to contemplate either a successful rebellion or the overthrow of a basic institution like slavery. Nevertheless the Church accepted the current hierarchical relations with apparent equanimity. Paul may have taken the sting out of slavery in his letter to Philemon, but the later Pastoral Epistles (I and II Timothy and Titus) accept the duty of the inferior to the superior without qualification. There are instructions on the obedience of wives to husbands, children to parents and slaves to masters, but nothing on the duties of the superior party. This distortion, so early in the church's life and in its sacred scripture had a grievous influence on later history, as Political Theologians are not slow to point out.

4. The role of the church in Political Theology. The institution of the church itself comes under scrutiny. The church has its own structures of power because it employs persons and owns property. Questions of authority, responsibility and accountability arise in these respects which are not usually faced by official ecclesiologies. For instance churches with a theology of the independence of each congregation may find themselves much influenced by wealthy lay church members, or even

controlled by them, or by officials of a central bureaucracy
(perhaps because of pension arrangements for Ministers), and
these are liable to be the more powerful because the less avowed.
The influence of the Church Commissioners on the outlook of the
Church of England is a study in itself, not least because they are
ultimately responsible to Parliament and not to the General
Synod. Money talks. Or in matters where doctrine and church
power politics are involved the influence of the Curia in the
Roman Catholic Church in implementing or holding up the new
insights of the Second Vatican Council is of enormous, almost
decisive importance, yet there is no mention of it in the
documents of that Council, and no study of its development,
composition and exercise of power exists.

Political Theology is also concerned to examine how the church
can best handle the political order. How can the element of
legitimate protest in the sentiment 'I don't like politics in the
pulpit' be met without impairing the integrity of the church's life
and witness? Obviously it can be the naive protest of someone
who does not want the *status quo* questioned. On the other hand
what is the role of the sermon? And what other channels of the
formation of Christian judgments on the contemporary scene can
be fostered? If the sermon is essentially a proclamation of the
different facets of the disclosure of God to us in Jesus Christ 'the
same, yesterday, today and for ever',[17] how can church members
be helped to wrestle with the bearing of the perennial gospel on
the changing features of social, economic, industrial and political
issues? To refuse to take these up because they might cause
dissension and spoil the fellowship is an abdication of responsibility, and a thoughtless support in fact for the *status quo*. Yet this is
how many congregations allow themselves to go on year after
year. Sermons need supplementing but they, too, need to move
from the perennial to the contemporary. In a visit to Russia I
heard four sermons in one weekend. They were all on the theme
that Jesus Christ is the friend, unlike human friends, who will
never fail you. True. But suppose you are fed year in and year out
with nothing but such pious reflections! Would it not be the
religious opium castigated by Marx?

This leads to the question of how conflicts of opinion on
contemporary issues can be contained within the church and the
task of reconciliation not be let down. For there is no question that

if Christians abandon the task of forgiveness and reconciliation they abandon the gospel. It is no use in the midst of a conflict saying, 'Let us get this settled and then we can begin the process of reconciliation.' Remarks like this were heard in the 1939–45 war. Reconciliation must be pursued even in the midst of conflicts. Of course we must do all we can to prevent situations getting so polarized that irreconcilable positions are taken. Christians are continuously and properly looking for mediating possibilities which will prevent this happening. They can be naive in this but they need not be. But what if such efforts fail? There is no escape from going with one side or the other. Neutrality is not possible. This is a hard saying. But war is the clearest example of the truth of it. If it breaks out even a pacifist attitude can only be taken by courtesy of the rest on whom the pacifist must depend. In this extreme case moral criteria must not be abandoned in the effort to win, and reconciliation must be sought even in the midst of warfare. This is not impossible, but it is very hard to achieve. Many in Britain fought to destroy Hitlerism in the last world war without hating Germans. Since then there have been many examples of frightful dilemmas arising in guerilla warfare, when terrorists to one side have been freedom fighters to the other, and it is easy to be deceived by the rhetoric of either side. In South Africa it looks as if the situation has got, or is rapidly getting, so polarized that it is beyond what the reformists on either side can influence. The church cannot be above the conflict. Either she will side with the whites (even if reformist and not extremist) and offend the consciences of the blacks, or she will side with the blacks (even if reformist and not extremist) and offend that of the whites. How to act with the necessary realism and courage and still work for reconciliation in doing so will tax church folk to the utmost.

Political Theology must shed light on these tense situations. If there had been more awareness of it when the Programme to Combat Racism of the World Council of Churches was first announced in 1969 we would not have had so much outcry from Western Christians who were not pacifist against support for social, medical and educational purposes of some black groups who were engaged in violent action against their *de facto* rulers, such as the Portuguese. Their own countries have had long histories of wars backed by the churches, and are clearly contemplating the possibility of more in the future (not necessarily nuclear ones, which is another issue), and the churches do not oppose this in principle; they have not adopted a pacifist position. Then why must blacks be required to do so?

Questions of violence are the most tricky of all; they require a deeply thought theology of power if they are to be clarified. Political Theology helps the churches to be critically responsive to these and other social-political issues put on the agenda by the world, and not to be frozen by positio..s taken in the past. Fixed constants are always being sought in Christian faith and life, but there are none other than the reflection of the people of God themselves on what they have inherited from the past in the light of their reading of the signs of their own times. It may be an untidy process, but that is the way God works with his people. It is in the light of such reflections that the people of God today are reminding themselves to look beyond the manifest brotherhood of believers to the latent brothers of Christ in the poor and oppressed, as the allegory of the sheep and the goats in St Matthew's Gospel makes clear.[18]

5. Political Theology is important for a renewed Christian-Marxist dialogue which must eventually come. To some extent it is happening in Latin America, as we shall see in the next chapter, but not as much as one might expect from the themes of Liberation Theology. In Europe its brief post-cold-war life came to an end with the Russian invasion of Czechoslovakia.[19] It has not been renewed. Marxism has had a direct influence on utopian elements in theologies of Hope, which will be considered later, but direct discussion is almost paralysed. It will not be easy for either side. Marxism will find a revision of traditional Marxist attitudes to all religions (not just Christianity) requires a fundamental reorientation, because the criticism of religion is the keystone of Marxist theories. However Marxism is as much a plural phenomenon these days as is Christianity, so that there should not be too much difficulty in making a start. Russian Marxists and Russian Christians will have the most difficulty; the Christians because they have been insulated for seventy years from modern intellectual movements, the Marxists because the political authorities have insulated them from all but caricatures of Christian doctrines. On the Christian side the influence of

Political Theology will be vital in a renewed Marxist-Christian dialogue. Those who are uninfluenced by it will see nothing but a complete opposition between them and no basis for dialogue.

6. The ultimate claim of Political Theology is that only a theology of the kingdom of God can be sufficiently self-critical to cope with the modern world. It is not a 'death of God' theology, as John Shelley claims in his introduction to Sölle's 1974 book. 'Death of God' theology was an aberration which hit the USA in the 1960s and faded almost as quickly as it came to the fore. There are indeed metaphysical problems connected with Christian theism which cannot be ignored. In Britain they have been eloquently expressed by Don Cupitt in books and television programmes,[20] to take one example. This is not the occasion to discuss them because they have not figured prominently in the writings of Political Theologians. They are believers in God and his kingdom as taught and lived by Jesus. As against Marxism the Christian knows less and not more than such an ideology claims to do about the temporal future of humanity. In the present his or her allegiance is to the kingdom of God as it challenges established institutions now, as it should have done more effectively in the past, and will undoubtedly go on to do in the future. This challenge in their view needs to be vindicated today and put at the centre of the theological task. To change the institutions requires investigative inter-disciplinary work in order to understand where we are now, together with innovative models to help us formulate where we are trying to go. In so far as these are based on Christian criteria such as the worth of persons, the solidarity of persons, the freedom of the person, or openness to the future, to quote some that have been proposed, there is no great difficulty. But some models of creative expectation use the mythological language of apocalyptic to free us from being time-bound to the present, and have utopian strains whose relevance to immediate decisions is hard to see. This will concern us in the next chapter.

IV

The influence of Political Theology extends far beyond the few who self-consciously use the term. It presents a sharp challenge to traditional theological methods, which have been sociologically innocent. Kee's anthologies show the variety within the category: for instance black theology, feminist theology and ecological theology as well as liberation theology (which is a development of political theology). In so far as these are partial they need placing in the fundamental perspective we discussed earlier in this chapter. It crosses confessional boundaries. Many of the new strains in Roman Catholic theology since the Second Vatican Council are open to it, especially the Pastoral Constitution *Gaudium et Spes* (The Church in the Modern World). It has been implicit in the 'Life and Work' side of the Ecumenical Movement from the beginning, and became more explicit in the World Council of Churches from the Geneva Conference of 1966 on 'Christians in the Technical and Social Revolutions of our Time', which itself was a conscious successor of the Oxford Conference on 'Church, Community and State' of 1937.[21] At a joint conference between the 'Church and Society' section of the WCC and the 'Faith and Order' section at Zagorsk in the USSR in 1968 the latter side of the Ecumenical Movement was brought in. And in subsequent years the advent of more Third World theologians and church leaders reinforced its influence.

Its effect on the traditionally conservative Lutheran theology of Germany has been striking. It was a second stage reaction. Dissatisfaction with it was first expressed by some who followed Karl Barth, the Calvinist. The Lutheran reaction was spearheaded by Bultmann. He stressed a personalist, existentialist self-knowledge as a necessary pre-understanding before the gospel message can be appropriated. This, when it is appropriated, leads to authentic personal living. This, however, can be no better than the old style individualistic Protestant pietism, spuriously apolitical and ahistorical. Sölle, and one thinks especially of her, maintained that a 'corrective' was needed to this. That is to say she did not completely repudiate it, but said that a social and economic-political pre-understanding is also needed before the gospel message can be appropriated. Then one realizes that no one can be saved alone, and that the social order is not some vast, inexplicable and in the end irrelevant backdrop to Christian living, but is intelligible and transformable by human beings. Bultmann was one of the leading Form Critics, who examined how the gospel tradition was shaped by the needs of the early Christian congregations, as fragments of it circulated by word of mouth before the gospel writers put it together in a connected narrative. He should have carried this investigation into the pre-understanding involved in appropriating the gospel to a more thorough study of the 'political' milieu (in the wide sense of Political Theology) of those Christians. Such studies have begun to be made in the years since Bultmann's death.[22]

Theology and church life in Britain has remained largely untouched by explicit influences from Political Theology. In some ways it may even have regressed. William Temple spent much time in explaining why the church should 'interfere' with politics (to quote a pejorative word often used) and could not be apolitical. By the time of his death the point appeared to have been largely made, and it seemed no longer necessary to go back to the beginning and argue it all over again. But now it seems necessary to do so. Bourgeois individualistic attitudes flourish in church life and Boards for Social Responsibility and the like have an uphill task.

Political Theology has, of course, its dangers. Its new form could be as uncritically biased to the Left as that traditional form of it which sees God as the great conserver was to the Right. This is nicely expressed in the General Thanksgiving in the 1662 Book of Common Prayer which thanks God for our 'creation, preservation and all the blessings of this life'. There is in it no thought of social change. Indeed it was part of the conservative restoration of the monarchy in 1660, ignoring the social and economic changes which were proceeding apace, which were to be more marked in the next century, and which are still proceeding. Even recent liturgical revisions have not caught up with this. No wonder it is hard to relate public worship to the structures of life in which we are placed. But change is not to be divinized. It needs to be evaluated and guided. Political Theology needs to draw out the right criteria.

A weakness of it is that it has little to say about celestial hopes. There is not much in it of the note that 'here we have no lasting city'.[23] Some reticence about our knowledge of life beyond the grave is wise in view of the exuberance of the details with which Christian preaching in past ages has embellished the theme. But it is a sure hope of those who worship God through Jesus Christ, and it needs relating to the terrestrial causes in which we must engage, if we are not to get them out of perspective. Political Theology is apt to suspect that thoughts of celestial hopes will cut the nerve of terrestrial effort. It could do, and it has done on occasion. All Christian doctrines are liable to, and have, suffered corruptions. The task is to guard against them. The kingdom of God, inaugurated by Jesus, is a present reality and a future hope. Political Theologians accuse those who stress the present reality and the need for obedience today (since our powers of forecasting the future are so limited and our vision of a consummation beyond the present space-time world bears only indirectly on present decisions) of preaching an individualistic and a-historical faith.[24] But this is by no means necessarily the case; no more than a stress on the future kingdom and final salvation need be, though it often is. The former has a salutary awareness of the ambiguities of history, which maintains an eschatological reserve in relation to even the most plausible current policy without losing an eschatological optimism that God will complete the good work he has begun in creation and renewed in Christ.

It is precisely the question of an eschatological reserve which is one of the main criticisms by Liberation Theology of Political Theology. It is this much more radical criticism than the caveats advanced here which leads to an appraisal of Liberation Theology, to which we turn in the next chapter.[25]

11

Liberation Theology: an Appraisal

Liberation Theology originated in Latin America. Like Political Theology, of which it is a development, it refers to theology in its totality in relation to its social milieu and as directed to transforming it. Hitherto theologians, like philosophers according to Marx, 'have only interpreted the world in various ways: the point is, to change it'.[1] In the view of Liberation Theology a new post-bourgeois society is on the way in which the hitherto marginalized, deprived and de-humanized persons will come into their own. It provides the basis for commitment to the process by which God is bringing this about.[2]

Latin America is the only major area in the world where there has been a colonial version of the Christendom situation.[3] In the classical colonial period Roman Catholicism provided the theological backing; church and state were clearly allied. In the neo-colonial era Protestantism arrived, mainly from the USA, with an ideology which fitted well with capitalism and allied itself with dominant entrepreneurs and financiers. In the course of the 1960s disillusionment arose with *desarrollo*, the developmentalist theory of economic growth according to which newly created wealth trickles down through the economy to the poor. Latin America developed the first indigenous theological movement to come from outside the bounds of 'Western' Christianity, though most of the leaders were at least partially trained in Europe in biblical studies, philosophy and theology.[4]

It is a well populated but unstable area. Half the Roman Catholics in the world are found in it. In Brazil the cities have doubled in population in ten years. The contrast between the extremes of wealth and the misery of life in the shanty towns is grotesque. In El Salvador twelve families are said to own most of the land. Political instability is marked. For example Argentine has recently shaken off a dictatorship, and Brazil has rid itself of one which seized power in 1974, but Chile still suffers under the Pinochet regime which, with covert help from the USA, overthrew the Allende government in 1973. Liberation Theology dominated the 'Christians for Socialism' conference at Santiago in Chile that year. At that time there was an optimistic note in it, with much stress on the Exodus as a paradigm of liberation which was being re-enacted. Since then the right-wing political backlash caused the leaders to be scattered, and Mexico became their chief centre, where they held a conference in 1975. The theme of Captivity came to the fore, of patience under suffering, but yet with hope even though revolution may not be possible this century. In either case their method has been described as nothing less than a new way of doing theology, 'on the edge of humanity'.[5] The milieu of the leaders has in fact been that of the university and the middle class, which sociologically considered is likely to be the most mobile and creative section of society, but lately there have been developments at the grass roots, as we shall see.

The influence of Liberation Theology grew quickly, notably at the second general conference of Roman Catholic bishops of Latin America (CELAM) at Medellin in Columbia in 1968.[6] Before long it spread to the rest of the Third World.[7] It began to be noticed in the USA, whose lines of communication with Latin America are strong, and after that in Europe.[7] In Britain the name has become familiar, but it is doubtful whether many understand exactly what Liberation Theologians are saying, though the general impression that they are politically radical and stand in the name of the gospel for 'a preferential option for the poor' is accurate enough.

I

Liberation Theology begins with a critique of 'Western' theology. This thinks of itself as being objective, scientific and universal. In fact it has been overwhelmingly produced and consumed by a small and economically comfortable section of that society. No theology can be as objective as these claims suppose. It is always partial and in need of an ideological critique.[8] Liberation Theology differentiates itself from all alternative theologies on offer. We will mention six of them.

1   Christendom Theology

Criticisms of this are the same as those made by Political Theologians discussed in the previous chapter.

2   New Christendom Theology

In Roman Catholic circles this refers to an outlook embodied in what is often known as 'Catholic Action'. Its theological basis is found in such sources as the Papal Encyclicals *Quadragesimo Anno* (1931) and *Mystici Corporis* (1943). It is held to have flourished from about 1931 to the Second Vatican Council (1962–5). It is said to represent a shift from a theology of the landowning class to a reformist theology of bourgeois developmentalism. It overlooked the fact that the economic development of Latin America was quite different from that of nineteenth-century European capitalism. W. W. Rostow's well known thesis of the five stages of economic growth did not apply.[9] Instead a neo-colonial dependence on the USA was the outcome. In social theology writers like Congar and Chenu, who refer to 'Christian principles' as a guide to society, work within what Gutierrez calls 'a distinction of planes', that is to say a false separation between a churchly sphere and a temporal sphere.[10] This in practice means adopting a political pluralism in an attempt to be neutral. However we do not need reformers, we need a commitment to liberation; it is a qualitative leap to this from a reformist 'social concern'.

3   Vatican II Theology

This is a development from New Christendom theology. It is seen in the effort of the Pastoral Constitution, *Gaudium et Spes*, to discern the signs of the times by taking seriously the struggle for humanity wherever in the world it is taking place. Some of its best expressions include the Encyclical *Populorum Progressio* (1967), the Pope's words in Columbia in 1968 that 'development is the new name for peace', the Medellin statement the same year which acknowledged built-in structures of injustice in society, and the statement on 'Justice in the World' made by the Synod of Bishops in Rome in 1971. Yet this theology is still held to be a mixture of political reformism combined with a preoccupation with internal church renewal. Liberation Theologians say that revolution, not development, is the new name for peace. The text of *Populorum Progressio* does not explicitly rule out revolution. It says that it will do more harm than good 'save where there is manifest long-standing tyranny which would do great damage to fundamental personal rights and dangerous harm to the common good of the country'.[11] The Bishops at Medellin defined revolution not in terms of violence but of people participating themselves in change as subjects, which was radical in terms of the Latin American context, and wise in that revolution is not necessarily bound up with violence but signifies drastic and rapid change.

Vatican authorities have been wary of Liberation Theology, not rejecting it but stressing dangers. A recent document from the Congregation for the Defence of the Faith criticizes it, but refers to a preferential option for the poor whose aspirations are fully justified. 'The scandal of the shocking inequality between the rich and poor – whether between rich and poor countries, or between social classes in a single nation – is no longer tolerated.' It says that its criticism of Liberation Theology must not be taken as any approval of those who profit from human misery. These criticisms are that it tends to (i) an implication all sin is social, (ii) an exclusively political reading of the Bible, (iii) an emphasis on class struggle (which in fact slows reforms and aggravates poverty and injustice), (iv) a use 'in an insufficiently critical manner, [of] concepts borrowed from various currents of Marxist thought' which is rooted in an ideology incompatible with the Christian faith.[12] How far these are plausible criticisms will emerge in the course of this chapter.

4 *Political Theology*

This is criticized for not being sufficiently 'scientific'. By this is meant not Marxist enough. It is forever concerned with the prolegomena to action but not with action itself. It still maintains a distinction between dogma and ethics. It attacks all kinds of absolutisms, including ecclesiastical triumphalism, but under the guise of the critical function of theology it opts for liberal reformism. It says it 'inclines to the Left'. But who will give his life for an inclination to the Left?[13] It claims a false autonomy for theology, as if it could take a middle course between Right and Left on the basis of some centrally situated reason, fortified by a doctrine of justification by faith. Its 'eschatological reserve' is without élan. Knowledge does not come from 'applying' political theology but from commitment to action on behalf of the poor. It is too preoccupied with the secularized European unbeliever when in fact the scandal is the marginalized, de-humanized poor person. The Enlightenment has led to the former, Marx drew attention to the latter. Moreover in Latin America, with 90 per cent of the population nominally believers, the church has power. How does it use it? These criticisms of Political Theology are not entirely fair to it, as the previous chapter has shown, but there is enough substance in them to be taken seriously.

5   The Theology of Revolution

Even this will not do. It was first heard of by a wider public at the Church and Society Conference of the World Council of Churches on 'Christians in the Technical and Social Revolutions of our Time' at Geneva in 1966. It was introduced, to the astonishment of most of those present, by church elders and others from Latin America, who are usually thought of as somewhat staid figures, arguing that all other alternative forms of bringing about social change and remedying gross injustices were blocked. A revolution was needed. However in the view of Liberation Theologians this understanding quickly became Europeanized and theoretical. It became abstract, lacking any basis in concrete practice.

6   The Theology of Hope

This replaces a Theology of the Beyond (trans-temporal), which has been endemic in Christendom, with one of God's future, but in practice it scarcely links with the struggle for liberation in the unjust present. Moltmann is particularly in mind. His stress on God as Promise, supremely seen in the Cross, as the source of absolute freedom is held to suggest that suffering is to be sought, and to underplay the participation of people in their own liberation. It is not true, however, that Moltmann is a Liberal in the political sense; in European terms he appears to be a Democratic Socialist. But in Gutierrez' categories he is undoubtedly a reformist. However Gutierrez approves of Moltmann's contrast between a calculable, foreseeable future and a desirable *avenir* which cannot be calculated but only anticipated (like the *parousia*).[14] However, there is reason to query the use of this distinction in making detailed ethical decisions, as distinct from contributing to the motives in making them.[15]

II

There are two basic starting-points in Liberation Theology; they are a prior commitment to the cause of the poor, and the need for a 'scientific' analysis to know how to implement it.

Liberation Theology holds that without active commitment to the cause of the poor authentic biblical and theological reflection cannot start. God is revealed in the actual historic context of the struggle of the poor for liberation. Without commitment to that what is arrived at will be the product of 'false consciousness'. It will be distorted. It will reflect a false ideology. The only valid truth is that which contributes to the struggle for liberation, not truth abstractly conceived in a study. Orthodoxy requires orthopraxis before it can be arrived at. We can discover the meaning of the gospel only by 'doing the truth', as St John's Gospel constantly stresses, and this means the *opción preferencial*. It is this pre-understanding we must bring to the gospels, not the individualistic existentialist one of Bultmann. Every theology is conditioned by the class position and class consciousness of the theologian, whether it be that of the bourgeois élite, the petty bourgeois or the grass roots poor. Nevertheless Liberation Theology shares in the Marxist assumption that some can transcend their class position and throw in their lot with the poor. Why this is so, in terms of the theory, is not clear. At any rate middle-class theologians are needed as technical advisers at the moment, for instance on the Bible, but they should seek to make themselves redundant and hand over the 'means of production' (in theology) to the poor. Since about 1975 Liberation Theologians have taken more seriously the poor themselves as actors, and have come to a more positive view of the Christianity expressed in the folk religion of Latin America, hitherto regarded as largely superstitious, and are willing to be taught by it.[16]

In a sense Liberation Theology has turned the Augustinian and Anselmian teaching on faith seeking understanding into commitment to the poor seeking understanding. If, for instance, one has this commitment one sees the Exodus as a political event which is a paradigm of the whole historical struggle for liberation (rather like Chairman Mao's perpetual revolution). In the New Testament Jesus will be seen as letting loose an active and vigorous messianism, which is a revolutionary force continually seeking the liberating opportunity, however partial it be. We cannot expect to avoid all errors and dangers in this struggle, nor that all evident defects in existing socialist systems will be avoided in the new order we are striving to bring about.

The second starting-point of Liberation Theology is its insistence on the need for a 'scientific' analysis of the contemporary situation. If we do not know what is happening we cannot effectively implement our preferential option for the poor. 'Political action calls for a scientific analysis of reality; there is a continuous interrelation between action and analysis.'[17] By 'science' is meant Marxism. Bonino is typical in assuming that it has shown that there is an irreversible movement of history towards socialism.[18] By this is meant (i) the common ownership of the means of production, (ii) the ending of a class-divided society, (iii) the de-alienation of work. There is no discussion of the basic economic problems of any society, such as the allocation of relatively scarce resources, and of how they are to be tackled in a post-industrial revolution economy.

To find out 'what is going on' as accurately as we can is certainly necessary. It is not sufficient to 'mean well'. If we stop there we easily make decisions which are irrelevant, or even harmful, to what we want to achieve. The trouble is that Liberation Theologians assume that the Marxist social and political analysis is a 'science' or 'scientific rationality' in understanding the direction of history. (Dussel is an exception.) They accept too readily the Marxist claim to have discovered the laws of 'scientific socialism', in the sense of being a satisfactory basis for prediction. In fact a certain selection from Marxist theories is being made, but without discussion of what and why. The intention is to be critically Marxists and to be 'a permanent critical consciousness at the heart of the revolutionary process'.[19] Assmann says that Christians are bound to raise questions about fellowship, sacrifice and death which Marxism hardly faces. What sense is there in the radical act of dying for others? Marxism is not drawn upon for basic doctrines. There is no illusion about its atheism and no intention of accepting it. It is, however, assumed that its economic and political thinking is a 'science' which corresponds with 'the facts', and that these can be divorced from its ontology. This is a hazardous assumption to make because those Marxists who most affirm its scientific status are the ones who most regard it as a seamless web from which it is impossible to remove the critique of religion without bringing down the whole system. Indeed they are likely to say that the criticism of religion is the heart of the structure.[20]

The use by Liberation Theology of Marxism as a 'master of suspicion' or, in other words, as an unmasker of ideologies is in line with what we have considered in discussing Political Theology.[21] Its use of the theory of the unity of theory and praxis will be considered in the next section. Here something further needs to be said of its use of Marxist economic theories to explain the neo-colonial dependence of Latin America. I do not doubt that in the situation of Latin America the Marxist explanation of this dependency seems plausible. The trouble is that the practitioners of Liberation Theology seem not to be well equipped to deal with economics and they do not realize how far from 'scientific' the theories are as a basis for prediction. They were led astray into imagining there was a revolutionary situation in the early 1960s. This is only one of the latest of many failures in Marxist prognosis. It has a history of startling mistaken forecasts. Here are some examples. (i) That the working class would become absolutely more impoverished. (ii) That the first socialist revolution would take place in the most industrially developed countries. (iii) That socialist societies would be free from internal contradictions. (iv) That there would be no conflicts of interest between socialist governments.[22] Explanations in Marxist terms have, of course, been given of all these falsified predictions, but they have all been advanced afterwards to justify the theories. It is doubtful whether they have ever predicted a significant new factor.

Several basic Marxist economic theories were adumbrated by Engels in 1844 before any of Marx's economic writings.[23] He assumed technical progress allied with the division of labour would lead to the abolition of scarcity and would make communism possible, and that his theories were 'scientifically' certain. Marx was later to accuse bourgeois economists of being 'hired prize fighters', and to claim that his theories were akin to those of

physics. According to him the 'natural laws of capitalist production' are working with 'iron necessity towards inevitable
results'.[24]

There are no such inevitable laws at work in society. That
means that there is no inevitable move to socialism, as Bonino
and most of the Liberation Theologians suppose. Capitalism is
much tougher than the theory allows for.[25] The economic
theories are the weakest part of Marxism, weaker than its
sociological theories. But all of it, whilst containing useful
insights, is sufficiently flawed not to be a basis for prediction. It
drew attention to factors either hitherto unrecognized or which
were being neglected in the nineteenth century. It is impossible
to return to a pre-Marxist way of thinking. Yet Marxism is not
'scientific' in the sense claimed. It is a pity Liberation Theologians
have not subjected the claim to more serious examination.
Among other things it leads them to an over-confident, if
somewhat imprecise, stress on the role of utopias (or ideologies
in the sense of co-ordinating ideas) as instruments for not only
denouncing what is, but for announcing what will be, because of
the irreversible movement towards socialism.[26]

III

The main theological themes which emerge from Liberation
Theology concern (i) the method of reading the Bible; (ii) the
doctrines that derive from that reading, especially concerning the
significance of Jesus Christ; (iii) the role of the church; (iv) the
relation of all these to life under God in the world.

1. Segundo gives one of the best accounts of the way Liberation Theologians approach the Bible, with his account of an
'hermeneutical circle'.[27] Assuming commitment to the poor
before reflection on the Word of God can start, one begins with an
'ideological suspicion' of the present economic and political
reality and goes on to a similar suspicion of the superstructure of
thought associated with it, including theology. This leads to a
suspicion of current biblical exegesis and thus to a new way of
understanding (or hermeneutic) of Scripture. In Britain Bishop
David Sheppard of Liverpool has attempted a somewhat similar
schema.[28] His steps are: (i) examine what critical factors affected

the biblical writers. What glasses did they wear? That is to say, what conditioning factors affected them? (ii) ask ourselves what glasses we wear; (iii) commit ourselves to action in obedience to what we believe God is saying in our particular situation, and to critical reflection on those actions; (iv) let the biblical text speak to the questions we then bring to it. Political Theology rather than Liberation Theology is the background of this, and it may well be none the worse for that. There are questions one would ask of both as to the type of illumination on current issues one is to expect from the Bible, and the intermediate steps between that illumination and the text if it is to be more than a general insight and refer to specific conclusions and actions in any given context. Both assume that there is 'a reserve of meaning' at the heart of the Scriptures which cannot be shut up in the immediate context of their production. Indeed without that biblical study would be merely of historical interest. Sheppard's schema fits more readily into current scholarship in biblical studies, provided it is prepared to face the questions raised by the sociology of knowledge. Segundo's schema seems a more abrupt break with it because of its apparent stricter tie to the theory of the unity of theory and praxis.

To the Christian there is a difficulty with the Marxist theory at this point. It is one which is reflected in the New Testament itself. On the one hand there are statements like this one from the Sermon on the Mount, 'Not every one who says to me "Lord, Lord," shall enter into the kingdom of Heaven, but he who does the will of my Father who is in heaven',[29] or the continual emphasis in St John's Gospel that doing the truth is the condition of knowing it. This stresses the unity of theory and praxis. On the other hand there are verses which say that we all fall short of what we know we ought to do, and are never beyond the need for God's forgiveness. St Paul is caught on both sides of this dilemma. In the Epistle to the Romans, his greatest sustained theological reflection, he argues in the first four chapters that no one, neither Jew nor Greek, can claim acceptance by God because of his or her moral achievements. The good news of the gospel is that Jesus Christ has shown that God accepts us in spite of our sins. The next four chapters go on to work out in a series of metaphors and similes the meaning of this relationship with God through Christ. The burden of them is a paradoxical exhortation

which amounts to saying 'Since you are in this new relationship
with God because of his boundless graciousness you cannot
possibly sin any more – therefore don't sin'! The graphic account
he gives in the seventh chapter of the divided self which finds
itself doing what at bottom it knows to be wrong and does not
want to do, can be interpreted as applying only to the pre-
Christian self. But from what St Paul says elsewhere of his
Christian pilgrimage as a striving towards what he has not
attained,[30] and from Christian experience down the centuries
(including that of those we consider the most 'saintly'), it is much
more plausible to interpret it of the permanent human state.
Faced with the demands of the gospel of God's love, the human
response in love, as for instance St Paul pictures it in I Corinthians
13, is inexhaustible. The more one knows of love the more one
finds there is to know. There is an inevitable gap between theory
and practice in the Christian life, a contrast we all experience in
our own case between what is and what ought to be.

In practice the exegesis of the gospels in Liberation Theology is
quite conservative in terms of current biblical scholarship. It
tends to accept the substantial historicity of the chronology of
Jesus' ministry in the synoptic gospels, including a crisis in
Galilee in the middle of it.[31] The stress is on the kingdom of God
in the life and teaching of Jesus, which all accept as the key to his
ministry. Liberation Theologians are likely to say that the
crucifixion of Jesus crowned a life in the service of justice; that he
established the poor as the messianic people; that he was not a
political figure like a Zealot, but that he summoned the poor to
form his kingdom, and only from their standpoint do we grasp
the radical nature of his liberation.[32] It is possible to chip away at
such statements and to point out, for example, that Jesus was
concerned with all society's rejects, not only the literally poor
(and including that one of the two sexes oppressed by the other –
women), but substantially the case is made: but it is not necessary
to start where the liberation theologians say we must in order to
accept it. That is to say, it is possible for one who was not
previously aware of the radical nature of the kingdom of God,
and may have etherialized it into a purely inward stance, to see
that in fact it does demand a looking at life 'from the underside of
history', and a radical eschatological dissatisfaction with the
social *status quo*; and the radicalization can be arrived at *after* the

study rather than because of a commitment to the poor made prior to it.

In approaching the Bible, and the Christian faith derived from it, the unity of theory and practice is not a doctrine that works. There must be some theology of the need to take the Bible seriously, some awareness of the ideological factors in knowledge, and some analysis of the present scene, and some commitment to action. There is no order of importance between these four; they all need to be present and to be related to one another. That relation is a reciprocal one. This is the never-ending reciprocal movement, each continually reacting with the other. Those who take Marxism very seriously want to use the word dialectical of the relationship. This term, with its Hegelian background, refers to the alleged pattern by which life and thought moves by a process of thesis setting up its opposite, an antithesis, so that out of the tussle between the two a new position is arrived at, a synthesis, embracing elements of both thesis and antithesis at a 'higher' level. This becomes a new thesis, and so the process goes on. Sometimes thoughts and processes may plausibly be held to develop like this, but there is no plausibility in maintaining that they always do. An understanding of a reciprocal relationship is what is needed.

Theologians who do not accept the extent to which Liberation Theology has adopted the Marxist view of the unity of theory and practice, and who doubt the justification of calling Marxist economic-political analysis 'scientific', have nevertheless to produce their own analysis of 'what is going on' today and what in the light of it they must do to respond to the gospel's concern for the poor. They will need to work with, and draw upon, the experience of others who have something relevant to contribute, including experts at certain points. They cannot find it out from the Bible or the Nicene Creed. The result will usually be some differences of judgment among equally committed Christians, simply because there is no 'science' in the Marxist sense to tell us. Continued discussions must go on within the church. I have written elsewhere on this matter, and will not add to or repeat it here.[33]

2. We can pass over quite quickly the doctrines which arise from the Bible, because the same considerations apply. Libera-

tion Theologians have not shown much interest in classical and ongoing theological problems such as how to understand today the doctrine of the Two Natures of Christ as formally expressed in the Definition of Faith of the Council of Chalcedon in 451. What they are interested in is how classical doctrines, such as those of the Incarnation and Atonement, have been used and are being used in a social context. They point out that popular teaching about, and representations in painting and sculpture of, the tortured, anguished and dead Christ are used to inculcate the acceptance of domination and suffering, making no distinction between sufferings which are remediable and those which are not, and accepting structures of domination uncritically. The Russian Church was a striking example of this for centuries, and it has paid a penalty ever since 1917. Soteriological images need to be translated from the eternal world to that of human history, so that redemption is seen as the opening of a new way to be truly human. Christological 'poetics' need to become a source of hope and inspiration for the liberation of human beings.[34]

3. We turn to the church (which is of course itself a key element in a biblically derived Christian doctrine). The church in Latin America is powerful. It needs liberating from false ideologies. It needs to become post-Constantinian and to abandon its clinging to a Christendom situation. Segundo says it has no need to be primarily concerned with its own institutional preservation for it is aiming to be a minority who know God's plan and are prepared to take responsibility for others. The church is not over against humanity but is part of it. It is not a community of the saved, nor is it necessary to be in it to be saved. Sentiments such as these are not peculiar to Liberation Theology, and their cogency can be discussed without drawing upon it.

That theology show no interest in traditional ecclesiological discussion of the 'marks' of the church as, for instance, in the Papal Encyclical *Immortali Dei*. It is concerned with the actual working of the church as an institution. It was Leonardo Boff's criticism of the centralized and authoritarian structures of the Roman Catholic Church which got him into trouble with the Sacred Congregation for the Defence of the Faith.[35] Liberation Theology is particularly associated with what are commonly known as 'basic communities' of which there are said to be

anything between 30,000 and 60,000 in Brazil alone. They vary
considerably, but mostly they consist of 20–30 men and women
getting together once a week to reflect on the Bible and their faith
in its bearing on their own situation. The overwhelming majority
are poor; 'basic' in the title refers to 'the masses' in the sense of the
poor. They are lay. Priests, or perhaps a social scientist, are
usually to be found in them, but they do not act as paternalistic
animators. Rather they function more like 'organic intellectuals'
in Gramsci's theory, who help to produce a critique of the church
for allowing itself to follow the ruling class in the struggle for
hegemony by imposing its conception of reality on the lower
classes and thus achieving an ideological consensus.[36] These
groups take up immediate social issues such as land tenure or the
absence or complete inadequacy of social services. Much of their
strength comes from the fact that they are among the very few
effective grass roots bodies in society, quite unlike the situation in
a 'Western' democracy. They pose problems for the church, but
they *are* the church in their context; they are not a sect, but their
relation to the traditional church structures is one which ecclesiologies of the past have never had to think about. Their method
is to begin with pressing immediate problems facing the community, then look at the questions raised in the light of a biblical
passage, often with the help of a person with some theological
training to explain the meaning of a text in its context. Then they
work collectively at what the meaning of the text is for themselves
today, and lastly decide what to do practically about the
questions from which the collective process of reflection
started.[37]

The 'official' church is caught in an awkward situation. In
many Latin American countries it is living under authoritarian
regimes who have a concept of a 'national security state' which
regards defeating internal dissidence as important as defending
its frontiers, indeed as a war in itself. Right-wing groups for the
defence of Tradition, Family and Property have been formed in
the church in several countries. The hierarchy is faced with these
on the one hand and the basic communities on the other. It wants
to preserve the unity of the institution whilst helping victims of
oppression, without what is pejoratively called a politicization of
the church.[38] In 1968 the Medellin conference of Bishops took the
social reality of Latin America, not that of Europe, as its starting-

point, and made a major step in pinpointing the evil of institutionalized violence. The Puebla Conference in 1979 faced all ways
and settled nothing. It stressed the hierarchical nature of the
church, the need to preserve the common life and participation of
all its members, the need for the liberation of the people, and that
the priests should keep out of politics.[39] Meanwhile the Protestant churches, still predominantly apolitical in a spurious sense,
reached a turning-point for some of them at an Evangelical
gathering in Mexico in 1978 when they made an explicit statement on the need for emancipation from colonialism, and for
concern for the structures of life in which human beings find
themselves willy-nilly, and of their need for reformation.

4. The theological point which relates all these considerations
to life under God in the world need not occupy us at length. It is a
stress on men and women as co-creators with God in nature and
history. Christ as our representative enables us to renew our co-
creatorship under God. This is not an affirmation peculiar to
Liberation Theology. That theology does not reflect any of the
unease about human technological prowess, or about ecological
issues, which has been shown by many Christians in Europe and
North America and other affluent areas of the world in recent
years.[40] Neither has it had anything particular to say about what,
beyond death, may transcend the present order of time and
space.

IV

Although some critique of Liberation Theology has been embodied throughout this chapter in commenting on its background, a
more explicit section is needed. Conventional criticisms are easy
enough to foresee: that the church is concerned with the salvation
of individuals; that the church's creativity is exercised in its own
life and not in the world; that men and women must learn to live
with some poverty, oppression and suffering because in a fallen
world they are irremediable; that violence can never be used with
Christian approval; and that Liberation Theology is only a
passing fad. I do not propose to discuss these.

More weighty is a critique maintained for many years by a
Belgian Jesuit, Roger Vekemans, now in Bogota, who was an

adviser to the Frei government in Chile. He publishes a journal *Terra Nueva*.[41] Associated with him is Bishop Lopez Trujillo, now President of CELAM (the Conference of Latin American Bishops), who did his best to keep Liberation Theology at arm's length at Puebla. Neither is an advocate of free market capitalism, and both agree that the church cannot be apolitical, as Nazism showed. They contend that faith is prior to praxis; that since there is no inviolable centre of a social organism as there is of a human person, social and personal ethics cannot be identified; that Liberation Theology subsumes faith in political practice; that it is uncritical about Marxism and therefore utopian; and that gospel values should certainly inform doctrinal statements on society, but that the application of these to detailed situations is indirect – through the media of ideological and political criteria – and then not by the church or the clergy as such, for the job of the clergy is to forge unity among its members at a level beyond political divisions.

I hope it is clear from this chapter that most of these criticisms can be answered though they cannot be brushed aside. The most plausible is the charge of being uncritical about Marxism. It is not wholly true. Segundo, for instance, has a section on 'The Oversimplification of Marxist Sociology'.[42] But in so far as it is true it illustrates a problem which is not peculiar to Liberation Theology, and one which has already been referred to in this chapter, that of moving from affirmation of Christian faith to detailed ethical decisions and policies. Empirical evidence is needed to understand the present situation, and there are problems in obtaining it; and no complete certainty in doing so, and in assessing it when obtained, is posssible. Theologians are rarely experts in the various secular disciplines involved. When grass roots experience is attended to, experts are still needed to put it in a wider context and assess wider implications of possible actions. But experts often differ or speak beyond their competence. In the end non-experts have to evaluate the evidence of experts. In this case Marxist analysis has to be vindicated and not merely appropriated. There is good reason to be grateful to it for valuable insights which more and more seep into general consciousness (as do those of Freud), but it is not a 'science' in the sense it claims. It is more like a faith, which becomes dangerous as a pseudo-science. Because there is no such science of society as

Marx claimed, there is rarely an unambiguously 'Christian' social policy. Perhaps it is a desire for one that frequently leads Christians to accept some 'expert' theory when strong plausibility is against it. Major Douglas's Social Credit theories misled many Christians in the economic depression of 1929. Many have recently been misled by the first Report of the Club of Rome, *The Limits to Growth* (1972). Liberation Theology, like Political Theology, is afraid that one cannot be dedicated and activist and at the same time provisional in politics.[43] Unfortunately it has abundance of evidence to back this fear. Yet that is precisely what Christians are called to be and to do.

Nothing written here is meant to preclude co-operation between Christians and Marxists. It may well be necessary. However, in co-operating, Christians need a well-founded political theology. They need to discriminate the truth and error in such reasons advanced for collaboration as (i) Marxism provides the unique scientific analysis to understand past history, present reality and future trends, and is therefore the right guide to social change; (ii) Marxism provides the best basis for a radical criticism to overcome false consciousness (ideologies) and arrive at objective reality; (iii) Marxism is the only valid viewpoint in interpreting Scripture, because it is faithful to the biblical promise of total salvation and its bias to the poor; (iv) Marxism is flexible and pluriform, and can be made more so if Christians discard anti-communist hysteria and work with it; (v) there is no viable alternative to the present economic-political order except the Marxist-Communist one, and even if it should be repressive it would not be worse than the present; (vi) we should co-operate with Marxists as a sign of our trust in God, who will give the church power to survive under a Marxist regime and to modify some excesses (since some are pretty sure to follow a revolution); we do not expect to usher in the kingdom of God in its fullness.[44]

One criticism of Liberation Theology is that there is an element of élitism in it. There is some truth in this. The left-wing guerillas of the 1960s and 1970s, who attracted a number of Christians, were a cultured élite which failed to arouse the masses. That is why the Basic Communities have been so necessary. In the process of liberation there seems to be an élite which is outside the grass roots, and which by practising Freire's 'pedagogy of the oppressed' is impressing on them a view which it is sure is right because it is 'scientific'. The intellectual is once again a person apart, of a higher class, able to criticize both the oppressor and the oppressed. Not too much should be made of this. The contribution of the intellectual is in fact to take a wider view, especially in considering the possible secondary consequence of the options for action that are available, and not acting only on what is immediately in front of one's nose. Nevertheless the danger of élitism is one to guard against.

Lately a more substantial criticism has arisen from the attack of Liberation Theology on dualism. Salvation history is made coterminous with universal history. There is one kingdom and one history. The sacred and profane are the same. In so far as this is directed against a spurious pietistic otherworldliness it is to be welcomed. The words of Dom Helder Camara, formerly Bishop of Recife in North-east Brazil, are often quoted, 'I am trying to send men to heaven, not sheep. And certainly not sheep with their stomachs empty and their testicles crushed.' Yet there is a serious flaw in the attack on dualism. In the Old Testament there is one kingdom, one history, one church and state combined. In the New Testament the kingdom of God has burst the bounds of one state and is universal. Henceforward there are two kingdoms, two cities (St Augustine), two realms (Luther), and a Christian lives in both at once. There is a civil righteousness (Luther), and a common as well as a saving grace (Calvin). The political and social responsibility of the Christian and the church lies precisely in how they relate these two kingdoms. It is false to dismiss dualism of this kind as necessarily anti-revolutionary. It delivered us from the omni-competent church of the Christendom era (which was a relapse into the one kingdom position), though it needed the help of the Enlightenment, and the secularization process which followed from it, as an ally. It makes it more difficult for the British or the Americans or the Boers to claim that they are God's chosen people. Moreover monism has unfortunate results. It has led to religion being seen as an individual human projection (Feuerbach) or a social one (Marx). We see in place of religion a sacralization of politics in the messianic overtones of Marxist theories, attaching to themselves both the prestige of science and the sacred dimension of religion. Liberation Theology thinks of God as fully disclosed in solidarity with the struggle of the poor for liberation. Rather there is a sense in which God is always partly hidden, but nevertheless summons us to a struggle which will never totally be completed in history.[45] Giving political causes too unqualified a divine sanction takes too lightly the dimension of reconciliation at the heart of the Christian faith. This must never be lost even in the middle of desperate conflicts, even though much piety is an obstacle to serious political commitment. The distinction between the two kingdoms found in the New Testament, patristic, medieval and reformation sources must not be jettisoned.

V

What is the significance of Liberation Theology for British Christians and those from other parts of the relatively wealthy world? One of the few attempts to apply it explicitly to Britain was by Alistair Kee in 1973. His points were (i) disillusioned radicals abound, so the need is for Christians temporarily to withdraw from the political struggle and build up alternative life-styles based on eucharistic communities; (ii) these will have greater staying power than disillusioned political groups, they will exemplify what they preach more than purely political groups, they will not be as utopian as such groups, and they will have a different emphasis from them and not merely echo them; (iii) individuals are easily picked off one by one, hence the need for groups; (iv) it may be that the monastic tradition has strengths on which to draw.[46]

There is always room and need for communities such as these but, unless all possibilities of political action are closed in a truly desparate situation, relying solely on such a tactic is far too limited a response. Liberation Theologians would think it an evasion of political responsibility, and rightly so. The British situation allows scope for many-sided political activity. The questions that arise concern the most appropriate ways for the church and for the Christian to be involved. The questions posed for the church are the same as those posed by recent Political Theology. Can it accept the attack on pseudo-piety and acquiescence in remediable evils? How far does it appear in the priorities of the churches and the way they handle their own institutional arrangements that they stand for a preferential option for the poor? What would a British church which took this seriously look like? What would be the milieu of its theological thinking and formation of clergy and laity? Could it make its own Rubem Alves' modified version of utopianism as 'not a belief in the possibility of a perfect society but rather the belief in the non-necessity of *this* imperfect order'?[47] If so it would have to modify its attitude of 'critical solidarity' with the government which Giles Ecclestone, a former Secretary of the Board for Social Responsibility of the Church of England, has said has been the tradition of that Church.[48] This is to put the most favourable construction upon it: many would say that the solidarity has been much more marked than the criticism in the last four hundred years. The Church of Scotland and the other mainstream British churches, from the perspective of Liberation Theology, have been little different. As it happens there have been recent signs of a more critical attitude by the churches to government policies. A recent instance is the Church of England report on Urban Priority Areas, which is equally critical of church and state.[49]

As for an analysis of our present situation it is evident that we cannot learn from the acceptance by Liberation Theology of Marxism as a 'science'. Euro-Communists have largely dropped it. The USSR, where its ideological hold is theoretically strongest, finds in practice large numbers of its citizens alienated from it; and there is widespread disillusion, even in Marxist circles, with its lack-lustre economy and repressive political order. To vindicate this critique of Marxism it is necessary to work through the major Marxist economic and political doctrines and show how each is sufficiently flawed as to not be a 'scientific' basis for action. There are six main ones; (i) the Labour Theory of Value; (ii) the Theory of Capitalist Evolution; (iii) the Theory of Capitalist Crisis; (iv) the Theory of the Class Origins and Nature of the State; (v) the Theory of Class Struggle; (vi) the Materialist Conception of History. Theologians as such have no particular competence in doing this, though they may well have insights from their faith which sharpen their perceptions of what is significant in assessing each of these theories.[50] Liberation Theology will make us see the necessity of a renewed Christian-Marxist dialogue, and not to be blind to it because of the weakness of organized Marxism in Britain; but it does not contribute any resources to it other than what is already available in Europe.

Our problem is that the simplicities of the New Right, the

paternalism of the traditional Right, and most of the traditional Christian and socialist criticisms of capitalism no longer carry conviction. To analyse our present situation we need a co-operative effort. Churches within the Ecumenical Movement are attempting to do this, together and separately. The new method of procedure of the Roman Catholic Bishops of the USA in promoting widespread public discussion on the way to issuing Pastoral Letters on current affairs is a good illustration.[51] It draws on widespread expertise and experience, and is ecumenical in tone. The voice of the poor is still, however, heard only spasmodically. Meanwhile church structures and traditional practices are resistant to change, and liable to accept it only when the situation has already moved on. The vitality of Liberation Theology must be a challenge and an encouragement to churches in an old world which seems to lack resilience.[52] But whereas Political Theology contributes an essential foundation for this renewal there is nothing peculiar to Liberation Theology to which we must turn.[53] In particular it does not transfer easily from an area which is saturated with folk religion to a Europe where the churches have never made much of an impact on the industrial worker, where the majority are relatively affluent and the poor a minority, and where a powerful middle class is conceptually minded. We must work at 'the preferential option for the poor' in our own way.

12

The Politics of Imperfection and the Politics of Hope

At the time when what we call the Industrial Revolution was involving Britain in rapid social change and leading to a new kind of civilization in the history of the world, the French Revolution brought to a head the dissatisfaction of the commercial bourgeoisie and the urban population with the *ancien régime*. The violent development of that revolution sent a shudder of horror through those in possession of political and economic power in Britain. In 1790, well before the violence that was to come in France, Edmund Burke produced a conservative response, *Reflections on the Revolution in France*, which emphasized historical continuity and respect for the past, the value of status and hierarchy, and the limited role that politics should take in the life of society. It was so well written that it has far transcended the situation which produced it, and it has been the background of a good deal of conservative political philosophy ever since. Embedded in it are perennial insights into the nature and nurture of the human social order. However, this organic conservative emphasis was already being opposed by a liberal, individualistic, *laissez-faire* political philosophy which fitted in well with the giant strides made by industrial capitalism in the nineteenth century. In this century, with the rise of Labour as the main opposition party, these two other elements have gradually come together, so that the modern Conservative party is an uneasy mixture, rather than a fusion, of hierarchical organic and liberal individualist elements.

It is generally assumed that the outlook going back in modern times to Burke must lead to a politics of the Right. It will stress human imperfection and the limits on what politics can achieve. It is also generally assumed that a politics of the Left will have the opposite characteristics; it will stress human perfectibility, and exhibit a utopian expectation of what politics can achieve. There is indeed much evidence that this is the case. In this chapter, however, I argue that those on the political Left need to discard a great deal, but not all, of the utopian elements in their outlook, and that they need to appropriate a great deal, but not all, of what those on the political Right say about the politics of imperfection. Indeed they make a mistake in allowing the Right to assume that arguments from human imperfection must lead in their direction.[1]

I

The Politics of Imperfection has had an intellectual revival since the check to economic growth in the West after the quadrupling of oil prices by OPEC in 1973. There are six main elements in it.

1 A stress on human sin

Sin is a term which belongs in a religious context, and by no means all the political philosophers of the Right who stress it are Christian, or religious, in outlook. Anthony Quinton and Michael Oakeshott are not.[2] Theologians obviously are, and so is the historian E. R. Norman who makes much of the depravity of human beings in his religious-political writings, and argues that it leads to a limited view of the competence of the state beyond preserving order and promoting conditions necessary for religious practice.[3] Reinhold Niebuhr, who was in fact heavily involved in politics of the Left all his life, gives in his Gifford Lectures probably the most searching analysis of sin of any theologian of this century.[4] Those on the political Right, who know some theology, are likely to refer approvingly to the doctrine of Original Sin. Nigel Lawson did so in 1980 in claiming that Conservatives are those who understand it and whose policies allow for it.[5] They draw from it that a strong mixture of the carrot and the stick is the key to good government. The carrot provides rewards in economic life for successful entrepreneurs as they pursue profitability and outstrip competitors, whilst poverty and unemployment, with its accompanying stigma, is the punishment for failure. This is accompanied by another strong stress on law and order, and an assumption that severe punishments deter. There is also a tendency to accept the belief that people cannot be trusted to respect or make good use of communal provisions, epitomized in the phrase that used to be quoted (with only a touch of caricature), 'If you give them a decent home they only keep coals in the bath.'

2 *A stress on human ignorance*

It is clear that people in many parts of the world, and especially in the technically advanced economies, are wanting to organize, plan and control much more of their future as they have become more conscious of the technical sources available to them. The political framework within which this is to be done is, of course, much disputed. The 'new Right' has made an aggressive come-back; and the centralized, Soviet type of economy is discredited. However humanity is not confined to these two options, and the next decades will be characterized by the search for a reasonably workable political-economic model which can handle the problem. I say 'reasonably workable', because no model will work without frictions and with no disadvantages. And I say that the model will be sought because it is inconceivable that there will be an option for the Soviet-model and, in my judgment, the 'new Right' will not maintain its momentum. Much of its rhetoric may remain, but the reality will be greater 'interferences' with market forces, as ideally conceived, in crucial parts of the economy. The reason is that the ideal model of the free market is so removed from social and political realities that it is impossible to implement. Neither management nor worker nor the electorate will stand for it. They are not willing to allow crucial decisions affecting their well-being to be decided by impersonal forces over which they have no control, unless there is a very strong framework of social support which sustains family income and circumstances during period of adjustment, and this is precisely what supporters of *laissez faire* jib at.

The supporters of minimum government, therefore, have a hard task in the long term. Nevertheless they put forward some powerful arguments concerning human ignorance which must be taken into account. The first concerns the uncertainties in economic forecasting, and therefore of planning for the future; uncertainties with regard to technological innovations and their economic and social consequences; and indeed uncertainties with respect to social policies decided in the light of what is already known. In the early 1970s it was confidently expected that economies would continue to grow as fast as they had between 1950 and 1970. Then after the oil price rise of 1973 they only grew half as fast for the rest of the decade, and fell off further at the end of it. On the other hand unsuspected innovations occurred. Who in 1970 had heard of brain scanners, video games, personal computers, word processors, and optical fibres, to name a few new products? New methods of production also came to the fore. Robots and numerically controlled machine tools are becoming more common in production lines; and computers enable small units to make a wide range of products with small production runs at costs close to those of mass assembly lines.

Another uncertainty is population forecasts. Human beings have largely concealed from demographers the factors which influence their propensity to reproduce themselves. Post-war estimates of population growth proved exaggerated, and the estimated world population at the end of this century has several times been revised downward.

There are various trends in economic forecasting. Herman Kahn and the Hudson Institute[6] suggest that in 200 years time the industrial revolution will be completed, and that by the year 2000 there will be a slow down in the industrial world, not because of scarcity but because of affluence. A varient of this is W. W. Rostow's qualified optimism[7] provided that the rich economies can sustain a growth rate of 4½ per cent per year and will admit manufacturing exports from the poor countries. He has estimated that by 2000 absolute poverty could be eradicated from middle-income countries, and be confined to no more than 13 per cent of the population of low-income countries, provided that the rich countries achieve a low inflation rate, substantial free trade, and that the balance of payments is kept in equilibrium. Clearly these forecasts require a political more than an economic optimism. The difficulties in getting even the countries in the European Economic Community to work together are notorious, yet they are hamstrung if they act separately, as was shown by the effort of France under President Mitterand to break away on its own from the policies which have brought so much unemployment to Western Europe.

On the other hand there have been pessimistic economic forecasts. The first two of the Club of Rome's reports, *The Limits to Growth* (based on 200 equations), and *Mankind at the Crossroads* (based on 100,000 equations) are examples of this.[8] Much of it was unfounded. Even more hazardous is Kondratieff's theory of a long cycle of economic growth with peaks every fifty years, of which 1970 was the last.[9] A caution of a different kind came from Fred Hirsch's *The Social Limits to Growth*.[10] It would have been better entitled 'The Social Limits to Private Consumption'. It advances the thesis that the incentive to private accumulation, which worked well in the early days of capitalism, works less and less well in its advanced stages because the advantage of the 'positional goods' which private accumulation enables one to acquire depends upon relatively few possessing them. The more widespread they become, with rises in the general standard of living, the less enjoyable they are, and they may even become self-stultifying. 'When everyone stands on tiptoe no one sees any better.'

There seems no economic reason why the relatively affluent 'Western' economies should not opt for a policy of a high rate of economic growth combined with a reduction in the level of inequalities between rich and poor countries, so that the standards of living in the two-thirds poor world grows much more rapidly than in the one-third rich one. The difficulty is the political will. It would be in the long-term interests of all, but short-term national, and within states sectional, vested interests prevent the adoption of policies which would lead to it. Governments subject to dismissal by an electorate need to work hard and continuously to create a climate of opinion favourable to constructive policies, and the kind of domestic social reconstruction they would require. They do not show much will to work in this direction.

Many of those who stress human ignorance suggest that it is beyond the power of governments to do much, and that is why they draw a pessimistic conclusion from the politics of imperfection. Little can be done in their view to improve the social order. Hayek has long had a political philosophy more influential with the public than his economic theories. He regards human society as a miracle of social cohesion, which generates its own order. Attempts to plan it will come to nothing because of our lack of knowledge.[11] Popper stresses the complexities of social life and urges that the aim of social policy is best seen as piecemeal, rather than utopian, 'engineering' and that social policy should aim at the least amount of remediable suffering for all, a kind of negative utilitarianism, instead of the traditional utilitarian aim of maximizing human good (usually defined in terms of happiness).[12] Oakeshott[13] stresses that politics is concerned with complexities so great that the aim must be to rule and to keep going. 'In political activity men sail a boundless bottomless sea. There is neither harbour for shelter nor food for anchorage, neither starting place nor appointed destination. The enterprise is to keep afloat on an even keel . . .'

3 A stress on human irrationality

This is a serious constraint on politics. People are liable to see only what is in front of their noses. They do not consider longer-term considerations. They need the guidance of experienced political élites. Even if it is true that one contribution of intellectuals, such as the products of universities, to the body politic is the ability to take into account the secondary consequences of possible courses of action, they have only a minor influence in society. Moreover they are prone to imagine that they themselves are free from the blinkers of the non-intellectual majority, when in fact they are quite capable of using their mental powers to follow more intelligently short-term ends. Hayek thinks that it is best if power is so dispersed that human irrationalities cancel one another out, so that no person and no group has enough power seriously to damage another. Furthermore, if the delicate political balance is upset, and the coercive framework of society eroded, we end with the politics of 'the mob'. Shades of the French Revolution again. The mob notoriously lashes out blindly. Any movement in which it is involved is either manipulated from the beginning by outsiders, or is taken over in the course of disorders by a group with well defined aims. The upshot is not what was intended, however inchoately; and the whole event is a warning against upsetting the steady process of political rule which keep the social order in a doubtless imperfect, but nevertheless indispensable, equilibrium if order is to flourish with liberty.

This stress on the irrationality of the public is combined with a confidence in the role of those in control of quite central public policies. One of the most alarming features of various scenarios advanced in connection with defence policies, particularly those involving nuclear weapons, is that the games theory which lies at the back of them presupposes rational decisions under extreme pressure and in the few minutes available if an incident appears to have broken out.

4 A stress on the insolubility of many problems

This follows from the previous stress. Many people do not understand the genuine difficulties and constraints within which governments operate. They assume that if only the right people are elected and pursue the right policies (to which they may have been pledged in opposition), and are not waylaid by the compromises and sweets of office, major abuses can be swept away and society set on a course free from the entails of the past. Disappointment when this does not happen leads to an unreasoning backlash, and a suspicion of politics and democratic processes. Once again there is a danger of society becoming ungovernable. Many of the analyses within the Labour Party after its defeat in 1979 were of this type.

5 A stress on the value of impersonal mechanisms

A deep suspicion of politics lies behind this. It is seen as an unprincipled auction for votes at elections, and a bending to the most effectively organized vested interests when in power.[14] By contrast, if decisions are made by an impersonal mechanism, where no one person or group has the power to make a decisive difference because they are made purely as a result of a multitude of independently operating decision-makers, the log-rolling of politics is avoided. What applies within nation states applies between them. That is why some advocate a return to the Gold Standard. Governments would then no longer be able to manipulate the value of their currency because of dubious aims or shortsighted pressures, the decisions would be made automatically in terms of the balance of trade and in relation to a standard of value as relatively stable as gold.

All of this type of reasoning abstracts from the social relations between citizens, other than an impersonal economic nexus, and from a moral underpinning which a social order requires unless it can be held together solely by force. It leaves human beings as isolated units in society, or at least together with their immediate families, perhaps subject to a fail-safe net in case of direct penury. It assumes that human beings are infinitely malleable. Labour can be treated in as impersonal a way as can land and capital. It can 'get on its bicycle' and move itself about the country or – in a free trade and labour market world – from country to country in search of work, or the work with the best pay and conditions, in accordance with the ever changing higgling of the market.[15]

6 A stress on the traditions of the past

Two different approaches are mingled in the stress by the Right on the politics of imperfection. The liberal-individualist approach did not think much of tradition. It was the source of effete privilege. The polemics in favour of the free market in the nineteenth century took on the aspect of a crusade against the bumbling inefficiency of traditional élites. A society of contract and not of status was to be a sign of emancipation from them. On the other hand Hayek, as we have seen, puts a high value on the delicate balance achieved by established social institutions, though he thinks conservatives are too subservient to the past. Quinton stresses more strongly the value of experience and tradition. The 'old Right' does so still more strongly, but it softens the sharpness of the politics of imperfection by a stress on the organic ties which bind society together, and which involve an attitude of *noblesse oblige* by those at the top of the established hierarchy towards those below them. Society, it is held, is kept going by the traditions of the past, and if they disintegrate it cannot keep going. Then we arrive at anarchy and no one can achieve any sustained purpose.

However, whether the stress is on more traditional hierarchies which should not be overthrown and only gradually modified (if at all), or whether it is on the impersonal mechanisms of a free economy, the result is an emphasis on the desirability of minimum government. Getting government off the backs of the people is the popular phrase. Defence, law and order and the enforcement of contracts are its main spheres with, these days, the provision of a minimum social safety net added. Such is the general position of the politics of imperfection.

II

The Politics of Imperfection is important as against a Politics of Perfection with its utopian strains. Theologically the idea of perfection has played a persistent but subordinate role in Christian theology. The issue is whether the gospel call to perfection is realizable in this life or not. General Christian opinion has been that it is not. John Wesley is the most prominent British church leader and theologian in modern times who maintained that it is. But his position rested on an insufficiently subtle idea of sin, and it has in practice been abandoned in Methodist theology today.[16] In any case it was expressed in terms of individual character. Those who thought of it corporately tended to set up, or advocate, Christian communes separate from the give and take, the here a little and there a little, of everyday politics.

The politics of utopia ignores this and thinks it is possible to transfer a view of human perfectibility direct to the area of politics and economics. On this view it is only the structures of human life which are wrong. It is they that stifle human beings. Remove the corrupt structures and the natural goodness of men and women will flower.

Anarchists are the chief example of the politics of utopia. It is latent in Marxist theories. Anarchists share with Marxists the hope of the abolition of the state and the replacement of imposed forms of government by the voluntary co-operation of individuals and groups. Most Marxists expect the communist society of complete human freedom and co-operation to arrive only after a considerable period of development, after the capitalist state system has been overthrown by the vanguard of the proletariat acting on behalf of the masses; only then will the state wither away. Anarchists tend to expect the utopia to arrive spontaneously once the present corrupt institutions are overthrown. Direct action is the way to bring this about, perhaps peacefully but perhaps violently, in order to make them unworkable. Anarchist Marxist groups are thus well to the left of Communist parties.[17]

Anarchist illusions are extremely dangerous. They imagine that to make the present system unworkable will be to inaugurate the new era. Nothing could be more mistaken. It is far more likely to lead to an authoritarian order imposed by the political Right.

Utopians rightly stress the human capacity to yearn and struggle for better things. There is a strong moral thrust in their desire for a humanizing of society, as against a purely managerial attitude to men and women which hinders proper relations between them, and in their vision of a non-competitive and communal life and of world peace. But they underestimate human sin and finitude. They present impossibilities as possibilities. This leads to zealotry, and either disillusion when they fail to achieve what they intended (and many ex-utopians become fanatics against their own past), or to the desperate maintenance, against all the evidence, that since the revolution has occurred it must have been successful. This was the position of many apologists for Stalin's Russia.

Political anarchists cannot succeed. Apolitical ones are usually found in communes, some of them Christian, on the margins of society. We are told that the task of Christian Ethics is the liberation of the human imagination, so that it can build utopias different from all current models of society, and therefore capable of contemplating the liberation of the world. It is said that if utopias are not imagined we are shut up in the established systems of the present. It is said we need to give names to what is not yet present but which will break the power of what is present. It is said that if we do not create utopias we shall lose our will to shape history.[18]

This is dubious doctrine. Rather, we need a Politics of Hope which can take on board all that is negatively relevant in the Politics of Imperfection, and then go further in the search for creative change. One can if one wishes call it a 'hard-nosed utopianism'.[19] It will prevent us from accepting policies that involve very high human costs now, perhaps even physical terror, in return for the promise of the mirage of an ideal future to be realized as a result of it.

III

More could be said on the politics of utopia, but it is not the focus of this chapter. We are not concerned with a Politics of Perfection but with a Politics of Hope. This needs to take Original Sin seriously, but also to take Original Righteousness equally seriously. These are traditional terms in theology which appear to be outworn, as depending on the literal belief that we are all descended from Adam and Eve who were originally righteous before Eve ate the forbidden fruit, and are all originally sinful since. In fact the terms stand for a fundamental reality in human existence and experience which is of great significance for politics.[20]

The subtlest point about sin is that it feeds on virtues. This is what Wesley overlooked.[21] The dramatic sins of temper, robbery, sexuality and violence are obvious. We can be delivered from them. The same applies to less dramatic ones like sloth or meanness, or some in the realms of sexuality. They, too, can be overcome. It is the pride of virtue which is the snare. The subtle sins are the hardest to recognize or admit, and they are the ones which corrupt virtues. This is what those whom we regard as the most saintly have always known; the gulf in their own lives between what is the case and what ought to be. The more they have entered into love, as interpreted in the New Testament, the more they have found there is to know and to realize.

This is to speak of individuals. In the case of collectives within states, and states in relation to other states, the very virtues which enable them to hold together and cohere make it harder for them to express a concern for other groups or states to the extent to which it is possible for individuals to do in their personal relationships.[22] Since conflicts of interests are endemic in society and between states it is folly to expect a social order without them. The task is to find a way of dealing with them that will produce the most creative outcome of the conflicts and minimize harm. That is the essential task of governments within their own territories, and collectively as they seek some sort of international order, however tentative and precarious. It is also the reason why any political or social gain which may be secured cannot be assumed to be permanent. Each generation has to face its own moral challenges. It cannot presume on the achievements of its predecessors. Good family and social and political structures can help, by giving each of us a milieu which promotes our moral insight from childhood onwards, but they cannot ensure that we shall continue a moral progress. Each of us can be set on the right road by our parents, but in the end we have to make our own decisions and may fall away badly. Societies too can develop corruptions. Indeed if a social gain is made which requires a greater moral co-operation of citizens to work it than was needed before, and it fails, the result may be worse than if the gain had not been made. In this century Nazi Germany is the supreme example of this. German culture was in many ways a leader. As late as 1930 it never entered the heads of those in other countries that it could succumb, and so easily, to the Nazi horror. This was aptly described as a synthetic barbarism. So much was this the case that many for a long time did not believe that it was no longer the case, and gave it the benefit of the doubt long after the evidence was in fact overwhelming. Even today it is hard to take in the enormity of the holocaust. Germany has now happily recovered. The point is that there is no immanent law at work in history leading us to expect permanent social and moral gains. There will always be a struggle to maintain any that have been made. And solving one problem is likely to reveal a new one.

Hope must not triumph over experience. But neither must it give in to a pessimism which says that there is no hope for a better social order. All the notable theologians who stressed the politics of imperfection, Barth, Brunner, Demant or Reinhold Niebuhr to name only four diverse ones, adopted varying degrees of radical attitudes to the *status quo* as they experienced it. For Original Sin is not the heart of the Christian gospel. It is not good news. There is in that gospel the concept both of Original Righteousness and of a new hope in Christ. Human beings may be 'very far gone from Original Righteousness', as the ninth of the thirty-nine Articles in the Book of Common Prayer of the Church of England maintains, but that is not the end of the matter. There are adumbrations of a sense of justice as fairness, as well as of the great triad of faith, hope and love in human life, on which it is possible to build and without the presence of which to some degree it would not be possible for human life to cohere, nor for the gospel to be intelligible. That gospel offers great encourage-ment. From it we understand that God's graciousness is present everywhere and at all times. Moreover it is a free grace. It does not have to be earned before it is received. And it is constant and not rare. Christians believe they know more about it because of what they have learned through Jesus Christ and have, therefore, through no merit of their own, greater possibilities of drawing upon it within the life of the Christian church. But their joy is to recognize signs of it at work in the multitudinous life of human beings. Christians do not live in an alien world where God's grace is not operative until they bring it. This is the basis for a Politics of Hope.

It is a realistic basis. Not all the explicit theologies of hope are in fact sufficiently realistic. It is possible so to stress the newness of the eschatological renewal brought by Jesus as to overlook its roots in the past, and to understate its present reality in concentrating on the future which it is heralding. We find assertions like the following. (1) The historical future will not arise from the past. This is the utopian idea of the total and radical break. It was expressed secularly by those Paris students in 1968 who had no idea what was to replace the existing corrupt structures which they held they must destroy. Only then it would be possible to see what should replace them. If the break is total and the future does not arise from the past, we cannot have any idea what it will be, as we either wait for something new to happen or destroy the present order in order to force the situation. (2) Humans are defined by their openness to the future. It is important that they should be. It is hard to exaggerate how hindered we are by a fossilized attitude to the past in both state and church, which prevents us taking moral purchase over the rapid social change which is what in fact we are facing. In the state we need social institutions which will carry citizens through inevitable changes, without allowing these to produce economic crises in their lives and the lives of their families so that they cling desperately to obsolete structures and ways of work. In the church, which can easily become a refuge for those who, finding change everywhere else, hope to find fixity there, we need not merely more flexibility in organization and in the deployment of resources, but we also need liturgies which root basic sacramental rites and the insights of the gospel in the kind of universe in which we know we live, with all its immensities and its minute features, and with its rapid social changes. Liturgical revision is too content with the recovery of third- and fourth-century models. It moves within the assumptions of God's preservative activity as experienced in relatively static social orders, and has not caught up with his transforming activity which is what we are so dramatically experiencing. But when all this is said, human beings cannot be *defined* by their openness to the future. They are equally defined by their appropriation of the past. In Christian terms the kingdom of God was inaugurated by Jesus, is experienced in the present, and points to the future. All three aspects are brought together in every eucharist. (3) God is ahead of us; he is the power of the future mastering every present. This is true in the sense that the gospel leads to a radical eschatological dissatisfaction with the *status quo*, and empowers us to work for its reform; but it is also true that God is the power of the past who has brought us to where we are. This point is a variant of what has already been said in discussing openness to the future. (4) Sin is devotion to the past, and social sin is a fixation in the structures of the past. Enough has been said already about sin, and of the necessity of relating to the past whilst being open to the future, to indicate the one-sidedness of this assertion. (5) Christ in his resurrection is a proleptic revealer of the future. Perhaps exaltation may be a better term to use than resurrection, which gives rise to many differences of interpretation, but (to continue to use the term) it does indeed reveal that God can bring a victory out of the worst that human beings could do in crucifying Jesus. It shows that his purpose will triumph, and that nothing worthwhile in the long saga of human life, in which we all share, will be lost. That is certainly good news. But there is no suggestion that it will be achieved in our world of time and space any more than Christ's resurrection was. Still less does it give any clue to what new initiative to expect from God in the conspectus of the present situation within which we have to make decisions. (6) Salvation is equivalent to a socio-historical temporal future which is the kingdom of God, either in its completion, or arriving for the first time (if one assumes, as a few do, that it was heralded by Jesus but not inaugurated by him). Enough has been said already to indicate that this is a mistaken equivalence.[23]

The stress on hope in these six affirmations is apposite. It is needed because just as the naive optimism which developed during and immediately after the first world war was quickly quenched in the years following 1919, so the more qualified optimism which followed the second world war has come to an end. It was more qualified partly because we had learned from the disappointments after 1919, partly because the war ended with the explosion of two terrifyingly new weapons, nuclear bombs, which cannot be disinvented and which we knew it would be hard to keep in check. In fact they have proliferated vastly in number and size, and threaten to do so in ownership. Nevertheless the economic growth rate until 1973 was so great that hopes had something to latch on to. But now this has been severely checked. Hope is in short supply. There are few technological optimists left. Political and economic aims have been cut down. Boldness is lacking. So hope needs its proper stress, together with faith and love. Adumbrations of it in the secular world need identifying and fostering. In the church it should lead to a less defensive style of theological thought and Christian life.

However, hope needs to be well based. It needs to be realistic. It must be willing to harness self-interest in structures which will promote the common good. Much of the talk of participation in decision-making by 'the people', a desirable aim, assumes too easily that the decisions will be wise, made in time, and without serious conflicts of interest or a residue of disgruntled minorities. The concept of 'the people' has been idealized. Hope needs to discern real possibilities, which means acute analysis, rather than stressing expectations of new divine initiatives not arising out of the present of which we can know nothing, and which can therefore play no part in making our decisions. The Politics of Hope can accept all that is well said in the first five stresses of the Politics of Imperfection described in the first section of this chapter. It draws from them not the minimum politics of the 'new Right' but the challenge of a radical conclusion. The world is unfinished. There are possibilities of improving it. Christian discipleship involves commitment to political action to improve its structures, just as it does to the transformation of personal character towards our full maturity in Christ.

What the Politics of Hope cannot accept is the sixth stress of the Politics of Imperfection. Societies are not kept going by the traditions of the past. If these traditions are inflexible and block change they will produce an explosion. The wisest conservatives have seen this and accepted adjustments in time. People today have 'come of age' in advanced industrial societies, and are not willing to be treated as needing tutors from traditional political élites. Nor will they subject themselves in matters vital to them to impersonal processes of decision-making over which they have no control.

There are indeterminate possibilities of improvement. No barriers have been laid down by God which set limits to what human beings can achieve if they are faithful, hopeful and loving. But no utopia is promised. Human nature will not change fundamentally. It will face the same moral struggles. History will remain ambiguous, but under God's providence. There is a prophetic-eschatological base for a vision of proximate goals, and a source of mercy and renewal for redefining these in the light of our successes and failures. We need to draw on this, especially when the going gets tough, and there is no progress or even regress. Insights of both a radical and conserving kind are found in the gospel, but the conserving ones must not prevent us from trying to humanize existing structures when they are de-humanized. They must not cut the nerve of action. There must always be moves in the direction of universalism as against racism, towards communities of greater mutuality in giving and receiving, towards a greater concern for those society is neglect-ing or rejecting, and in vigilance to check abuses of power by those who possess it. There is no warrant which allows a Politics of Imperfection to ride lightly to these criteria. They will always be of significance for a Politics of Hope.

In implementing it in detail those who stress a theology of Hope are prone to broad, impressionistic and dramatic analyses of our present situation, even if they often come to a relatively humdrum and conventional 'progressive' conclusion on what should be done. A more probing analyses is needed, of an interdisciplinary character, and drawing upon collective work in groups. Preoccupation with the eschatologically new and future divine initiatives leads to abstractions. A good deal is said about this throughout this book. There are inevitable hazards and uncertainties. The final ground of a Politics of Hope is that what God has begun in Christ he will complete, and that our labours in the realm of politics are not limited to maintenance work; on the contrary our striving to improve it will not be in vain in the Lord.[24]

13

Social Theology and Penal Theory and Practice: the Collapse of the Rehabilitative Ideal and the Search for an Alternative

A theological contribution to a discussion of penal policy must begin by recognizing that Christians as such have no special access to the details of criminological problems unless they happen to be professionally or voluntarily engaged in the activity of the apprehension, trial and treatment of criminals (as of course many Christians are), in which case they have their own experience on which to make a contribution to public discussion. But all Christians have the duty as citizens to share in the communal responsibility for criminal policies, for this is a test of the quality of our communal life and insights. This chapter therefore makes no claim to expertise in the field of penology beyond that of the concerned citizen. In an effort to reflect responsibly on the issues it must rely to a considerable extent on the expertise of those who have specialist knowledge and experience. This includes the experience of those involved in legal processes, the whole complex of prison services (including that of prisoners), and experts in relevant fields of study such as law, psychology and sociology. Expert evidence has to be examined critically, partly because experts often differ, and partly because value judgments will be explicit or latent in it and need to be assessed. In the last resort, however what will settle the matter is not expert evidence but the policies which the moral judgment of the public will support or at least not actively oppose. We must try to make it as informed and sensitive as we can.

In the present context we are told that the rehabilitative model for the treatment of offenders is in the process of breaking down, and that the growing awareness of this is producing something of a crisis in British penology. I do not doubt that there are differences of opinion on this matter among criminologists (no academic discipline is without them); but this chapter assumes that the breakdown has been substantially established and agreed, and attempts to reflect on this collapse, using insights from the Christian tradition. It will also consider in view of the breakdown of the rehabilitative model, the justice model which is offered as an alternative to it. Further the chapter seeks for some common moral ground on which social policies can be built, a task which cannot be avoided in our increasingly plural society.

Problems in Making a Theological Contribution

In a plural society it cannot be assumed that the nature and limits of a theological contribution to a discussion of penal policies are commonly understood. In particular, two difficulties arise, the first out of the position of the Christian faith in this country, and the second out of the nature of the faith itself. Because of our long Christian tradition we have inherited in Britain the remains of a 'Christendom' situation which less and less corresponds to the reality. For centuries the church was influential and a broadly Christian understanding of life was accepted and publicly assumed. A country where this is still the case is the Irish Republic. For centuries Christianity and commonwealth went together, and Christians were deeply involved in penal policies and institutions. Now, however, Christians have become in this and most traditionally Christian countries what Peter Berger calls a 'cognitive minority'.[1] When it comes to questions of public social policy they can no longer assume that common ground exists, and they have to search for it with those of other faiths and ideologies, including a considerable number of humanists who have absorbed much of the classical-Christian ethical tradition. Among other things the contribution of moral philosophy must not be neglected in the effort to clarify moral issues involved in public policy. The question is: what are the penal institutions and practices which our highest common moral insight requires, and what sort of society do we need to sustain them? How far can distinctively Christian insights contribute to this? How can we work towards such a society? And at any given moment, how far can the state go in such a penal policy and still carry the support of the man in the street or in the Clapham omnibus?

The second difficulty arises from the nature of the Christian faith itself, which is not focused directly on the institutions of civil society but derives from the ministry of Jesus and his teaching on the kingdom or rule of God. The ethic of the kingdom of God is paradoxical by the standards of commonsense morality because it is non-reciprocal, and transcends embodiment in social institutions whilst also challenging them. The teaching on forgiveness is a key example in our present context. When the disciples suggest that seven times is the most that any human being could possibly be expected to forgive an offender, Jesus puts the whole question in a different dimension by demanding forgiveness seventy times seven.[2] The basis of this demand is that this is the way God in his graciousness treats us, so this is the way we must treat one another.[3] The gospel ethic starts with the graciousness of God as its fundamental presupposition, which means that hope arises from faith or trust in this God, and both are expressed in love. The Christian gospel is that the gracious and loving God, whose paradoxical way of ruling the world Jesus believed himself to embody in his life and in his teaching on the kingdom of God, goes on forgiving the crimes and follies of man 490 times, that is to say without limit.

At one level there is a realism which some would call pessimism in the Christian faith because of its understanding of human waywardness ('sin' is the theological term).[4] Nor does it think that a Christian has been translated out of this double condition of great moral possibilities and tragic failures. Rather it sets his face in the right direction, assures him of renewal and forgiveness, and that God has set no limits to what he may achieve. Nevertheless he remains in Martin Luther's words *'simul iustus et peccator'* (at one and the same time 'justified', i.e. forgiven, and a sinner); he is still prone to do what he ought not to do and leave undone what he ought to do. This is especially the case because the more subtle sins are not the flamboyant ones – the ones most likely to get one into a criminal court – but those which are the corruption of good qualities, such as the pride of the 'unco guid'. The gospels are thus as much concerned, if not more, to expose a taint in the motives of the 'good' as they are to rebuke the 'bad'. This is not because they take in a simple sense either an optimistic or pessimistic view of Man, but that they expose Man as he is in his mixture of good and bad, and rejoice in God's graciousness towards him despite it. The sting of the situation is that the good are not as good as they think themselves, and the bad are not as bad as the good think them.

This teaching is in the setting of one-to-one relationships. How can it be related to social relationships and social policies? The problem of corrective justice is not raised in the gospels, because the problems of ongoing civil society are not the focus of attention. Jesus' mission was other than that, and of perennial significance transcending any particular embodiment in civil society. The fact of the state, and that it has legitimate claims is admitted, indeed stressed, but how to work out what is God's and what is Caesar's and what related to both, is not gone into.[5] From the time of the earliest Christians, such as St Paul, until now that problem has remained with the Christian community. The radical gospel insights are not related to the details of social problems in the gospels themselves, and cannot be related directly to the problems of penology. Nevertheless they must not be allowed to become irrelevant to them.

In practice this is precisely what has happened. Radical Christian insights have been bypassed. There have been two characteristic ways of doing this. The first has been to make a separation between the moral precepts incumbent on all, and the counsels of perfection to which a few are specially called (and these are termed 'the Religious' with a capital R). The second has been to make a very sharp distinction between the two realms, that of the church and that of the state and civil society, and in effect not to allow the radical Christian writ to run in the latter.[6] But that is not the whole story. At their best Christians have wrestled with problems of justice – including penal justice – and tried to see how they are related to love (with varying emphases and varying success).[7] They found in the Greek ethical tradition an understanding of justice as 'rendering to every man his due' (*suum cuique*), and in the Old Testament a witness to God's concern for social justice and for the vindication of the poor and oppressed. The love of which the New Testament speaks was seen to require not less than these two even though it goes beyond them. The story of Christian reflection on justice in society is long and complicated, but in general it has led to a stress on the coercive authority of the state under God for the common good. Classical Protestantism has talked of the state as an 'order of creation'; and classical Catholicism of it as expressing man's social nature. Nevertheless they have an even stronger doctrine of the person as in the last resort transcending the authority of the state, not least because in the Christian view the person has an eternal destiny.

In the course of dealing with the problem of justice and the state, Christians have joined moral philosophers in elaborating retributive, reformative and deterrent theories of punishment, though as a rule they have seen dangers in going along unequivocally with any one of them. At their worst Christians have so let go of their radical insights that they have discussed penal questions on society's own terms and shared in its inveterate self-righteousness. In particular they have supported current social institutions and structures of authority uncritically. 'Throne and altar' became a byword. It is this attitude which is being increasingly criticized amid the political stresses of the twentieth century.

The danger for Christians is therefore of having a radical ethic which is neutralized in practice. The problem is how to bring at any given time an ethic so radical as to transcend the possibility of complete empirical embodiment alongside current theories and institutions, and to make a creative contribution to current problems. This means calling the current situation into question in such a way that possibilities of creative change are enhanced without what is advocated being so far ahead of current opinion as to be impracticable, yet doing it in such a way that the further challenges of radical Christian insights are not forgotten. In doing this the Christian finds himself in an ambiguous relation to the history of his own past. He has the problem of distancing himself to some extent from its unsatisfactory features whilst affirming its deepest insights. It is not surprising that in a plural society he is frequently misunderstood, and may indeed find it hard to get a hearing. At all events if it leads him to a sense of the provisionality of what he says and the avoidance of all pretension in relation to his own tradition, it is likely to lead him to be sensitive to all pretensions in the discussions of penological issues and to the provisionality of practices proposed. Indeed this may be a significant contribution he can make to the public discussion of them, but it is not easy to achieve. There can be a temptation to criticize everyone else from a 'perfectionist' gospel stance which in effect evades the responsibility of tackling the immediate problems. More common, perhaps, is that the realization of the complexity of making a Christian contribution leads in effect to a silence on the matter, of which the upshot is to give an irresponsible, because tacit and unthought-out, support to the *status quo*.

Rehabilitation, Retribution and the Christian Tradition

The breakdown of the rehabilitative model is presented by some with a certain amount of zest as the overthrow of an idol which had pretensions to knowledge which it could not sustain, which led to a coercive form of reformation hidden under the guise of concern for the person, and which resulted in grave injustices in the treatment of different persons who were convicted of the same offence. It means the exposure of institutions (such as prisons) which are incapable of fulfilling some of their alleged aims. There is no reason for the Christian to cavil at the exposure of pretension in institutions or theories. Indeed more traditional theologians such as Emil Brunner[8] pointed out the dangers of leaving prisoners relatively at the mercy of would-be reformers (pejoratively referred to as 'do-gooders'), who were free to decide if and when they were rehabilitated and suitable for release. In particular, without being obscurantist, Christians will be glad that the mystery of the person has proved elusive to those social scientists who thought that the antecedent causal conditions of criminal behaviour, whether in the psyche of the criminal himself or in his social environment, were so established as to be an 'objective' scientific matter. They will also be glad that the hidden value judgments in rehabilitation have been called in question. If one asks: rehabilitation in terms of what?, the answer must presumably be the norms of society as incorporated in its legal systems. Yet while some of these norms may be (and indeed are) acceptable, a good number at any time may well need questioning. Infringement of them may even be praiseworthy. In any case there is cause to raise objections to custodial sentences, indeterminate within wide limits, where release depends on the prisoner showing himself to have been rehabilitated in the eyes of experts whose expertise is itself under scrutiny, and may indeed differ. For it is not uncommon for practitioners in different behavioural sciences to work with incompatible theories, or indeed for different practitioners in the same discipline to do so.[9]

Yet from a Christian point of view there is a certain element of tragedy in the breakdown of the rehabilitative model. A great deal of Christian idealism went into it, a great deal of care for the offender and of courage in defending him against philistine public attitudes. This itself was a reaction against what was felt to be an excessive Christian insistence on retribution among the three traditional justifications of punishment.

Christian partiality for a retributive view was on three grounds. First, assuming that the criminal code reflected God's moral laws, offenders against it ought to be punished. Second, a retributive code avoids sheer vengeance by setting public penalties for crimes. Third, in its concern for justly deserved punishment such a code does justice to man's responsibility for his actions and therefore to his dignity. His punishment – assuming that he is correctly convicted and is responsible for his actions – is itself a witness that he is treated with proper respect. Augustine, Aquinas, Luther, Calvin, Hooker and Butler – to name six very different key figures – are on the same side in this respect. The theological backing for this preference probably lies in the classical Christian view that although God shows himself as signally gracious and forgiving in the ministry of Jesus, the fruit of forgiveness must progressively issue in right moral conduct; for in 'the end', at the 'last' judgment, God can no longer continue in this way but will judge every man according to his works, and human penal justice must do the same and give every man his due, which in the case of a sane, properly convicted offender, is punishment.

However there have been other strains in Christian theology, and one in particular has grown in the last century or so. This holds that a Being (God) who is both good and rational cannot inflict punishment for the sake of retribution and nothing but retribution. If God cannot be thought of as doing this, men must not do it either. It is those who take this view who have been sympathetic to reformist theories of punishment, and more critical of the institutions of civil society and aware of the ambiguities of the state. Many of them have been active in the prison service – one obvious name is that of Alec Paterson. Nevertheless although it is clear that the influence behind the rehabilitative model in the last twenty years or so owes much more to the theories of social scientists than to Christians, the breakdown of the model represents a tragedy for much not altogether uninformed Christian idealism, which often showed real care and concern, even if it did not pay enough attention to the warnings of more retributive-minded theologians, especially concerning the elements of paternalism and injustice in efforts to reform a person who is in a coerced situation.

However if the model has broken down, facts must be faced. We must not ignore evidence, if it is clear, and allow ourselves to be buoyed up with false hopes. On the other hand we need to be sure that the model has not been given up too easily; that with more care there are not elements of value in it; that it really is the case that any element of coercion in the situation frustrates the possibilities of success from the start. Indeed what is meant by 'success' needs careful thought unless we are working in purely mechanistic terms. A religion which has a cross at its centre is at least alert to possibilities of evaluating success and failure which might ask questions of commonly accepted criteria. When Jesus told us to love our enemies he did not suggest that by this means we should always win our enemies over and have none. We cannot give up a rehabilitative concern because its success is much more doubtful and the conditions it requires are much more subtle than we thought. What Christians must not give up is a critical concern for the needs of offenders, nor a concern for a social order which works towards the fulfilment of person-in-community rather than hinders it, one which tends to foster rather than frustrate the common good.

A Critique of the Justice Model

The critics of the rehabilitative model are in different ways mostly advocates of what may broadly be described as the justice model, but they appear to fall into at least three main and incompatible groups.

(i) Liberal humanitarians or radical liberals. They stress the oppression of individuals under the practice of the rehabilitative model, and are particularly concerned with justice as fairness.[10]

(ii) The radical Left or liberal radicals. These stress the oppression in all pre-socialist societies. Many of them are libertarian Marxists verging on anarchists and almost all are utopians. Some would hold that what the liberals are concerned with is only 'formal' justice, characteristic of imperfect societies. When the perfect society comes it will be irrelevant. In any event even now proletarian justice is more important. Sometimes the Chinese form of communal correction is favoured, with the minimum of formal law.[11]

(iii) Those of the political Right. Not many of these as yet have realized the breakdown of the rehabilitative model. For one thing they have had little or no sympathy with it. When they do realize its breakdown they will press for longer and harsher sentences in the interests of law and order, and rejoice in the collapse of what they regard as mostly sentimentalism which is more bothered about the criminal than his victims. In this attitude they will represent the majority of the electorate. Critics of the rehabilitative model need to realize that they are playing with fire, and their exposures of it need to take account of this.

A number of the advocates of the justice model seem to me – though I may misunderstand them – to try to 'bracket out' the divergent attitudes of the critics of the rehabilitative model by making punishment as much as possible a regulative and technical matter. Of course they realize that there must be some moral-political base to it, and they sometimes refer to a minimum 'social contract' theory of the state. This is akin to the attenuated version of the traditional Natural Law theory of society as presented by H. L. A. Hart.[12] This refers to the minimum level of common agreement to enable human society to survive, to moral rules which any state must enforce if it is to be viable. It includes restrictions in the use of violence and bodily harm, a system of mutual forbearance and compromise as a basis of legal and moral obligation, a limited requirement of altruism, a minimal form of property (not necessarily private), the recognition of promise-making as a source of obligation, and some system of sanctions to ensure that those who obey these minimal requirements are not sacrificed to those who do not.

In this view the law sets out in rationally articulated rules the basic conditions for human life and co-operation to be possible.

Criminal activity therefore presupposes the human co-operation on which the law insists, and the criminal has secured an unfair advantage by undermining the system which secures to everyone (himself included) basic goods necessary to human corporate life. Punishment, therefore, redresses the balance of advantages which the criminal has unfairly swung in his favour.[13] So far so good (though it is doubtful how far the Marxist will accept this view of society and therefore of punishment).

But there are difficulties in this position which in my view need further thought. An impression can be given that punishment is verging on being seen as a purely regulative matter like the 'sin bin' in ice hockey, or library fines, or (perhaps) the growing attitude to shoplifting. At first the obvious point occurs that the state is a very different institution from ice hockey, in that one cannot get out of it whereas no one need take up ice hockey. That is to say the state is much more morally significant. If one were to take a purely technical view of the juridical system one would have to take an even more minimal view of the state than Hart's attenuated Natural Law approach, a view such as that of the sociologist Bryan Wilson who refers to society as being held together 'by non-human mechanistic forms of control such as the conveyor belt or parking meter'.[14] But this may not be what is presupposed, and we can leave Wilson's remark aside as a rhetorical exaggeration. Nevertheless Hart's view and the minimal social contract view is a very 'thin' view of the state. Its heyday was the break-up of the old mercantilist system and the early stages of modern industrial society. It was the foundation of a *laissez-faire* view of the state and its tasks which had serious theoretical and practical defects. It is not suitable to enlarge upon them in this context, except to say that it gravely underplayed the corporate and organic as against the individualistic aspects of human life, and in my view is quite inadequate as the basis for an advanced industrial society. Is it wise, then, to base a view of punishment on such an inadequate view of the state? We cannot be content to think of the state as being concerned with no more than the question of how we can make the necessary technical arrangements to survive together; it must be concerned with richer, more common, human values than this.

Moral considerations also enter into the justice model of punishment in connection with the boundaries and the range of severity of the fixed penalties which are imposed. Crime and sin are not identical. There are many sins (and the most subtle ones) which are not crimes and there are crimes which are not sins. Nevertheless crime and sins do overlap. Obviously the area and scope of penalties reflect a preference for order rather than anarchy. But beyond that they may be more or less related to a particular social order which is more or less worth defending. A concern for human fulfilment must not be lost in concern for the justice model. It remains legitimate to raise the question in connection with any law and penalty for infringing it, 'In whose interests is this being enforced?' Frequently it is the common good that is involved. Not infrequently, however, as the history of social reform shows, the law needs criticizing in the interests of a wider common good; it is too tied up with the interests of a particular class, or race, or group. It is not hard to think of instances where disobedience to law may be a moral duty, a way of bringing creative moral criticism to bear on the social order.

Again, legal penalties must be exacted humanely. This brings prison conditions under scrutiny. In this connection we may mention those criminals thought to be sufficiently dangerous in one way or another to require incarceration for a long period or permanently. It is evident that there are such, but that it is not at all easy to establish with accuracy who they are. The evidence is that the tendency is to put many more into this category than is necessary, perhaps in order to err on the side of protecting the public, which is understandable. Moreover the breakdown of rehabilitative theories of human conduct casts doubt on the adequacy of the theories by which permanently dangerous criminals are classified as such. There is thus a moral challenge both to improve methods of classification, and to administer this 'prisoner-of-war' type of imprisonment for dangerous offenders as humanely as possible. 'Out of sight, out of mind' is the temptation of society as far as they are concerned. If classification cannot be improved, society has to face the problem whether in order to be sure of locking up those who are dangerous it will agree to locking up perhaps twice as many in addition who will not be dangerous, for lack of any means of identifying which is which.

Although society is prone to oversimplify penal questions (a point to which I shall return), it is surely right in thinking that much crime is morally blameworthy, and that the criminal deserves punishment. (I assume in saying this that he is properly convicted and is properly held responsible for his actions.) This brings back the 'classical' retributive element, and is an indication that the area within which crime and punishment can be treated as primarily a technical and regulative matter is limited.

Prudence, Proportion and Theories of Punishment

Nothing that has been said so far seems to me to remove the necessity of wrestling with the three traditional models of punishment, retributive, deterrent and rehabilitative. Indeed much of it requires us to do so, as does the ideal of 'respect for persons'. (The traditional wisdom is that it is unwise to follow any one of them to the exclusion of the other two.) Christians have come to encapsulate their concern for human beings in the phrase 'respect of persons', and adherents of other faiths and ideologies often agree with them. In doing this they realize that persons must not be seen as isolated individuals but as persons-in-community. They also realize that this concern relates to all three common theories of punishment but cannot be satisfied with any one of them alone:

(i) Persons must be treated as responsible, the onus being on those who wish to qualify this in particular cases. If they offend, punishment must be deserved and legitimate (retribution). But once paid society should wipe the slate clean, something it signally fails to do.

(ii) In certain cases the common good of persons-in-community may require an element of deterrence. I state this with caution because of the inveterate tendency of the public to exaggerate the deterrent effects of punishments. In most cases we have no deterrence except community attitudes. Deterrence, however, is not the focus of attention in this chapter and I shall say no more about it.

(iii) Because of the ambiguities of society in causing crime and in punishing it, a rehabilitative attitude is needed. That is to say that punishment on solely retributive grounds with no other consideration in mind will not do. An intention actively to promote the good of the offender is also required. This should not mean adding a further and indeterminate length to a retributive sentence purely for rehabilitative purposes and under coercive conditions.

In this connection it is suggested that rehabilitation should be available to the criminal but entirely on a voluntary basis, with no explicit or implicit coercions in the shape of a hidden threat such as 'if you don't accept treatment you won't get parole'. Those who refuse to have anything to do with it would be free to ignore it. A partial analogy with Alcoholics Anonymous has been suggested. There would seem much to approve of in these proposals. They are certainly compatible with many Christian ideas and insights. There is less pretension, more mutual respect, greater readiness to recognize 'solidarity in sin', and that what human beings have it in them to become is something to be discovered together rather than announced by the 'good' to the 'bad'. It is also more realistic to recognize that many do not choose to be 'cured', at any rate by this means. One would like to see a serious effort put into a scheme of voluntary rehabilitation. It will certainly not require less resources than the present system. It would need to guard against the same kind of coerced 'soul transformation' which it has criticized in the rehabilitative model, but its advocates seem quite aware of this.

One of the main problems will be the attitude of society. In my view the bulk of the electorate has never accepted rehabilitative policies, let alone realized their collapse. Reformers in the Home Office, often accused of obtuseness, have pushed ahead of public opinion. This remains appallingly self-righteous and revengeful, amounting at times to the view that we should do to others at least what they have done to us, if not more so. There is much hypocrisy in punishment. Is it not significant that the vast majority of those in prison (perhaps 90 per cent) come from the social classes four and five, whilst white-collar crime, like fraud, embezzlement and bribery is liable to escape prison? We are often keener to deter offences against property than against persons. Moreover all the traditional theories of punishment have been advocated in simplistic ways. High-sounding retributive theories are put forward in a society which fails to fulfil its side of the theory and pervasively discriminates against prisoners once the penalty has been paid. Similarly advocates of rehabilitation have overlooked the fact that it involves what amounts to experiments on human subjects in a milieu of coercion. Advocates of deterrence have had an unfounded belief in the deterrent effects of fierce punishments. Candour forces the Christian to admit that he finds many examples of these distorted attitudes in members of the Christian community, and that is a reason why any comment he makes must be made with due modesty.

Clearly the traditional virtues of prudence and proportion are required in threading one's way through the intricacies of penal policy. They are the virtues of practical wisdom. Prudence relates basic insights to the weighing up of the pros and cons of different theoretical and practical considerations, each of which has to be allowed for, but never to the exclusion of others. Proportion considers the details of each proposed policy in relation to the weight of the various considerations embodied in it. For instance mandatory sentences appear indiscriminate, and discretionary ones appear arbitrary. Is there not a cleft stick between consistency and discrimination? Does this not indicate that one must not be pursued too far without reference to the other? This is one of several questions which could be put to the advocates of the justice model.

Hopes, Aims and Policies

I turn in the final sections of this chapter to the wider question of the nature of the society within which penal policy operates, and to some suggestions for changes in policy which Christians should support. They will require a great effort by men of goodwill if they are to carry public support. Human justice in the Christian view corresponds neither to the paradoxical justice of God now, as Jesus affirmed it, nor to the ultimate judgment of God (however this is understood)[15] but is between the time of these two, and therefore provisional. Its task is to restrain the 'natural' justice of aggrieved individuals and groups by institutional procedures, to see that the procedures themselves are just, and that the state which sets them up pursues personal and social justice. The Christian understanding of justice makes it necessary to speak relatively of the penal system. Punishment will always be ambiguous because persons and societies are always ambiguous, and will be, short of the *parousia*.[16] In particular what are suitable punishments, and the relative seriousness of different offences are relative matters.

However this ambiguity is no reason for not attempting to improve things. The Christian in one sense is pessimistic in that he expects neither a perfect society nor a perfect penal system, if only because success can be a subtle source of pride and therefore of corruption. After all it was a combination of flagrant and subtle sins that brought Jesus to a cross. On the other hand the Christian is an optimist because he is not prepared to set any limits to what might be achieved by a humanity which is alert and sensitive. He has a large hope, and that allows him to hope against hope when provisional hopes are dashed.[17] Indeed if God and the world are as Jesus said they are he must needs hope, because the nature of things is with him. He can understand, because he shares, disappointment that the rehabilitation models have not worked. He will not be surprised at the breakdown of what is provisional, and he will not seek to put his hope in an illusion. He will look for fresh initiatives. At the same time he cannot give up hope for the criminal, not even for those in long-term or permanent confinement for security reasons. He will seek what is possible for their full humanity for them too. He cannot allow society to forget the criminal in the process of dealing with his crime.

It should be evident that hope does not destroy critical powers. It can even enhance them. It should encourage a cold eye to be cast on the element of pretension in punishment and on the social conditions which encourage crime. Some recent theorists suggest that a strengthened sense of neighbourhood and community is the best hope of diminishing crime. It seems very likely. But this is an immense task which no advanced industrial society has solved: it is as much a problem to the USSR as to us. Community has become a catch-all word which has to be unpacked.[18] Demands for it reach us on all sides, witness the growth of community development or community work concerns in the last decade. To achieve an improvement here requires the co-operation of a variety of different people with different skills, theoretical and practical. Perhaps it is worth noting in this connection that the churches have a large number of full-time paid agents and potential part-time voluntary ones, and a lot of plant (although much of it is the wrong sort) which could be very useful, if the struggle to keep them going at a time of inflation could be sufficiently successful to allow concentration to move from the needs of the immediate worshippers to those of the neighbourhood in which the worship takes place.

Mention of neighbourhood and community leads to a consideration of the nature of the wider society within which penal practices operate. At the end of his critique of John Rawls' *A Theory of Justice*, Brian Barry says that there are three basic models of society – hierarchical, liberal-individualistic and altruistic-collaborative.[19] I think he is right. Many are advocates of one model only, but just as the Christian faith relates to, and asks questions of, each of the three traditional theories of punishment, it does the same with respect to these three models of society. It relates to the hierarchical one because there will always be a division of interest between the givers and the receivers of orders, between the managers and the managed, in any society. It is the mark of utopian thinking to suppose otherwise, however skilfully methods of participation in decision-making are devised. It is necessary to work for power structures that are just and humane, that provide for checks on the abuse of power, and in particular to be actively concerned for those who are less powerful or powerless. The Christian faith relates to the liberal-individualist view because self-interest must be harnessed yet controlled for the common good. It relates to the altruistic-collaborative model because men and women need to give as well as to get, and are only truly themselves in a community which expects and encourages mutual giving and receiving. The task is to achieve the best 'mix' of these elements at a given time, and it requires both a critical and a sustaining role from the Christian community. The third one needs fostering because it is the weakest of the three. Human sin favours the first two. A continually renewed vision is required to strengthen the third.

This vision has to be married to practical steps which are capable of being realized, in the sense of winning enough public support, or at least tolerance. In the immediate context there are some things which it is certainly worth working for:

(i) An attempt to deal with as many convicted offences as possible by non-custodial penalties, which is one of the aims of some advocates of the justice model. The evidence suggests that as many as 80 per cent of those in prison at present ought not to be there. It does not protect the public and it actually harms rather than improves those imprisoned. The system is unfair and inefficient, indeed monstrous. It will not be easy to shift public opinion on this, but if I were an Old Testament prophet I would feel like saying 'Thus says the Lord; cursed be a society which tolerates this prison system; away with it; it is an abomination to me.'

(ii) Efforts to make claims on an offender, in terms either of personal restitution or of community service, as being suitable to his dignity as a responsible person and fellow citizen. I do not think that the charge that this is paternalistic cuts much ice. It is possible that such a practice might prove reformatory but that would not be the reason for adopting it. Vigorous pursuit of this might also help the public to see that there is concern for the victims of crime and not only for the criminal, which is a widely held view.

(iii) Beginning a system of voluntary rehabilitation, as has already been mentioned.

(iv) Scrutinizing more closely the crimes of the powerful with the aim of securing as much attention to them as to those of the less powerful.

(v) Continuing to wrestle with the problem of containing the 'mad' and the 'bad'. Not only must containment be humane, but efforts at restoration must not be given up even if they are unpromising.

To return to where this chapter began, we note that in advocating these policies and in general discussions of penal policy the Christian will seek to relate himself to an ongoing public discussion, especially among those with the greatest concern and with special expertise. He will hope that their ideas will not be a denial of his own even though they cannot achieve all that he would wish for in penal policy. He will be prepared to use relevant arguments devoid of any special Christian basis, though they may accord with Christian insights. One of these is the attempt to get the public to see beyond the immediate facts and short-term interests to the secondary consequences of actions and long-term interests. This is on the basis that the Lord needs to use any suitable weapons that he has available to coax or propel men into more humane ways of behaviour. It is aptly expressed in the prayer which ends 'save, Lord, by love, by prudence, and by fear'. Positively the Christian will hope to extrapolate from common human experience and see how far he can take it in public policies. Thus it is only the very unfortunate who have no experience at all of what it means to be unconditionally loved and forgiven in family life or its equivalent. The Christian gospel takes this experience, however fragmentary it may be, and expands it to cover the whole dimension of the ways of God with men. It is not utopian to hope that there can be sufficient understanding of it in society at large that glimpses of it may illuminate penal policies and practice.

At times it is the hopeful side of the Christian understanding of life which speaks most powerfully, at others the realist; it depends on the context. It is not easy to express both together. W. H. Auden and Louis MacNeice[20] do not quite achieve it in these lines, but they do express a good deal of what I have been trying to say of the way Christian insight may be brought alongside contemporary problems of penal theory and practice and illuminate them:

> And to the good who know how wide the gulf, how deep
> Between Ideal and Real, who being good have felt
> The final temptation to withdraw, sit down and weep,
> We pray the power to take upon themselves the guilt
> Of human action, though still as ready to confess
> The imperfection of what can and must be built,
> The wish and power to act, forgive and bless.

14

Bryan Wilson on
'The De-moralisation of Modern Society'[1]

I

Wilson's argument is a subtle blend of description and value judgment so I begin with a summary of it.

1. *Social cohesion* depends on shared values and mores.

2. *Previous societies had this.*

(a) *Traditional societies* were held together by sanctions and common sentiment which worked together, and were local in operation. The moral and the sacred were mingled. No distinction was made between public and private life. Many of the rules were arbitrary but their value was that they were symbolic and shared.

(b) *Industrialized societies* were still largely moralized, but they were too complex for effective old-style communal local control. Individuals had to be moralized in respect of their work which required honesty, pride and punctuality. But this had to arise from self-regulation rather than communal surveillance. Public morality therefore depended on a private moral foundation.

3. *Post-industrial society* has a diminished reliance on morality. Rather it relies on technology and rational bureaucracy, and the disciplines of classical economic theory are less and less limited by lingering non-rational residues of traditional morality. Neither the worker nor his children needs moralizing. Rational procedures are applied at the cost of 'community morality – of those arbitrary proscriptions and prescriptions that were rooted ultim-

ately in local, national, religious or ethnic prejudice'. Irrational bonding (the bond of communal morality) is replaced by planned, contractual relationships.

(*a*) *Private morality in post-industrial society.* Since it is not bothered about, because not required, there is a freedom unbridled by moral inhibitions and an hedonistic unbridled right to consume; at the same time there is a fear of surveillance by those in authority acting in their amoral social roles. True, the need to deal with people abstractly as interchangeable units has led to health and unemployment insurance etc., but this is less an indication of individual moral concern than of an abrogation of personal responsibility and increased moral insensitivity. Personal faults are blamed on the system. 'Once salient distinctions of personal worth – age, sex, race, nationality, local origin – are no longer significant criteria.'

(*b*) *Yet social control is needed, and it is achieved by:*

(i) *Role requirements.* These are more and more precisely specified, and the demand is made to lay aside everything, including moral competence, irrelevant to the rational procedures required. Even clergy, teachers and social workers are told to be professional, and affectively neutral. As morality in public life is so much less relied on the upshot is impersonality, anonymity and permissiveness, e.g. traffic control systems and computers are rational, de-personalizing and egalitarian innovations, which 'discount morally justified social distinctions'.

(ii) *A politicization of morals,* e.g. legislation on racial and sexual equality. The economy requires universalization. It cannot afford to wait for the process of socialization which is slow because there is no stable, homogeneous base from which a moral consensus can arise. So it legislates – against the persisting moral dispositions from the communal past, 'loyalty, group identity, preference for one's own and their own way of life'.

4. Traditional community morals were sometimes quite arbitrary, yet to eliminate their prohibitions is de-moralization, for their latent function was to reinforce social cohesion. Indeed the moral prohibitions of a people are in a sense arbitrary but they are needed to reinforce group identity.

II

1. Obviously there are features in this analysis of our society which we can recognize, but it is flawed because it ascribes to post-industrial society what was more characteristic of industrial society and it does this not because ours is de-moralized but because Wilson's moral values are different.

(a) To some extent the argument is a familiar one, drawing in particular on the work of Tonnies, Durkheim and Weber. Another way of putting it is that the liberal, individualistic industrial society, with its *laissez-faire* economic system elevated into a philosophy of social life, involved changing the place of the citizen in society from one of status to one of contract. It dissolved social ties (at least beyond the family), except for an economic nexus. In fact it needed a basic morality to support it – honesty, truthfulness, promise-keeping, etc. – which it did little to foster but presupposed; and it was parasitic on a pre-industrial moral tradition, aided by the Protestant work ethic. However contract, though at first a liberation for some, proved too exposed a position, and in this century we have been moving back to a citizen status society, of which the Welfare State is an uncompleted exemplar, with common rights and responsibilities. Wilson's picture of *post*-industrial society applies more to industrial society. 'Thatcherism' and 'Reaganism' are a reversion to this, but it is questionable how far they will succeed, because neither management nor worker (for good and bad reasons) is willing to submit established economic and social ties to the automatic decision of market forces, and insists on political intervention.

(b) Another feature of liberal society is the loosening of the tie-up between crime and sin. Traditionally they largely overlapped. Now they are largely separated. Many sins are not thought to be wisely treated as public crimes. Hence Wilson's talk of private morals. The arbitrary nature of what was included in the tie-up in the past does not worry him. It helped to enforce group identity and to hold society together.

2. His account of current private morality is very onesided.

(a) There has in fact been a great increase in pastoral care. His illustration from the universities is the reverse of the truth.

Whereas when I was an undergraduate there was virtually none, now it is well established. I think the reason is that before the expansion of universities the assumptions were set by upper-middle-class students, who predominated, and because of family ballast were expected to cope; now lower-middle-class ones predominate with little family ballast behind them. Professionalism is urged to guarantee standards, and as a safeguard against personal idiosyncrasies, and 'affective neutrality' is better thought of as 'non-attached sensitivity', and something considered essential in medicine is now seen as equally so in the caring professions.

(b) Consumerism is not necessarily hedonistic. The 1929 depression and the 1939 war revealed the extent of deprivation in Britain. Many born before 1945 will remember it. We have had only a short period in which the majority of the population has shared in the 'affluence' which the professional and managerial classes have taken for granted.

(c) A much more positive view could be taken of private morality both in its particular manifestations and its basic reality. Those who talk as if we have no common basis of moral discourse and understanding seem to me to exaggerate wildly (see below). Wilson writes as if the challenge to traditional sexual morals means unlimited licence, when much of it comes from a realization that a good deal of it was due to a fear of human sexuality compounded with masculine dominance. And was not 1985 the year of Bob Geldof?

(d) Roles involve more than the rational procedures Wilson stresses. They involve the handling of conflicts of rules and loyalties, attitudes to people and sensitivity in the use of power, together in many cases with the ethical implications of professionalism.[2]

3. Wilson is rightly preoccupied with morality and its necessity for social cohesion, but in the cause of social cohesion he favours a narrow 'little England' backward-looking moral stance, the maintenance of which he claims is of more importance than concern for 'abstract social justice'. He talks of 'salient distinctions of personal worth', and 'morally justified social distinctions'. This results in approval of a morality based on prejudices (local, national, religious, ethnic) and one in which personal

worth arises from distinctions of age, *sex, race, nationality*, local origin (my italics). In view of the many elements that have gone into the making of Britain, including its Empire, and of the evils nationalism and racialism have brought in this century, this is a breathtakingly simple and nasty list.

4. There is lacking in Wilson any conception of Natural Law morality, that is to say that morals are 'natural' to human beings, and at a certain level provide for the basis for a common (but not necessarily universal) moral discourse. Since he does not look for it he does not find evidence of it, but only of institutionalized rational procedures at the cost of a common morality, and assumes that there is no basis in our society for the process of socialization to inculcate it, because it is a plural one and not a 'little England'.

There is no question that a social morality is needed. It will involve the affirmation that every citizen counts (either because humans are made in God's image, as in Christian belief, or in humanistic belief because they are rational creatures, or because 'nature' has made them basically alike); it will also involve established social customs (which are subject to moral scrutiny); and rationality, consistency and fairness in administration and social structures. It also needs fostering and sweetening by what Wilson in other writings has called 'disinterested good will'. He has been preoccupied as to where it is to come from; at one time he thought religious sects might be a source, but he has given that up, and failing to find any other has become more and more pessimistic.[3] He seems to me now to have reached a position which is descriptively dubious and morally repellent. Instead of a closed and backward-looking society we need to strengthen the basis of an open and plural one. Wilson is no advocate of the 'new Right' but rather of the 'old Right', but he shows how easily a necessary stress on the organic element in human societies can spill over into a dangerous racist, nationalist (and sexist) outlook.

Epilogue

15

Reflections on Leaving the Chair

Invited to reflect after retiring from a University Chair, my mind casts about for some model for guidance. The only one I can think of is an article by Barbara Wootton on resigning the Chair of Social Studies at Bedford College, London, to pursue her academic work in other ways. This article, however, is for a church constituency, and so I propose to raise four issues which between them relate church and university, and church and social and political issues.

I

What is the relation of the academic theologian to the church? In my experience there is quite a widespread lack of interest in theology in the church. Once I have been asked to preach on the place of the professional theologian in the life of the church, but that is all. I notice that the constitution of the Synod of Manchester Diocese has no place for a member of the Faculty of Theology of the University, although it is one of the largest and best developed in England. (I am a member of the Synod as a Bishop's nominee.) Indeed the lack of interest verges on suspicion that theologians perversely raise sceptical questions which upset the faithful. The lack of encouragement to serious theological reflection on the part of churchgoers is shown in my experience by University Extra-Mural Lectures. The vast majority of those attending courses on religious subjects are regular churchgoers. Yet in the discussions which are such a valuable part of them, as the course proceeds it becomes clear that the questions asked go back to the first principles of the subject rather than to the specific topic of the course. We do not seem to be able to get beyond the elementary stage.[1]

Another example of the relative indifference to theology is the low standards we are content with in Anglican theological colleges. This is partly because we cut down the time available to a minimum on financial grounds, but even more because we insist on having many small colleges. This in turn is because we allowed them to be formed on a private 'party' basis so that they fossilize a particular ecclesiastical situation of the last century, and the effect is to put party interest above theological quality. Because they are small the teaching staffs are not large enough properly to cover the necessary range of theological study. They have to cover too wide a field. Staff are usually young and stay for only a few years. They do not have time to develop their own studies, yet the best teaching at tertiary level usually comes from those who are engaged on some research of their own. We constantly see promising young men on the staffs who disappear after a few years into other kinds of job, and are not given the chance to develop as scholars. All the colleges together would hardly make one reasonable sized College of Education. The rapidly growing cost of them may make us ask questions which a concern for theological standards has not made us ask.

If the standards were higher and such colleges as are necessary were suitably situated, a more fruitful liaison would be possible with University Faculties and Departments of Theology. The church is realizing only slowly how much theology has developed as university study. Recently when preparing a lecture to commemorate the seventy-fifth anniversary of the Faculty of Theology of Manchester[2] I came across the text of a speech made in 1908 by Professor T. F. Tout, the historian, to a Church Congress in Manchester drawing attention to the significance of this for the church. Little notice was taken of it. If the money for theological training were better spent there might be less pressure to cut down the time, more concern to encourage well-qualified graduates in other subjects also to graduate in theology (a matter of growing importance because of the need for interdisciplinary work at every level, including that of the parish), and a greater willingness to sponsor those qualified to work in depth for a period on research projects.

One development which ought to get much more church

backing than it does is the effort to establish Pastoral Theology as a serious academic discipline, important for the study of theology as a whole. It is becoming widely understood that the old 'hints and tips' type of Pastoralia is outmoded. Indeed various models of pastoral care involving both individual counselling and group therapy procedures are on offer, but they are not always subject to sufficient theological – and indeed sociological – scrutiny. Universities need persuading to put more resources into this field. Only Birmingham, Manchester and, to a lesser extent, Oxford in England have made a modest start so far, and it is not going to be easy to convince them in the present economic climate. It would be helpful if church concern were less tepid, because here there is potentially a most fruitful relation between church and university.

The academic theologian is not, of course, a servant of the church, any more than a Lecturer in Politics is the servant of a particular political party, even though he is parasitic on the church for having a field of study in the first place. However, church and university ought to have a fellow feeling for a deeper reason. Both have an ambiguous relationship to the community in which they are set. They both depend heavily on public support for their continuance. Yet if they do their job properly they are both called, among other tasks, to a critical appraisal of that community. Both are asking the community to pay them to be critics of it. It is not an easy role to sustain. Neither always tries to sustain it. The easiest way for the church to be popular is to side with current national causes; the easiest way for the university to sell itself is as the producer of the technical skills which will increase the Gross National Product. Neither of these courses is necessarily to be deplored, but both are inadequate. The Editor of *Crucible* has recently characterized the attitude of the Church of England to the public authorities as one of 'critical solidarity', and this is right provided that equal emphasis is given to both words, and that we remember, as he observed, the neglected biblical witness to God's special concern for the marginalized.[3]

Although the church is often classed by sociologists of religion with law as a primary buttress of society, that is to underplay the prophetic strain in the Judaeo-Christian tradition. Indeed current social strains in the world have brought to the fore the questions asked by the Latin American theologian, J. M. Bonino,[4] 'Who does theology?' and 'Who consumes it?' His answer is that a limited section of a particular social class both does it and consumes it, and that theology must find a way to overcome this class captivity. Similarly if a university does its job properly it will produce not merely technical experts but graduates who are trained to ask critical questions of their subject, their teachers, themselves and their society; and they will have been required to examine critically the critical basis on which the critical questions are asked. Moreover it is too simple to say that the university stands for intellectual virtues and the church for moral ones, for the two are closely related and both need both.

Obviously the community needs deep, sustaining resources for its well-being, but not lack of criticism; otherwise there will be petrification and in the end violent change. But it is a sophisticated community which realizes its need to pay for its own critics, and both church and university have to educate their paymasters. In a time of inflation and recession both are under pressure. The church must avoid merely appealing to the most conservative attitudes of its faithful in order to raise its increasing diocesan quotas and parochial expenses so that everything may continue as before, with priorities unchanged; and the university must beware of selling itself merely as a producer of profitable technological innovators. They should shed their mutual suspicions – the church its unease that the university fosters disaffection and irresponsibility in the young, and the university the latent feeling (surprisingly widespread) that the church if it got the chance would like to resume control of universities and impose intellectual and perhaps moral controls. In short, that the church cannot be trusted.

II

In my experience the change in the composition of the student body reading theology in the university is striking. When I began to teach it was largely made up of ordinands, together with some intending teachers in Religious Education, and they were predominantly male. Today I doubt if more than one quarter to one third are ordinands; and about the same number teach. The remainder enter a wide variety of occupations in industry, commerce, the social services, administration, journalism. Half at least are women, and these among the best. Nor are they all professing Christians or adherents of other faiths. Some are agnostics or atheists who nevertheless think religion a highly significant element in human life and worthy of serious study. It means that questions arising in a lecture may come from very varied points of view and it is not always clear at first which. Reading theology is no ivory-towered activity.

Theology should be seen as a group of interrelated disciplines which together form the basis of a good education, since they give scope for almost all types of ability except experimental laboratory work. Theology is a vital humanistic study and I think every university should have it represented. It is only possible to think this if one has moved away from regarding theology as essentially a training for ordinands. The fact that many universities today do not include theology reflects the restricted idea of it in the academic community and often among theologians themselves. Also the link with classical studies has been too exclusive. Theology needs to relate as much to the Social Sciences (including Law), as to the Natural Sciences (including Technology), to Medicine and to Education. Practical difficulties of timetabling make much of this difficult, but we are a long way from getting to the point when we might even consider how to overcome them. However, beginnings are being made.

Another change in the theological student body is that Roman Catholics are now appearing at both undergraduate and postgraduate level. Hitherto Roman Catholics have opted out of university theology in the United Kingdom and created their own institutions. Roman Catholics are also beginning to be appointed to university teaching posts in theology, and there would be more if more suitable candidates were available, for the university will seek the best candidate, in terms of its criteria. This change is a welcome one for the future of church and university, for it is not good that Roman Catholic higher education in theology should be confined to relatively isolated institutions. In the field of Colleges of Education (with which in this article I am not concerned) the process has gone further.

III

Once employed by a university the theological don finds himself caught up in the same arguments about pay and conditions of work as among other professions and wage earners, and in the growingly similar attitudes of both in an age of inflation and recession. Indeed medical folk and miners have been the leaders in using industrial muscle to keep themselves at the top in salaries and wages. Clinical medical dons in universities have higher rates of pay than the rest, and this is a situation that the rest are resigned to but not happy about. Should one join the Association of University Teachers (which is now affiliated to the TUC)? My guess is that half the theological dons do not join. It may be that they are conscious that they are much better paid than parish clergy and ministers (more in terms of the financial situation on retirement than cash available when working), and are reluctant to press for salary increases. It may be that they have assumed until recently that they are in no danger of redundancy or dismissal. It may be that they are individualists, lacking in a sense of solidarity. It may be that they are absorbed in their work and apolitical. If they do join the AUT, problems of solidarity quickly arise. The union keeps as sharp an eye on comparability as do other unions, in this case with the pay in the higher ranks of the Civil Service, in addition to other sectors in education. For several years dons have felt themselves unfairly discriminated against when compared with either. But, aside from medicals, university teachers do not have much industrial weight. They have what most people consider a desirable job, in many areas there is no shortage of applicants, and in some a don after a few years is almost unemployable in any other occupation. Yet only threats of unpleasant action seem to secure reasonable pay settlements. Negotiations dragged on, settlements were delayed. Exasperation grew. There were mass lobbies. Casting around for some sanctions the only ones dons could find was to threaten not to release marks of final degree examination scripts so that students could not graduate. This has happened twice in France. There was a serious possibility a few years ago that the AUT would call for this action here. Some theological dons, and others, said they would never do anything which harmed students. Others felt the call of solidarity, and also used a familiar union argument that firmness was in the long-term interests of students as well as staff. In the end what I expected happened. Faced with a serious threat the Government gave way and a settlement was reached. So the crucial strike question never had to be faced. The problem remains.

It is possible to hold, as I do, that an advanced industrial society must have an incomes policy, as one element of government strategy, and also to think that present differentials in pay between occupations need radical scrutiny, arduous as this will be. But the situation we were faced with at the time was that government policy seemed clearly inequitable as between different contendants, and chiefly influenced by those who used industrial muscle. It is a classical illustration of economic and industrial problems which are constantly arising in the political sphere. It may disconcert some that there are no easy answers, but it does seem incumbent on the theological don to wrestle with it. Those who did not bother with union affairs still benefited from its threat of strike action. To be thoughtlessly apolitical is to behave irresponsibly. The only remotely similar situation known to me in the life of the ordained ministry is the small number of Church of England clergy who have joined the ASTMS, presumably because they are not confident that in the peculiar way in which their pay is determined they will receive natural justice without some back-up support.

IV

Since my major interest has been in Christian social ethics I have been asked to reflect on the capacity of the churches to relate to social and economic issues. My impression is that at the centre they are better informed, and as a result more cautious. There are fewer egregious utterances by church leaders or representative church bodies, but less clarity on what it is appropriate to say and a greater tendency not to say anything. There is more awareness that few of these issues have clear, let alone peculiarly 'Christian', answers, and perhaps a growing appreciation that the churches themselves are not neutral observers, impartially issuing warnings and encouragements to all sections of the community, but often themselves part of the problem by virtue of their own stake in the current economic and social structures, and their natural connections with only some sections of the community. They are also, I think, more aware of the futility of pious-sounding general statements to the effect that if everyone behaved as he ought there would be no problem.

The years since the last war have seen the development of the Boards for Social Responsibility at national and diocesan levels (and the equivalent in other churches), of the British Council of Churches, and of the semi-independent Catholic Institute of International Relations, together with the work of the World Council of Churches which has helped to put British problems in a wider context. It means that there is a much greater amount of sifted material and analysis available to answer the question 'What is going on?', and to sort out the issues, necessary preliminaries to having anything to say. To take an example of the emotive issue of Strikes or the Closed Shop. The instinct of the General Synod is to side with the traditional middle-class individualist point of view (ignoring the growth of professional solidarity), but it is better briefed by the BSR, and also rather more aware of how extraordinarily unrepresentative it is of the wage-earning population of the country and that things do often look very different from that perspective. The result is that there are fewer ignorant, as well as foolish, utterances.

It seems clear that the Church of England can be relied upon much less to support government policy, including that of Conservative governments. The Sunday after the Attlee administration was voted into power in 1945 the celebrant at the service of Holy Communion which I attended said in his biddings to prayer, 'Let us pray for our King in the great sorrow that has come to him this week.' No doubt this was an extreme reaction, verging on the eccentric, but it represented a predominant tendency which is not nearly so marked now. It must have been unprecedented when the General Synod in February 1981 condemned the government's British Nationality Bill by 198 votes to 1. And this was on a detailed matter. One of the perennial problems is that general statements on ethical issues cut little ice, whilst detailed ones involve an assessment of evidence and of possibilities of action which inevitably have large elements of uncertainty, and about which agreement among equally conscientious Christians is unlikely. How far it is useful and possible for church bodies to operate at a middle level between the two is a matter on which experience is accumulating. However, even when agreement is not possible at other than a general level it is possible to list and analyse areas of disagreement, and let proponents of each policy address questions to fellow Christians who advocate a different use.

Differences on the basis and method of Christian social ethics remain to be worked at. Perhaps the chief of these is the use of the Bible. Because some still think that detailed and binding rules of a timeless kind can be drawn from it we have unresolved arguments on, for example, pacifism or homosexual actions. This lack of agreement on the use of the Bible remains an obstacle to coherent Christian utterance, but in principle this difference is resolvable if we work at resolving it. Differences arising from different judgments on the detail, and the evaluation, of empirical data are not in principle resolvable, but they can be reduced by the systematic attention given to current social issues which the growth of bodies like the BSR in recent decades has promoted.

This would be done even more efficiently if the churches pooled their scarce resources, Roman Catholic included, and did together all that conscience did not require them to do separately. We should also do better if we paid more attention to the global and ecumenical content which the Ecumenical Movement represents. If the British have lost an empire and not yet found a role, the churches are slow to realize the extent to which Europe is no longer the centre, and the Church of England that what it thinks is no longer decisive in the Anglican Communion.

But how much does discussion at the central level affect the parishes? Generalizations here are dangerous. One is thankful to know of many examples of vitality. Nevertheless I get the general impression that the effort to cope with inflation is driving congregations into themselves. Also that the greatly increased contribution made by congregations to current clergy stipends is giving them more influence, which is good, but in the immediate future that influence is likely to be in a conservative and conserving rather than an adventurous direction. The search is for comfort and for stability rather than for challenge. The church is strongest in middle-class suburban parishes. Lay people in them are prone to say that they spend their working life on executive activity and decision-making, and do not want to be troubled with more awkward issued in their church life. University dons who are faithful churchgoers do not want to be extended at work by challenging thoughts on the university, and their idea of university chaplaincy work is very much that of a supportive pastoral kind. Religious publishing is sharing in the economic difficulties of the day, but the more traditional denominational and biblical books sell, whilst admirable manuscripts on the world today do not. A weariness has set in which may be the equivalent of the *trahison des clercs*.

This is particularly serious because we are being faced with the question whether our type of political democracy is workable. Are we becoming ungovernable? The expectations of an advanced industrial society have become such that electorates are in danger of not giving governments enough manoeuvring room to cope with the problems that arise. We want full employment, an end to inflation, and free collective bargaining and the three are incompatible. Failing to face this we lurch into mass unemployment or a high rate of inflation; both produce mounting discontent. Participation in community politics at the local level, though highly desirable, will not solve this problem. Only representative democracy can do it, and that on the basis of a more informed public opinion, whether we live in a social democracy or a democratic socialist society rather than a different and altogether less pleasant form of authoritarian one. Also the representation has to extend more fully from the political into industrial structures. It needs a greater effort to see how inevitable conflicts of interest can be held within a more specific spelling out of the common good, and that in global and not merely national terms. The values of our type of democratic society are too important to be assumed or ignored. Christians can surely not be indifferent to these. They need to be cultivated, and it will not do for us to withdraw into merely cultivating our parochial gardens.

Notes

In writings referred to in these notes, the place of publication is London unless otherwise stated.

1 The Future of Christian Ethics

1. In this brief discussion I confine myself almost entirely to England. The Scottish, Welsh and Irish situations are different, and in different ways.

2. When I first came to Manchester there was only one full-time post in this area in an English university, the Chair of Moral and Pastoral Theology at Oxford, and one part-time lectureship at Manchester. This was so marginally paid that the holder had to have a full-time post as well. There was hardly any postgraduate research work. Now there are two more Chairs (London and Manchester), two lectureships (Birmingham and Manchester), several qualified part-time lecturers, and a considerable number of research students. University Extra-Mural Courses of various lengths have also increased considerably, and the experience of Manchester is that a three-year Extra-Mural Certificate in Religious Studies, in which there are strong components from Christian Ethics, attracts many excellent students. In the present era of financial cut-backs on universities, the churches might well consider whether to endow some posts in this and other areas of theology, as industry is being asked to do in science and technology, business firms in administration studies and management, and drug companies in medicine. Both the new Chairs were privately endowed, and it is hard to believe that the government, working through the University Grants Committee, will show much interest in theology. Although an excellent intellectual discipline, using all the major human skills, it does not bear directly on the Gross National Product; this appears to be the overriding criterion, and hardly even lip-service is paid to anything else.

3. There has for over 15 years been an Association of Teachers of Moral Theology, mainly Roman Catholic and mainly concerned with teaching in seminaries, but not exclusively so. There is some overlap of membership between it and the Society for the Study of Christian Ethics.

4. A Handbook for Teachers of Christian Ethics in Theological Colleges, 1964 (which was privately printed), and Teaching Christian Ethics: an Approach, 1974.

5. Cf. ch. 15 below for weaknesses of Anglican theological colleges.

6. The Report of the Archbishop of Canterbury's Commission on Urban Priority Areas, Faith in the City, 1985, raises this question in ch. 3, but does not thoroughly tease it out; the 'academic' and the 'committed' approaches to theology are left side by side as both necessary.

7. I have played a part in many over the years. Three recent examples are: (1) Adrian Speller, Breaking Out, 1986, the writing up of a Commission on

Penal Policy of the British Council of Churches; (2) *Not Just for the Poor: The Future of the Welfare State*, 1986, the report of a Working Party of the Church of England Board for Social Responsibility; (3) an ongoing Criminal Justice Panel of the same body. Diocesan Boards for Social Responsibility can also be active. Manchester, for instance, has a Social Concerns Research Group (among other activities), which tries to put national issues in a local context to inform congregational thought, e.g. on environmental issues or ethnic minorities.

8. Tribute should be paid to the work of Mark Gibbs over several decades in furthering the development of thought and action on the lay role in church and society; he is the linchpin of the Laity Exchange project in the USA and its British connection, the Audenshaw Foundation.

9. For example Garth L. Hallett, *Christian Moral Reasoning*, Indiana 1983; Ian C. M. Fairweather and James I. H. McDonald, *The Quest for Christian Ethics: an Inquiry into Ethics and Christian Ethics*, Edinburgh 1984; James Gallagher, *The Basis for Christian Ethics*, New York 1985; Robin Gill, *A Text Book of Christian Ethics*, Edinburgh 1985; Michael J. Langford, *The Good and the True: an Introduction to Christian Ethics*, 1985; and Vincent MacNamara, *Faith and Ethics: Recent Roman Catholicism*, 1985; three of these are from the United Kingdom.

10. *Report of the Committee of Enquiry into Human Fertilisation and Embryology*, 1984, Cmnd 934.

11. *Personal Origins*, the Report of a Working Party on Human Fertilization and Embryology of the Board for Social Responsibility, 1985.

12. Cf. I Cor. 11. 14ff.

13. Cf. Matt. 10. 8.

14. S. Hauerwas, *The Peaceable Kingdom: a Primer in Christian Ethics*, 1983.

2 The Development of Christian Ethics in the Church of England in the Twentieth Century

1. Cf.Bryan Wilson, *Religion in Secular Society*, 1976, *Contemporary Transformations of Religion*, 1976, and *Religion in Sociological Perspective*, 1982.

2. Owen Chadwick, *The Secularization of the European Mind in the Nineteenth Century* (the Gifford Lectures for 1973–4), 1975.

3. Cf. Alan Wilkinson, *The Church of England and the First World War*, 1978, and *Dissent or Conform? War, Peace and English Churches 1900–1945*, 1986.

4. Max Weber, *The Protestant Ethic and the Spirit of Capitalism*, ET 1930.

5. Cf. my Scott Holland Lectures, *Church and Society in the Late Twentieth Century*, 1983, ch. 1.

6. See W. Reason, ed., *The Proceedings of COPEC*, 1924; also the Reports of the COPEC Commissions in 12 volumes, 1924.

7. G. K. A. Bell, ed., *The Stockholm Conference*, 1925.

8. *Malvern 1941: the Life of the Church and the Order of Society*, 1941.

9. *Faith in the City*, 1985, is the latest.

10. *The Church and the Bomb*, 1982. It advocated a phased unilateral renunciation of nuclear weapons; the General Synod did not accept this.

11. Cf. the Scott Holland Lectures (n. 5 above), pp. 77–81.

12. William Temple, *Christianity and Social Order*, reissued with an Introduction by R. H. Preston, 1976.

13. Giles Ecclestone, *The Church of England and Politics*, 1980.

3. The Future of Protestant Ethics

1. For Luther's doctrine of the two realms, see 'The Two Kingdoms and Two Regiments: Some Problems of Luther's Zwei-Reich-Lehre', W. J. Cargill Thompson in his *Studies in the Reformation: Luther to Hooker*, 1980. Convenient discussions of Luther's ethics are found in Paul Althaus, *The Ethics of Martin Luther*, ET 1972, and H. Bornkamm, *Luther's Doctrine of Two Kingdoms*, Philadelphia 1966. A selection on ethics from the writings of Lutheran theologians is contained in K. H. Hertz, *Two Kingdoms and One World*, Minneapolis 1976.

2. R. H. Tawney, *Religion and the Rise of Capitalism*, 1929 edition, p. 88.

3. On Luther's doctrine of the Calling and the Office see Gustav Wingren, *The Christian's Calling: Luther on Vocation*, ET 1958.

4. Anders Nygren, *Agape and Eros*, revised ET 1953, p. 735; and p. 740 '(Man) becomes a "tube" which by faith receives everything from God's love and then allows the Divine love to stream out over the world.'

5. Recent Lutheran attempts to deal with this include the substantial *Theological Ethics* of Helmut Thielicke, Vol. 1, Foundations, ET 1968; Vol. 2, Politics, ET 1969; also *The Ethics of Sex*, ET 1964. There is also Supplement No. 2 to the *Lutheran World*, 1966, on 'Faith and Society'; and several essays in one of the volumes issued in connection with the World Council of Church's Conference in Geneva in 1966 on 'Christians in the Technical and Social Revolutions of our Time', *Christian Ethics in a Changing World*, ed. John C. Bennett: 'Luther's "Two Kingdoms" Ethics Reconsidered' by H. D. Wendland, and 'Natural Law and Social Ethics' by N. H. Søe. See also 'La Doctrine Luthérienne des deux Règnes' in the journal *Istia* (April–June 1972). The general tendency is to revise the doctrine of the two kingdoms by putting them under an eschatological critique, or by establishing social justice as a proper theological concern.

6. See A. S. P. Woodhouse, *Puritanism and Liberty*, 1983, which deals with the Army debates of 1647–9.

7. Cf. A. D. Lindsay, *The Essentials of Democracy*, 1932, and *The Churches and Democracy*, 1934, and note the remark of R. H. Tawney:'. . . it is probable that democracy owes more to Nonconformity than any other single movement' (op. cit., p. 272).

8. Cf. *Voluntary Associations*, ed. D. B. Robertson, Richmond, Virginia, 1968.

9. The debate provoked by Max Weber's *The Protestant Ethic and the Spirit of Capitalism*, ET 1930, is so great that what he said has been lost in the subsequent discussion. It is best to read Weber himself. An exposition, comment and bibliography is in Michael Hill, *A Sociology of Religion*, 1973, ch. 5, 'The Theoretical Background to the "Weber Thesis"', and ch. 6, 'Protestantism and Capitalism'; and an appraisal in Gianfranco Poggi, *Calvinism and the Capitalist Spirit*, 1983.

10. On Calvin's ethics see *La Pensée Economique and Sociale de Calvin* (Geneva, 1959) and *The Social Humanism of Calvin* (Richmond, Virginia, 1964) both by Andre Biéler, and on Calvinist ethics the chapter on that theme in Jürgen Moltmann, *The Experiment Hope*, ET 1975.

11. William Perkins, 1558–1602, *A Discourse of Conscience*, 1597; *The Whole Treatise of the Cases of Conscience*, 1611.

Joseph Hall, 1574–1656, *Resolutions and Decisions of Divers Practical Cases of*

Conscience in Continual Use Amongst Men, in Four Decades, 1650.

William Ames, 1576–1633, *De Conscientia, eius Juris et Casibus*, Amsterdam 1630 (ET *Conscience with the Power and Cases thereof*, 1643).

Robert Sanderson, 1587–1663, *De Obligatione Conscientia*, 1647; (ET, *Bishop Sanderson's Lectures on Conscience and Human Law*, edited by Christopher Wordsworth, 1877); *Eight Cases of Conscience Occasionally Determined*, 1674.

Jeremy Taylor, 1613–1667; The most considerable treatment of moral theology in his numerous writings is *Ductor Dubitantium*, 1660.

Richard Baxter, 1615–1691, *A Christian Directory*, 1673; Jeanette Tawney produced *Chapters from A Christian Directory*, 1925.

John Sharp, 1645–1714, *A Discourse Concerning Conscience*, 1673; *The Case of a Doubting Conscience*, 1685.

There is a broad survey of this whole area in Thomas Wood, *English Casuistical Divinity During the Seventeenth Century*, 1952.

12. Cf. C. F. Allison, *The Rise of Moralism*, 1966, for a treatment of this duality, particularly in Jeremy Taylor.

13. The best known was John Skinner, *Synopsis of Moral and Ascetical Theology*, 1882.

14. K. E. Kirk, *Some Principles of Moral Theology*, 1921; *Ignorance, Faith and Conformity*, 1925; and *Conscience and its Problems*, 1927; *The Vision of God*, 1931, has a wider theme.

15. Wilson lists Confessionist (e.g. Salvationists), Revolutionist (e.g. Jehovah's Witnesses), Introversionist (e.g. Exclusive Brethren), Manipulationist (e.g. Christian Science), Thaumaturgical (e.g. Spiritualists), Reformist (e.g. Quakers) and Utopians (e.g. the Bruderhof). See his *Sects and Society*, 1961, and *Religious Sects*, 1970.

16. Cf. J. H. Yoder, *The Politics of Jesus: Vicit Agnus Noster*, Grand Rapids 1972.

17. Cf. C. H. Hopkins, *The Rise of the Social Gospel in American Protestantism 1865–1915*, New Haven 1940. The last and most weighty theologian of the Social Gospel was Walter Rauschenbusch; see his *Christianizing the Social Order*, New York 1912, and *A Theology for the Social Gospel*, New York 1917.

18. There is no substantial treatment of the Protestant Pietist ethics, partly because there is not much to say. Traditional 'conservative evangelical' ethics can be studied in John Murray, *Principles of Conduct*, 1957; and an example of the many books indicating new strains in evangelical social theology is Alan Storkey, *A Christian Social Perspective*, 1979.

19. Cf. Thomas C. Oden, *Radical Obedience: the Ethics of Rudolf Bultmann*, Philadelphia 1964.

20. In Protestant circles it never lived down Pascal's attack in *Lettres Provinciales*, 1657.

21. Bernard Häring, *Free and Faithful in Christ*: Vol. 1, *General Moral Theology*, 1978; Vol. 2, *The Truth Will Set You Free*, 1979; Vol. 3, *Light to the World: Salt for the Earth*, 1981. The contrast can be seen by comparing with Häring two standard works of moral theology widely used in the Roman Catholic Church in Britain prior to the Second Vatican Council of 1962–5, both of which ran through several editions, H. Davies, *Moral and Pastoral Theology*, 1935, and T. Slater, *A Manual of Moral Theology*, 1908.

22. The report was published in *The Ecumenical Review*, 25. 4, Oct. 1973.

23. H. R. Niebuhr, *Christ and Culture*, New York 1951, 1952.

24. The problem of how precisely to make this contribution amidst the

technicalities and uncertainties of a rapidly changing social order is manifold, both for individual Christians and for churches as corporate bodies. I have discussed a central issue which arises in Appendix 2, 'Middle Axioms in Christian Social Ethics', in *Church and Society in the Late Twentieth Century*, 1983.

25. Matt. 10. 8.

26. E.g., the moral issues raised by abortion or by living as a Christian under an atheist government; on the latter see Trevor Beeson, *Discretion and Valour*, 2nd revised ed., 1982, which deals with the position of Christians in the Marxist countries of Europe. I discussed problems in using the Bible as a direct basis for ethical decisions in a previous Rylands Lecture, 'From the Bible to the Modern World', reprinted in my *Explorations in Theology* 9, 1981.

27. Cf. N. H. G. Robinson, *The Groundwork of Christian Ethics*, 1971.

28. Emil Brunner, *The Divine Imperative*, ET 1937, p. 71.

29. Dietrich Bonhoeffer, *Ethics*, ET, 2nd ed., 1971, pp. 3ff.

30. Karl Barth, *Church Dogmatics*, II. 2, ET 1957, p. 518.

31. It was percipiently summed up almost before the debate got going in an article by James M. Gustafson, 'Context v. Principle: a Misplaced Debate in Christian Ethics', *Harvard Theological Review* 58, No. 2, 1965, reprinted in *New Theology* No. 3, 1966.

32. Seen n.5 above.

33. This is so much taken for granted that Catholic-Protestant divisions are scarcely mentioned in Liberation Theology. How much is at issue between them in Western theology is covered in James M. Gustafson, *Protestant and Roman Catholic Ethics*, 1978.

34. Cf. David Little 'Calvin and the Prospects for a Christian Theory of Natural Law', in *Norm and Context in Christian Ethics*, ed. Gene H. Outka and Paul Ramsey, 1968.

35. Cf. Stanley Hauerwas, *Vision and Virtue in Christian Ethical Reflection*, Indiana 1974, and *Character and the Christian Life: A Study in Theological Ethics*, San Antonio 1975.

36. Cf. Knud E. Løgstrup, *The Ethical Demand*, Philadelphia 1971.

37. Cf. H. Richard Niebuhr, *The Responsible Self*, 1963.

38. For the Barmen Declaration and the Ansbach Proposals see Richard Gutteridge, *Open Thy Mouth for the Dumb: The German Evangelical Church and the Jews*, 1976. There is an extract from both Paul Althaus and Werner Elert in *Faith and Action*, ed. H. Thielicke and H. H. Schrey, ET 1970; and for Paul Althaus on *Volk* see his *Theologie der Ordnungen*, Gütersloh 1935.

39. Brunner, op. cit., Book 3. Some relevant sections from it were reprinted with an introduction by Vernon Sproxton in *Love and Marriage*, 1970.

40. Barth, Bonhoeffer, Thielicke and Troeltsch in the works already quoted. For Künneth see *Faith and Action* (n. 38), pp. 282–92.

41. Jürgen Moltmann, *Theology of Hope*, ET 1967, was a herald of this emphasis.

42. I have discussed 'possessive individualism' in *Religion and the Persistence of Capitalism*, 1979, ch. 4, 'Capitalism, Socialism, Personal Freedom and Individualism'.

43. There is little material, and still less of it good, available on Orthodox ethics; the first generally available survey is Stanley S. Harakas, *Towards Transfigured Life: the Theoria of Eastern Orthodox Ethics*, Minneapolis 1983.

4   *The Question of a Just, Participatory and Sustainable Society*

1. A full bibliography of the theme treated here would be very large, so in this and the subsequent notes I include only basic references. The history of the Ecumenical Movement is covered in *A History of the Ecumenical Movement, 1517–1948*, ed. R. Rouse and S. Neill, 1954; *The Ecumenical Advance, 1948–1968*, ed. H. E. Fey, 1970; and (more briefly) Ernst Lange, *And Yet it Moves*, 1979. In the first book chs. 11 and 12 are particularly relevant to this lecture and there is an important appendix by Dr W. A. Visser't Hooft, the first General Secretary of the World Council of Churches, on 'The Meaning of Ecumenical'.

2. *The Stockholm Conference*, ed. G. K. A. Bell, 1925.

3. There was an important preparatory volume for the Oxford Conference, *The Church and its Function in Society*, by W. A. Visser't Hooft and J. H. Oldham, part 3 of which is specially relevant to this lecture. Six volumes of theological essays in connection with the Conference were also published, each on a particular theme, of which the ones on 'The Christian Faith and the Common Life', and 'Church and Community' bear most on this le_ture. The report of the Conference appeared in the same format, *The Churches Survey their Task*.

4. Four volumes of essays in connection with the Geneva Conference were published earlier in 1966: *Christian Social Ethics in a Changing World*, ed. J. C. Bennett; *Man in Community*, ed. E. de Vries; *Economic Growth in World Perspective*, ed. D. Munby; and *Responsible Government in a Revolutionary Age*, ed. Z. K. Matthews. The Report of the Conference is *World Conference on Church and Society*, 1966.

5. Preliminary papers for the MIT Conference were published in *Science, Faith and the Future*, 1978; the many papers presented at it are in *Faith and Science in an Unjust World*, vol. 1, ed. R. L. Shinn, and the reports in vol. 2, ed. P. Abrecht, 1980.

6. For the first see, for example, E. Brunner, *The Divine Imperative*, ET 1937; for the second J. Fletcher, *Situation Ethics*, 1966; and for the third, Paul Tillich, *Love, Power and Justice*, 1954.

7. See especially E. Duff, *The Social Thought of the World Council of Churches*, 1956; and the chapter by E. de Vries in *Technology and Social Justice*, ed. R. H. Preston, 1971.

8. See Paulo Freire, *Pedagogy of the Oppressed*, 1972.

9. The first report was *The Limits to Growth*, 1972; the second *Mankind at the Turning Point*, 1975; the third *Re-Shaping the International Order*, 1977, and the fourth *Goals for Mankind*, 1977.

10. One of them is the University of Sussex study already quoted, *World Futures: The Great Debate*, ed Christopher Freeman and Marie Jahoda, 1978.

11. Aside from Christian discussions of the nature and status of the Genesis myths and broader questions of doctrine, there is a good general survey in John Passmore, *Man's Responsibility for Nature*, 1974. See also ch. 5 below.

12. Cf. ch. 12 below on The Politics of Imperfection and the Politics of Hope.

5.   *The Integrity of Creation: Issues of Environmental Ethics*

1. This is at the level of what are unfortunately, because misleadingly,

often called 'middle axioms'. Detailed policy recommendations give rise to much more complex problems. I have dealt with them in Appendix 2 of the Scott Holland Lectures 1983, *Church and Society in the Late Twentieth Century*.

2. There are now several sources available on the The Responsible Society, of which the earliest is Edward Duff, *The Social Thought of the WCC*, 1956, Part 4, ch. 4. Among the later sources is Paul Bock, *In Search of a Responsible World Society*, Philadelphia 1974, ch. 3.

3. The phrase Just and Sustainable Society was first introduced in a 'Church and Society' Consultation in Bucharest in 1974 on 'Science and Technology for Human Development: The Ambiguous Future and Christian Hope'. 'Sustainable' reflected the growing concerns of ecologists and environmentalists in the affluent world, and was a better because more flexible term than 'steady state equilibrium' or 'zero growth rate' which the most ardent ecologists were advocating. Participation was added later, largely through the insistence of the WCC Churches' Commission on Participation in Development which reflected the strong feelings of Christians in the Third World that they were excluded from power-sharing in economic matters by the affluent countries, and that many of their own governments were run by corrupt political élites. Justice has, of course, been a perennial criterion to bring to bear on the social order, though there have always been problems in seeing precisely how it relates to the gospel *agape* (love).

4. A lecture given for the Faculty of Divinity in the University College of South Wales, Cardiff.

5. In Britain incomes were up 100 percent between 1951 and 1973, for two hours a week less work and more and longer paid holidays (*Social Trends*, HMSO, 1973).

6. Including DDT in many countries. It did much good in preventing insect-borne disease, like malaria, and in improving crop yields. But it is not bio-degradable and accumulates in carnivorous birds and in the end, through the food chain, in humans.

7. The Mediterranean has been described as 'a sewer for centuries', but since 1960 the growth of tourism, of industrialization, and of dumping by ships is proving too much for it. It is tideless and its water changes with that of the Atlantic only once in 30–40 years (the Irish Sea by contrast changes every year). It is in danger of becoming a marine desert as oxygenation and photosynthesis decreases, accompanied by more indestructible plastic bags and containers. Co-operation among countries bordering on the sea is making efforts to rectify the situation. The Aswan High Dam in Egypt is a favourite environmentalist example of development gone wrong, but the evidence is ambiguous. There were certainly unforeseen harmful consequences but they do not appear to be beyond correction.

8. There is a devastating attack on the mismanagement of nuclear waste in the USA in Donald L. Bartlett and James B. Steele, *Forevermore: Nuclear Waste in America*, New York 1985. It amounts, according to a review in *The Economist* (19 October 1985) to a chronicle 'of scientific blunders, of criminal behaviour by industry, of ineptitude and cover-up by politicians, of incompetence and impotence on the part of regulators and lawmakers and of man's inability to recognize his limitations'.

9. Freedom to breed would be restricted in order that other freedoms could flourish. Further stipulations included a return to natural materials from

synthetic ones and the restoration of railways and canals as against road building.

10. The Club of Rome was financed by an ecologically concerned Italian industrialist, and made up of 17 natural scientists from Massachusetts Institute of Technology.

11. The first 4 reports of the Club of Rome were D. H. Meadows and others, *The Limits to Growth*, 1972; M. D. Mesarovic and others, *Mankind at the Turning Point*, 1975; *Reshaping the International Order*, ed. J. Tinbergen, 1977; and *Goals for Mankind*, ed. E. Lazlo, 1977. There is a critique of the issues by the Sussex University Policy Research Unit, *World Futures and the Great Debate*, ed. C. Freeman and M. J. Jahoda, 1978. Concentration has lately been on the north-south (rich-poor) relationship, and arguing powerfully against leaving aside problems of pollution, scarcity and famine for future generations to deal with. The trouble now is held to be not growth, as in the first report, but undifferentiated as against stable, organic growth. This is what the criterion of Sustainability has been concerned with.

12. Lynn White, 'The Historical Roots of our Ecological Crisis', in *Science* (USA), March 1967.

13. Cf. J. V. Taylor, *The Primal Vision*, 1963.

14. There is much evidence in Keith Thomas, *Man and the Natural World: Changing Attitudes in England, 1500–1800*, 1983.

15. Cf. Matt. 6 *passim*; Matt. 10. 29f.

16. Mark 10. 42–44.

17. Jer. 18; Rom. 9. 21.

18. Matt. 10. 8.

19. Cf. Gunnar Myrdal, *An Asian Drama: An Enquiry into the Poverty of Nations*, 1968. India's sacred cows enslave humans to nature.

20. Harold Hartley in giving the first Fawley Lecture at Southampton University, *Science and Society: The Problem of the Future*, 1954, forecast by extrapolation from current trends population, energy consumption and food production in the year 2100. All his forecasts were exceeded in 25 years.

21. The Joint European Torus (JET) research project at Culham, near Oxford, with its huge magnetic machines, is into its second phase of work. The Lawrence Livermore National Laboratory in the USA is rapidly developing an alternative short wavelength laser system of Internal Confinement Fusion (ICE). JET has been on the way for 30 years, ICE for 10. The latter has been progressing faster, although having had less investment, and the two are now neck and neck. The Japanese are also developing a variant of the second.

22. The only significant reference is on p. 251 of *Gathered For Life*, ed. David M. Gill, the official report of the Assembly (Geneva 1983). 'Jesus Christ is the life of the world. This life is to be expressed through justice and peace for the whole world and respect for the integrity of all creation. Growth toward full ecclesial, spiritual and political commitment to this expression by all member churches, in all dimensions, should be one of the purposes of all programmes of the WCC'. There is another reference to a 'caring attitude to nature' to replace Sustainability (p. 225). The main sources of previous work relating to the theme are the Reports of the MIT Conference *Faith and Science in an Unjust World*, Geneva 1980, especially Vol. 2, pp. 28–38, the report of the section on Humanity, Nature and God; and in *Anticipation*, No. 25, January 1979, an occasional journal of the Church and Society Sub-Unit of the WCC.

23. The Faith and Order Commission of the WCC at its meeting at

Stavanger in Norway in August 1985 produced a paper on 'The Integrity of Creation in the Light of the Apostolic Faith', which includes the statement that nature is not to be regarded as 'the neutral material for life, a mere theatre in which history is played out'.

24. Herman Kahn, William Brown and Leon Martel, *The Next 200 Years*, New York 1977.

25. Peter Singer, *Animal Liberation*, 1976. Singer is Professor of Philosophy at Monash University, Melbourne. His criticism is valid against the element in the Christian tradition which condemned cruelty to animals solely because of its bad effect on humans.

26. As an example G. F. Woods, *Personal Theological Explanation*, 1958.

27. James Gustafson, *Theology and Ethics* (Chicago and Oxford 1981) and *Ethics and Theology* (Chicago 1984).

28. Robin Attfield, *The Ethics of Environmental Concern*, 1983. Attfield draws on 140 books and 160 articles and essays on this theme, published in the previous ten years. Cf also Robert W. Kates, 'Part and Apart: Issues in Humankind's Relationship to the Natural World' in F. Kenneth Hare, ed., *The Experiment of Life*, Toronto 1983.

29. John Passmore, *Man's Responsibility for Nature*, 1974, 2nd ed., 1980. Passmore is not a Christian. Process philosophers and theologians (followers of A. N. Whitehead) are disposed to speak of consciousness as an essential aspect of the universe. Do bacteria enjoy their lives? But that still leaves ethical questions operating within the criterion already discussed. Three other books of the many that might be mentioned are: *Man and Nature*, a Church of England symposium edited by Hugh Montefiore, 1975; *Ethics and the Problem of the Twenty-first Century*, ed. K. E. Goodpaster and K. M. Sayre, 1979; and Mary Midgley, *Beast and Man: the Roots of Human Nature*, Hassocks, Sussex, 1979. She minimizes the distinction between humans and animals, unlike Passmore, and maintains that the world was not made for us but we for it. It is surely a case of 'and', not 'but'.

30. The issue here is too big to discuss. To give an example may clarify it. Quoting the human 'right to life' settles nothing. It cannot be treated as an absolute. If e.g. it is expanded to 'the right not to be murdered', we have to decide (a) what kind of killings we are going to classify as murder, (b) what are the characteristics of a human being to which we apply it. The issues covered by the Warnock Report on Human Fertilisation and Embryology (1984) illustrate the problems in applying these criteria.

31. 'The Integrity of Creation', see n. 23 above.

32. Briefly (i) it made too much of a claim to knowledge of the future; (ii) it was too pessimistic in assuming that things would get worse before divine intervention brought the new order into being; this easily becomes an ideology of the *status quo*; (iii) it was thus too indifferent to human history; (iv) its new order was too discontinuous with the human present; (v) its expounders were too certain of their own exclusive place in the new order.

33. C. Rowland, *The Open Heaven: A Study of Apocalyptic in Judaism and Early Christianity*, 1982.

34. A book from Western Christianity which makes an effort to come to terms with this is N. P. Williams, *The Idea of the Fall and of Original Sin*, 1927.

35. There is now a WCC position paper on this, David Gosling, 'Towards a Credible Ecumenical Theology of Nature', *The Ecumenical Review* 38.3, July 1986.

6 *Church and Society: Do We Need Another William Temple?*

1. 'William Temple: after Twenty-five Years', *Church Quarterly*, Vol. 2, No. 2, October 1969.
2. Introductory essay to a re-issue of *Christianity and Social Order* in 1976, 'Thirty-five years later, 1941–76'.
3. 'William Temple as a Social Theologian', *Theology*, Vol. 84, No. 701, September 1981, an issue containing several articles to commemorate the centenary of his birth. This article covers much the same ground but with further reflections.
4. David Nicholls, 'William Temple and the Welfare State', *Crucible* (the journal of the Board for Social Responsibility of the General Synod of the Church of England), October-December 1984.
5. E. R. Norman, *Church and Society in England, 1770–1970: a Historical Study*, Oxford 1976, contains 85 references to Temple in the Index and 40 pages of text concerned with Temple.
6. St George's House, Windsor is somewhat similar, but more concerned with clergy.
7. I refer here to his most substantial books. Some of his many smaller books still read powerfully, for example *Christian Faith and Life* (1931), his Oxford University mission adresses.
8. *The Nation* (New York), 11 November 1944.
9. E. R. Norman (op. cit.) says much the same of it; Trevor Beeson, however, sees the specific recommendations in Temple's Appendix as 'clearly socialist'.
10. Nicholls quotes p. 23 of the original Penguin edition of *Christianity and Social Order* as justification for this assertion, but in fact it does not refer to conflicts of interest but to the need for 'a spirit and method of reconciliation' in handling industrial conflicts. The two are not incompatible and indeed both must be held.
11. See Temple's essay in the Oxford Conference volume *Christian Faith and the Common Life* (1938).
12. In as article in *The Economic Review*, vol. 18, 1908, p. 199.
13. The debt which the twentieth-century church owes to Oldham is easily overlooked. It is much to be hoped that the biography of that remarkable and self-effacing layman on which Dr Kathleen Bliss has been working for some years will be completed.
14. William Temple, *Nature, Man and God*, 1934, p. 478.
15. Though he approved of provision for Conscientious Objectors during the war, and disapproved of punitive mass bombing.
16. *Christianity and Social Order* (1976 edition), p. 65.
17. I have discussed the scope and limits of economics in the Scott Holland lectures for 1983, *Church and Society in the Late Twentieth Century*, Lecture 2, 'Christianity and Economic Man'.
18. Conference on Politics, Economics and Citizenship (COPEC), Birmingham 1924, an early British ecumenical effort of which Temple was Chairman.
19. The Scott Holland Lecture 1, 'The Legacy of the Christian Socialist Movement in England', deals with all these groups.
20. 'Church, Community and State in relation to the Economic Order', in *The Churches Survey Their Task*, the Report of the Oxford Conference, 1937, and also issued separately because of the great demand for it.
21. *Malvern 1941: the Life of the Church and the Order of Society*, 1941.

22. This aspect of Temple's thought is fruitfully explained in an unpublished Ph.D thesis of Durham University by Alan M. Suggate (1981). It is the most thorough study of Temple's writings, and in its references to other unpublished research material bearing on the theme of this lecture. There is an article by him, based on it, 'Reflections on William Temple's Christian Social Ethics', in *Crucible*, October–December 1981, and one on 'William Temple and the Challenge of Reinhold Niebuhr' in *Theology*, Vol. 84, No. 702, November 1981.

23. Giles Ecclestone, *The Church of England and Politics: Reflections on Christian Social Engagement*, 1980.

24. COPEC, Vol. XI, *The Social Function of the Church*, 1924, p. 94.

25. Their Pastoral Letter on War and Peace in the Nuclear Age, *The Challenge of God's Promise and Our Response*, is available in the UK (1983); the final text of the one on the economic order is awaited.

26. I have dealt fully with the possibilities and limits of Middle Axioms in Appendix 2 of the Scott Holland Lectures, 'Middle Axioms in Christian Social Ethics' (cf. n. 17 above).

27. Though it is interesting to note that in 1916 Temple was envisaging the ordination of women (see F. A. Iremonger's life of *William Temple*, 1948, p. 452).

28. E. R. Norman, *Church and Society in England*, pp. 370f.

7 *The End of the Protestant Work Ethic*

1. Max Weber, *The Protestant Ethic and the Spirit of Capitalism*, ET 1930. This book has promoted an immense discussion, to such an extent that what it actually says has been in danger of being buried. In my view the points I have made from it are unshaken, and it is wise to read the book itself before drawing conclusions from discussions of it. It was reprinted in Germany with an Introduction by Weber in 1920, and this is included in the English translation.

2. Cf. H. K. McArthur, *Understanding the Sermon on the Mount*, 1960, for, among other things, twelve different types of exegesis of it.

3. Matt. 7. 12.

4. Matt. 18. 21ff.

5. Matt. 6. 14f.

6. Matt. 5. 24, 46ff.

7. Matt. 6. 19–34.

8. Matt. 6. 21.

9. Matt. 6. 2–18.

10. Luke. 18. 9–14.

11. *An Interpretation of Christian Ethics*, 1936, p. 68. Later Niebuhr wrote, 'I am not therefore able to defend, or interested in defending any position I took in (that book).' This was in a chapter entitled 'Reply to Interpretation and Criticism' in *Reinhold Niebuhr, His Religious, Social and Political Thought*, ed. C. W. Kegley and R. W. Bretall, New York 1956, p. 435. I doubt whether this was entirely the case, but in any event the problem of how to interpret the most radical element in Jesus' ethical teaching remains.

12. Cf. n. 2 above; and also V. P. Furnish, *The Love Command in the New Testament*, 1973, and Gene Outka, *Agape*, 1972.

13. I Cor. 1. 2.

14. I Cor. 1. 1 and Rom. 1. 1.

15. I Cor. 7. 18–24.

16. Cf. G. Wingren, *The Christian's Calling: Luther on Vocation*, ET 1958.

17. Cf. K. H. Hertz, ed., *Two Kingdoms and One World*, Minneapolis 1976.

18. The Catechism in the Book of Common Prayer of 1662, on which generations of English children have been instructed, is more dynamic: the child is told that his duty towards his neighbour includes 'to learn and labour truly to get mine own living, and to do my duty in that state of life unto which it *shall* please God to call me' (my italics). This reflects Calvinist influence.

19. Cf. André Biéler, *La pensée économique et sociale de Calvin*, Geneva 1959, and *The Social Humanism of Calvin*, ET Atlanta 1964. There is a chapter on 'The Ethics of Calvinism' in J. Moltmann, *The Experiment Hope*, ET 1975. A magisterial earlier discussion of both Luther and Calvin is found in E. Troeltsch, *The Social Teaching of the Christian Churches*, 2 vols., ET 1931.

20. Calvinism is not necessary to capitalism. Hong Kong is an example of a flourishing capitalist economy which probably rests on a Confucian family ethic, without recognizing it; but scarcely at all on Protestantism.

21. Cf. my Scott Holland Lectures, *Church and Society in the Late Twentieth Century: the Economic and Political Task*, 1983, ch. 2 Section 2. and for possessive individualism *Religion and the Persistence of Capitalism, and other Studies in Christianity and Social Change*, 1979, ch. 4.

22. Cf. Scott Holland Lecture 1.

23. The Parish of St John, Park.

24. Of Chalmers' many writings in this area three may be mentioned. *The Christian and Civic Economy of Large Towns*, Glasgow 1821–6; *Tracts in Pauperism*, Glasgow 1833; *The Sufficiency of a Parochial System Without a Poor Rate for the Right Management of the Poor*, Glasgow 1842. See also H. Hunter, ed., *Problems of Poverty: Selections from the Economic Writings of Thomas Chalmers*, 1912.

25. Report on *Social Insurance and Allied Services*, 1943 commonly known as the Beveridge Report.

26. In the spring of 1986 there were about 3,408,000 unemployed, according to government figures, which underestimated them, of which about 1,350,000 had been unemployed for over a year, and about 425,000 men had been unemployed for more than three years.

27. Cf. Report of the Church of England Board for Social Responsibility, *Not Just for the Poor: The Future of the Welfare State*, 1986.

28. Cf. F. O. Darvall, *Popular Disturbances and Public Order in Regency England, being an account of the Luddite and other disorders in England during the years 1811–1817 and of the attitude and activities of the authorities*, 1934.

29. An OECD Survey of the Economy of Industrial Countries 1950–80 showed the extent of economic advance. In this period there was a 100 per cent increase in the consumption of goods and services; 92 per cent of workers had three weeks paid holiday, as over against 4 per cent in 1950; the percentage of income spent on the basics of food and clothing fell from one half to one third in Britain and to one quarter in the USA; and personal incomes in Britain were 50 per cent higher in real terms. Jobs in services had risen as against those in manufacturing, and on average one-third worked in industry, one half in services and one-tenth in agriculture. There was a vast increase in part-time jobs, particularly in the services sector, where four-fifths of women at work are found. This has created a big demand for pre-school care, partly because of the increase of one parent families, partly

because of the still rigid sex roles, which have only slightly weakened, with respect to the husband's share in family care.

30. For instance micro-electric technology can be used in the Third World as a cheap and reliable control mechanism for small water power generation in poor rural areas.

31. I am informed that all Harvard graduates must show that they can write a two loop computer programme, a most elementary exercise. It is ironic to think that it was only in the 1920s that Oxford abolished the requirement that all graduates should take a Viva in one of the gospels. Commonly known as 'divvers' it was the butt of many irreverent jokes, such as 'Forgive us our debts as we forget our divvers.'

32. Cf. W. Leontieff, *The Impact of Automation on Employment 1983–2000*, 1985. It suggests that clerical work will be drastically cut, but that many blue-collar workers will be needed to produce and service new equipment for new industries. It stresses change and the need for flexibility.

33. The two Brandt Reports, *North-South: a Programme for Survival*, 1980, and *Common Crisis: North-South Co-operation for World Recovery*, 1983.

34. Cf. Roger Clarke, *Work in Crisis*, 1981; David Bleakley, *In Place of Work: the Sufficient Society*, 1981 and *Work: the Shadow and the Substance*, 1983; James Robertson, *Future Work*, 1985, argues that we should develop self-organized work at home or in the community, paid or unpaid. He calls it 'own work'. There are many more studies in this area, but they tend to assume too easily a general state of unemployment in the future, and do not specifically consider the case of the displaced unskilled.

35. For the confusing term Middle Axiom see the full discussion in Appendix 2 of my Scott Holland Lectures (n. 21 above).

36. Another possible middle axiom, that one would hope would in the end be agreed by most Christian opinion, is the necessity of some incomes policy. Implementing is a tricky matter. Companies, for instance, could be taxed if their wages bill shewed that they were above the norm; and there could be a regional Income Tax. But there are many possibilities which need thought.

37. *Christianity and Social Order*, first published in 1942 as a paperback, was reissued in 1976. The Appendix is called 'A Suggested Policy'.

38. Cf. Tony Walter, *Fair Shares? An Ethical Guide to Tax and Social Security*, Edinburgh 1985.

39. I have discussed economic efficiency in several places in the Scott Holland Lectures.

40. Some more exuberant prophets of the technological future talk of the abolition of the distinction between work and leisure; cf. Alvin Toffler, *The Third Wave*, 1980; Clive Jenkins and Barrie Sherman, *The Leisure Shock*, 1981. I take this with a dose of scepticism. Our powers of looking into the future are limited (cf. the chapter on 'The Politics of Imperfection and the Politics of Hope'). I have kept within what I think we may reasonably expect at the moment.

8 *The New Right: a Theological Critique*

1. P. Hennessy, S. Morrison and R. Townsend, *Routine Punctuated by Orgies*, Strathclyde University Press 1984.

2. J. Philip Wogaman, *A Christian Method of Moral Judgment*, 1976.

3. Walter Lippmann, *Men of Destiny*, New York 1927, pp. 49f., quoted by Daniel Jenkins, *Equality and Excellence: a Christian Comment on Britain's Life*,

1961, p. 21.

4. R. H. Tawney, *Equality*, 1931; 4th edition, with an Introduction by R. M. Titmuss, 1952.

5. *Church and Society in the Late Twentieth Century*, 1983, ch. 3.

6. *Religion and the Persistence of Capitalism*, 1979, ch. 4.

7. Iris Murdoch, *The Sovereignty of the Good*, 1970, p. 80.

8. Robert Nozick, *Anarchy, State and Utopia*, 1974.

9. There is an overlap here with ch. 12 (below) on 'The Politics of Imperfection and the Politics of Hope', where the matter is treated more fully.

10. Peter Townsend, 'A Society for People', in *Conviction*, ed. Norman Mackenzie, 1958, p. 118.

11. Norman Macrae, *The 2024 Report*, 1984.

12. Jo Grimond in *The Economist*, 29 September 1984.

9   Brian Griffiths on Capitalism and the Creation of Wealth

1. In 1985 Griffiths became Special Adviser and Head of the Policy Studies Unit at 10 Downing Street.

2. *Morality and the Market Place: Christian Alternatives to Capitalism and Socialism*, 1982.

3. 'Christianity and Capitalism' in *The Kindness that Kills*, ed. Digby Anderson, 1984, pp. 105–15.

4. *The Creation of Wealth*, 1984. See also his *Monetarism and Morality*, a Patrick Huber Memorial Lecture, 1985, published by the Centre for Policy Studies.

5. A. A. Berle and G. G. Means, *The Corporation and Private Property*, 1932; cf. A. A. Berle, *The Twentieth-Century Capitalist Revolution*, 1955.

6. Fred Hirsch, *The Social Limits to Growth*, 1977.

7. Cf. Denys Munby, *Christianity and Economic Problems*, 1956, *God and the Rich Society*, 1960, and *The Idea of a Secular Society*, 1963.

10   Political Theology: an Appraisal

1. See especially J. B. Metz *Theology of the World*, ET 1969, and *Faith in History: Towards a Practical Fundamental Theology*, ET 1980, and Dorothee Sölle, *Political Theology*, ET Philadelphia 1974.

2. *A Reader in Political Theology*, 1974, and *The Scope of Political Theology*, 1978. The first has no British contributions; the second three out of twenty-four.

3. A conveniently brief treatment can be found in S. L. Greenslade, *Church and State from Constantine to Theodosius*, 1954.

4. See the essay by Raymond Plant, 'The Anglican Church in the Secular State', ch. 13 in the symposium *Church and Politics: the Role of the Church of England in Contemporary Politics*, ed. G. Moyser, 1985.

5. See A. D. Lindsay, *The Essentials of Democracy*, 1929, and *Religion in America*, ed. W. G. McLoughlin and R. N. Bellah, 1968.

6. Among the accounts of the German Churches under Hitler are Gunter Lewy, *The Catholic Church and Nazi Germany*, 1964, J. S. Conway, *The Nazi Persecution of the Churches, 1935–1945*, 1965, and E. Bethge, *Dietrich Bonhoeffer: A Biography*, 1970. References in my text refer to the Ansbach Proposals of 1934 which were a reply to the Barmen Declaration of the Confessing Church earlier in the same year, of which Karl Barth was the theological mentor.

On the Lutheran doctrine of the two kingdoms and its changing interpretation since Nazism see K. H. Hertz, ed., *Two Kingdoms and One World*, Minneapolis 1976.

7. In *Agenda for Prophets*, ed. R. Ambler and D. Haslam, 1980, p. 105.

8. The term Sociology of Knowledge was first used by Max Scheler in 1924. Its impact in Britain was furthered by Karl Mannheim, *Ideology and Utopia*, ET 1936. Even he was disposed to exempt intellectuals from many of the conditioning factors he explored on the grounds that they are 'socially unattached'. See also his *Essays in the Sociology of Knowledge*, 1952.

9. John 7. 17 (RSV).

10. Mannheim, op. cit., p. 256.

11. See especially S. G. F. Brandon, *Jesus and the Zealots*, 1967. A detailed discussion of the issues is best found in the symposium edited by E. Bammel and C. F. D. Moule, *Jesus and the Politics of his Day*, 1984, ch. 1, 'The Zealots and Jesus', by J. P. M. Sweet, and ch. 2, 'The Revolution Theory from Reimarius to Brandon' by E. Bammel.

12. *Bias to the Poor* is the title of a book by David Sheppard, Bishop of Liverpool, 1983; for 'preferential options for the poor' see especially the Report of the Second Conference of Latin American Roman Catholic Bishops at Medellín, Columbia, 'The Church in the Present Day Transformation of Latin America in the Light of the Council' (ET New York 1968).

13. Rom. 12. 5 is a good example: 'we who are many are one body in Christ.'

14. See I Cor. 7. 1–16 and 25–40.

15. II Peter 3. 1–10.

16. I Cor. 15. 58.

17. Heb. 13. 8.

18. Matt. 25. 31–46.

19. See for example Peter Hebblethwaite, *The Christian-Marxist Dialogue and Beyond*, 1977, and James Bentley, *Between Marx and Christ: the Dialogue in German Speaking Europe 1870–1970*, 1982.

20. See Don Cupitt, *Taking Leave of God*, 1980, *The World to Come*, 1982, and *Only Human*, 1985.

21. There is a considerable literature on this, the best short treatment being in the essay by John C. Bennett, 'The Ecumenical Commitment to Transforming Social Justice', in the symposium edited by F. F. Church and T. George, *Continuity and Discontinuity in Church History*, 1979. For the Zagorsk consultation see *Study Encounter* (WCC) No. 2, 1968.

22. Two examples are Gerd Theissen, *The Followers of Jesus: a Sociological analysis of the Earliest Christianity*, ET 1978, and Howard C. Kee, *Christian Origins in Sociological Perspective*, 1980. This kind of study presents difficulties because of the extent to which data have to be inferred from the scanty sources. However the same has been true of Form Criticism itself, which has proved a worthwhile study. There is every reason to pursue these investigations as far as they can plausibly go. Note also B. J. Malina, *The New Testament World: Insights from Cultural Anthropology*, 1981.

23. Heb. 13. 14 (RSV).

24. Thus Jürgen Moltmann in *On Human Dignity: Political Theology and Ethics*, 1984, argues that the 'reduction of apocalyptic to the "eschatological moment" and the defamation of cosmic eschatology as a

"myth" is simply an expression of and justification for a Christian-bourgeois individualistic culture . . .' (p. 173). This is highly implausible.

25. Other books bearing on the theme of this chapter include:

J. L. Segundo, *Evolution and Guilt: a Theology of Politics* (Vol. 5 of 'A Theology for the Artisans of a New Humanity', 1972–4).

J. Moltmann, *The Church in the Power of the Spirit*, 1972.

J. M. Petulla, *Christian Political Theology*, 1972.

Charles Davis, *Theology and Political Society*, 1978.

J. B. Cobb, *Process Theology and Political Theology*, 1982.

J. M. Bonino, *Towards a Christian Political Ethic*, 1983.

Paul Lakeland, *Free in Christ: the Challenge of Political Theology*, 1984.

11. Liberation Theology: an Appraisal

1. The last (eleventh) of the *Theses on Feuerbach* (1845).

2. The best introduction by one of the Latin American theologians is still that of Gustavo Gutierrez, *A Theology of Liberation*, ET New York 1973, London 1974. A shorter one, which also covers Asia and Africa as well as Latin America and includes black and feminist theology (which at first were not on the horizons of Liberation Theology) is Theo Witvliet, *A Place in the Sun: an Introduction to Liberation Theology in the Third World*, ET 1985.

3. There are several minor ones; in Anglicanism Barbados for example.

4. Among the leaders one thinks of Hugo Assmann, originally from Brazil, and the brothers Leonardo and Clodovis Boff from the same country, Enrique Dussel originally from Argentina, Gustavo Gutierrez from Peru, Juan Segundo from Uruguay and Jon Sobrino, a Basque by birth but from El Salvador. These are Roman Catholics. Among Protestants one thinks of Rubem Alves from Brazil, and José Miguez Bonino from Argentina (who has been one of the Presidents of the World Council of Churches). Then there is the poet and priest Ernesto Cardinal of Nicaragua, a friend of Thomas Merton, who led a peasant community on the island of Solentiname, and, when the army of the dictator Somoza destroyed it, left to join the guerilla opposition, and is now Minister of Culture in the Nicaraguan government. For an account of gospel exegesis in the Christian community at Solentiname see Philip Berryman, *The Religious Roots of Rebellion: Nicaragua, El Salvador, Guatemala*, 1984. Ernesto Cardinal's Preface to Hugo Assmann's *Practical Theology of Liberation*, 1975, gives an indication of his (utopian) outlook.

5. A general theme in Gutierrez' writing.

6. *The Church in the Present-Day Transformation of Latin America in the Light of the Council*, ET Bogota 1970.

7. At first there was not much response from Asia and Africa whose situations were both varied and in important respects different from that of Latin America. However an Ecumenical Association of Third World Theologians (EATWOT) was founded. Its first meetings were at Dar-es-Salaam (1976), Accra (1977), Colombo (1979), Sao Paulo (1980), New Delhi (1981) and Geneva (1983). There are several books of essays available, some of them arising from these: *Frontiers of Theology in Latin America*, ed. Rosino Gibellini, 1974; *The Emergent Gospel: Theology from the Underside of History*, ed. Virginia Fabella and Sergio Torres, 1976; *Irruption of the Third World: Challenge to Theology*, New York 1983; and *Doing Theology in a Divided World*, New York 1984.

8. *This point is discussed in ch. 10 above on Political Theology.*

9. W. W. Rostow, *Stages of Economic Growth*, 1961.

10. Of their many writings one might select M. D. Chenu, *Pour une Théologie du Travail*, Paris 1955, and *Théologie de la Matière: civilisation technique et spiritualité chrétienne*, Paris 1968, and Y. M. J. Congar, *Lay People and the Church: a Study for a Theology of the Laity*, ET 1957.

11. *Populorum Progressio*, Par. 31. However the Pope said in Bogota in 1968 that it did rule out revolution.

12. *Instructions on Certain Aspects of the Theology of Liberation*, 1984. It has been associated with the summoning to Rome and temporary silencing of Leonardo Boff. His writings escape the first three of these charges, and in regard to the fourth he is one of a large company. In fact he appears to have been disciplined for his attack on the centralized and authoritarian structures of power in the Roman Catholic church in his book *Church, Charisma and Power: Liberation Theology and the Institutional Church*, ET 1985. This action is not formally incompatible with the affirmations of the *Instruction*, but it does in fact raise the question of how deep the commitment to liberation is. A further *Instruction on Christian Freedom and Liberation* was issued in 1986.

13. J. L. Segundo, *Discussion sur la théologie de la Revolution*, Paris 1972.

14. *A Theology of Liberation*, p. 241, n. 33. Moltmann has been much influenced by the Marxist Ernst Bloch's stress on hope and a completely open future, though as a Christian theologian he has to combat Bloch's view that God is the supreme obstacle to a completely open future because he leaves no room for human freedom. Prometheus is the patron saint of Marxism.

15. Cf. the appendix to ch. 5 above (pp. 95–8).

16. See, for example, G. Gutierrez, *The Power of the Poor in History: Selected Writings*, ET 1983, and *We Drink from our own Wells: the Spiritual Journey of a People*, ET 1984.

17. Cf. J. M. Bonino, *Revolutionary Theology Comes of Age*, 1975, Introduction, and Hugo Assmann, *Practical Theology of Liberation*, 1975, p. 104.

18. Bonino, op. cit., p. 99.

19. Assmann, op. cit., p. 144.

20. José Miranda is the writer in Liberation Theology who moralizes Marx: cf. *Marx and the Bible: a Critique of the Philosophy of Oppression*, 1971, and *Marx Against the Marxists: the Christian Humanism of Karl Marx*, 1980. The most Marxist of the theologians is the Spaniard A. Fierro, *The Militant Gospel*, 1978, who criticizes several Political Theologians, including Metz, Moltmann and Sölle, and Liberation Theologians, including Assmann and Gutierrez.

21. It is not necessary nowadays to be a Marxist to appropriate this. Paul Ricoeur is an example of a philosopher who advocates a 'theological hermeneutic of suspicion', cf. *La Symbolique du Mal*, Paris 1961, and *Le Voluntaire et l'Involuntaire*, Paris 1967. Indeed it is hard not to have absorbed something of this element in Marxism in exposing false consciousness.

22. With (3) cf. East Berlin (1953), Budapest (1956) and Prague (1968), South Yemen (1986). With (4) cf. the Russian and Chinese conflict. On this theme see Imre Latakos, *Philosophical Papers*, 1978 Vol. 1.

23. F. Engels, *Outlines of a Critique of Political Economy*, 1844. This included the theory of capitalist crises but not the labour theory of value or the theory of surplus value. Classical Marxism regarded science as the source of all certain knowledge; hence the necessity of a Scientific Socialism. Engels made more unqualified claims for this than Marx.

24. Preface to the first edition of *Das Kapital*, 1867.

25. Cf. my *Religion and the Persistence of Capitalism*, 1978.

26. On utopias, see ch. 12 below on 'The Politics of Imperfection and the Politics of Hope'.

27. Juan Segundo, *The Liberation of Theology*, 1976, ch. 1.

28. David Sheppard, *Bias to the Poor*, 1983, p. 91 where the exact wording, which I have not entirely followed, will be found.

29. Matt. 7. 21.

30. E.g. in Philippians 3.

31. I cite this because it has been the focus of discussion between more conservative British biblical scholars, like C. H. Dodd, and more radical ones, like Dennis Nineham, as to whether an historical chronology in Jesus' ministry is recoverable. The issue concerns the processes involved in the period of oral transmission before the gospels as we have them took shape.

32. Good examples of biblical exegesis are found in Jon Sobrino, *Christianity at the Crossroads: a Latin American Approach*, ET 1978, and Leonardo Boff, *Jesus Christ Liberator: a Critical Christology for our Time*, ET 1978; cf. also Leonardo and Clodovis Boff, *Salvation and Liberation*, ET New York and Melbourne 1981; Ferdinand Belo, a Portuguese, goes further in *A Materialist Reading of the Gospel of Mark*, ET 1981, and treats the messianic practice of Jesus as a resolute engagement in the class struggle, but much of his exegesis is conventional enough.

33. See e.g. my Scott Holland Lectures, *Church and Society in the Late Twentieth Century*, 1983 especially Appendix 2.

34. See especially L. Boff, *Jesus Christ Liberator*.

35. See L. Boff, *Church, Charisma and Power* (n. 12 above).

36. Cf. Antonio Gramsci, *Selections from the Prison Notebooks*, ed. and trans. G. Hoare and G. Nowell Smith, 1971.

37. For the Communidades Ecclesiales de Base see Alvaro Barriero, *Basic Ecclesial Communities: the Evangelisation of the Poor*, ET 1982, and John Eagleson and Sergio Torres, eds., *The Challenge of Basic Christian Communities*, 1981; and for an example of a church-inspired systematic teaching course in the spirit of them see *Vamos Caminando: a Peruvian Catechism,*, ET 1985 by pastoral team at Bambamarca. The method of CEB's is related to the process of 'conscientization' (conscientizacào) developed by Paulo Freire, which is in essence a process of literacy training which in itself expands the self-consciousness and political consciousness of marginalized people, and enables them to work together for social change, and no longer passively accept their marginalized position. Thus it fosters, and enables them to be ready for, a revolutionary situation. See Paulo Freire, *Pedagogy of the Oppressed*, ET 1970. Boff's further book, *Ecclesiogenesis*, New York 1986, has as its subtitle *The Basic Communities Re-invent the Church*.

38. Cf. D. H. Levine, ed., *Churches and Politics in Latin America*, 1974.

39. For a different view of Puebla see G. Gutierrez, *The Power of the Poor in History*, Part III (n. 16 above).

40. Cf. ch. 5 above, 'The Integrity of Creation'.

41. As early as 1972 Vekemans published an extensive bibliography in *Ecclesiastica Xaveriana* no. 22, following the publication of his own book *Iglesia y Mundi* in 1971.

42. Cf. Segundo, *The Liberation of Theology*, pp. 57ff.

43. This is a theme in Dennis P. McCann, *Christian Realism and Liberation*

Theology: Practical Theologies in Creative Conflict, New York 1981.

44. For the diversity in Marxism see Leszek Kolakowski, *Main Currents of Marxism*, 3 vols., 1978, or, in shorter compass, David McLellan, *The Thought of Karl Marx: an Introduction*, 1971, together with *Marxism after Marx: an Introduction*, 1979.

45. Cf. n.43 above.

46. In an epilogue to *Seeds of Liberation*, the report edited by Kee, of a Student Christian Movement conference in Huddersfield in 1973.

47. In an article in the New York journal *Christianity and Crisis*, 17 September 1973.

48. Giles Ecclestone, *The Church of England and Politics: Reflections on Christian Social Engagement*, 1980.

49. *Faith in the City*, 1985.

50. Cf. n. 44 above.

51. The one on 'Peace and War in a Nuclear Age' was published after three drafts as *The Challenge of Peace: God's Promise and our Response* (in Britain by CTS and SPCK, 1983). The one on the Economic Order is being discussed in draft but the final text is not ready.

52. A critique of Liberation Theology by an evangelical theologian who has had extensive contacts with it is J. A. Kirk, *Liberation Theology: an Evangelical View from the Third World*, 1979. Note also Issue 177 of the journal *Concilium*, 1984, devoted to 'The Ethics of Liberation and the Liberation of Ethics'.

53. 'Minjung' theology, which is being developed in Asia, is very similar to Latin American Liberation Theology; the term is from South Korea and means 'downtrodden'. Cf. The Commission on Theological Concerns of the Christian Conference of Asia, *Minjung Theology: People as Subjects of History*, New York 1983. Africa is dominated by the racist issue; cf. Allan Boesak, *Farewell to Innocence: a Socio-Ethical Study on Black Theology and Black Power*, 1972, which asks the questions, What does it mean to believe in Jesus Christ when one is Black and living in a world controlled by white racists? And what if those racists call themselves Christians also?

12 *The Politics of Imperfection and the Politics of Hope*

1. The theme of this chapter was first suggested to me when I read Anthony Quinton's *The Politics of Imperfection*, 1978, which goes back beyond Burke to Hooker. It was further stimulated by a paper by Paul Wilding, Professor of Social Administration in the University of Manchester on 'Christian Theology and the Politics of Imperfection' read to the Manson Society in the Faculty of Theology in that University, and subsequently published in *The Modern Churchman*, New Series, Vol. 27, No. 2, 1985. I mostly follow his analysis in delineating the elements in the Politics of Imperfection, but he does not see that these elements can lead to politics of the Left as well as the Right, and did in fact do so in the case of several theologians he quotes, who would not have agreed at all with him when he says that the essence of the Politics of Imperfection is 'the view that the human race has reached a stage of development from which no further avenues of social or political transformation open up' (p. 11).

2. Michael Oakeshott, *Rationalism in Politics and Other Essays*, 1962; for Quinton see n. 1 above.

3. E. R. Norman, essay on 'Christianity and Politics' in Maurice Cowling, ed., *Conservative Essays*, 1978, and *Christianity and the World Order*, 1979.

4. Cf. Niebuhr's Gifford Lectures, *The Nature and Destiny of Man*: Vol. 1, *Human Nature*, 1941; Vol. 2, *Human Destiny*, 1943.

5. Nigel Lawson, *The New Conservatism*, 1980.

6. Herman Kahn, *World Economic Development: 1979 and Beyond*, Hudson Institute, USA, 1979.

7. W. W. Rostow, *Getting from Here to There*, 1979.

8. The first (1972) edited by D. H. Meadows and others, the second (1975) edited by M. D. Mesarovic and others; cf. the comment in ch. 5 above, 'The Integrity of Creation'.

9. 'The Long Waves in Economic Life', reprinted in *Lloyd's Bank Review*, July 1978.

10. Fred Hirsch, *The Social Limits to Growth*, 1977.

11. F. A. Hayek has argued this in various books, notably a trilogy, *Law, Legislation and Liberty*: Vol. 1, *Rule and Order*, 1973; Vol. 2, *The Mirage of Social Justice*, 1976; Vol. 3, *The Political Order of a Free People*, 1974. In the second he maintains that the concept of *social* justice is meaningless; justice can be used only in connection with the relation between individuals.

12. K. Popper, *The Open Society and its Enemies*, 2 vols., 1945; *The Poverty of Historicism*, 1957.

13. Oakeshott, *Rationalism in Politics*, p. 127.

14. I have dealt more fully with the necessity of politics in the light of suspicions of it evinced by exponents of the Politics of Imperfection on the political Right in the 1983 Scott Holland Lectures, *Church and Society in the Late Twentieth Century: the Economic and Political Task*, chs. 2, 3 and 6.

15. See chapter 8, on the theological critique of the 'new Right'.

16. John Wesley's *A Plain Account of Christian Perfection* is the chief text. Of the writing on the doctrine of Perfection, the most useful is Newton Flew, *The Idea of Perfection in Christian Theology*, 1934. It includes an acute analysis of the defects in Wesley's understanding of sin, but moves uncertainly in assessing the Doctrine of Perfection as such. Basically he wants to maintain only that the Christian 'ideal' can be realized in part *in via*, that God has not set limits to personal moral and spiritual growth in this life, and that bondage to sin can be overcome. No Christian should deny this.

17. George Woodcock, *Anarchism*, 1962, and G. Woodcock, ed., *The Anarchist Reader*, 1977.

18. Cf. Barbara Goodwin and Keith Taylor, *The Politics of Utopia*, 1982. This makes a case for utopianism in the words '. . . the extending scope and predictive power of the social sciences now make future thinking, including utopianism, a more respectable and less hubristic enterprise than it seemed previously', which shows an excessive optimism about the social sciences, and adds, 'It is feasible, using economic projections, to devise a Good, in terms of resource use and corresponding social organization, for the next generation, and perhaps to manufacture a utopia – not in the sense of a "perfect society", but a utopia which is the best of all possible worlds in the circumstances' (p. 224). This is a much modified use of the term. The book ends by stressing the importance of optimism (p. 253), which is a thin humanist equivalent of Christian hope. A theological discussion of this in terms of utopian thinking is Rubem Alves, *The Theology of Human Hope*, 1970. He has modified his position since then to a stress on the non-necessity of the present social order. A minimal use of the term utopian is to refer to mobilizing ideas, such as that of the 'welfare state', as a guide to action; cf. ch.

10 above on Political Theology.

19. Cf. P. Berger, *Pyramids of Sacrifice: Political Ethics and Social Change*, 1976.

20. Cf. n. 4 above. The last two chapters of Niebuhr's Vol. 1 are on 'Original Sin and Man's Responsibility' and 'Justitia Originalis'.

21. Cf. n. 16 above.

22. This is the point of one of Reinhold Niebuhr's early and best known books, *Moral Man and Immoral Society*, New York 1932, London 1963.

23. Many of these positions are found in Jürgen Moltmann, *Theology of Hope*, 1967, and other of his writings.

24. I Cor. 15. 58.

13   Social Theology and Penal Theory and Practice

1. Peter Berger, *A Rumour of Angels*, 1971.

2. Matt. 18. 21ff. There is much more on forgiveness in the gospels, not least the necessity of those who would be forgiven being ready themselves to forgive, but it does not affect the main point of this chapter.

3. Of course only a man of faith sees this. Jesus appealed to the weather (the sunshine and the rain, Matt. 5. 43ff.) for evidence of God's graciousness. A sceptic could draw different conclusions. The evidence is ambiguous. But Jesus was a man of faith. Subsquently Christians, as men of faith, have appealed to the life and death of Jesus as a true indication of the nature of God, and his way of ruling the world and dealing with human sin.

4. The classical expression of this is the doctrine of 'original sin', which amounts to saying that there is no element in human nature, not even the reason, which is not 'fallen', because we are born into a sinful society; hence the persistence of our self-centredness and our continual need for renewal. Many have held that this is the one Christian doctrine which is empirically verifiable! However in the classical Western Christian tradition it became so caught up with St Augustine's views of sexuality that it is exceptionally difficult for the enquirer not to misunderstand it. So acute a theological moralist as Reinhold Niebuhr gave up using it for this reason and tried to state, as does this chapter, what the term implies without using it. (Cf. Niebuhr's Gifford Lectures of 1941–3, *The Nature and Destiny of Man* with his introduction in 1955 to his *Man's Nature and His Communities*.) The Doctrine is too often interpreted in an individualist way, when in fact it basically refers to the corruptions in society which affect the growing person from birth.

5. Mark 12. 13–17.

6. The first tendency has been specially characteristic of Roman Catholicism, the second of Lutheranism.

7. Some have held justice and love to be identical, some that they are antithetical, and the majority that love presupposes justice but points beyond it. The first group says that justice is love distributed as soon as more than two people are involved; the second restricts love to I–Thou relationships and thinks of it as warm, spontaneous and personal, while justice is impersonal, cool, and deliberate; the third says justice prepares for love and expresses it but cannot exhaust it.

8. Cf. Emil Brunner, *Justice and the Social Order*, 1945.

9. One thinks for example of Sigmund Freud and B. F. Skinner in psychology, both of whose theories have been widely reflected in penal practice.

10. For the most part they have not related their thought to the major theoretical work of John Rawls, *A Theory of Justice*, 1972, but there are significant links.

11. Cf. H. E. Pepinsky, *Crime and Conflict*, 1976.

12. H. L. A. Hart, *The Concept of Law*, 1961.

13. Cf. G. W. F. Hegel *The Philosophy of Right*, ET 1942, Sections 93–103.

14. B. Wilson, *Contemporary Transformations of Religion*, 1976, cf. ch. 14 below.

15. I am avoiding here the technical vocabulary of 'eschatological' (meaning the 'last things' in the sense of those of ultimate significance, which Christians hold to have already been disclosed in Jesus) and 'apocalyptic' (meaning the last things in chronological time). Christians look in some way for the final triumph of the former at the latter.

16. Another technical term; it refers to the 'return of Christ', and is a way of expressing the triumph at the end of time (however conceived) of what he embodied.

17. There does seem a tendency for secular humanism to ricochet from an over-confidence in human beings and in 'science' to despair when things do not work out as expected. H. G. Wells was a notorious example in my youth. Later we have had Arthur Koestler, who verged for a long time on insights which, if not explicitly Christian, were consonant with it, but never quite achieved them, in his book *Janus* (1978) adopting a deeply pessimistic view of humans. Their brain is alleged to have evolved too fast, so that we are only now coming to terms with the inherent sickness and paranoia of character which is bound to destroy us. There could be a similar pessimistic rebound when the failure of the rehabilitative model is realized. The Christian should have resources in the faith which guard against this, and he or she will need to deploy this for the good of all involved in penal policies.

18. Cf. Raymond Plant, *Community and Ideology*, 1974.

19. Brian Barry, *The Liberal Theory of Justice*, 1975.

20. W. H. Auden and Louis MacNeice, *Letters from Iceland*, 1937, p. 258.

14　Bryan Wilson on 'The Demoralisation of Modern Society'

1. An article in *The Salisbury Review*, Vol. 4, No. 1, October 1985, abridged from the 1985 Hobhouse Memorial Lecture, the full text of which is in *The British Journal of Sociology*, Vol. 36, No. 3, 1985, under the title 'Morality in the Evolution of the Modern Social System'.

2. For a very different view of social roles, see Dorothy Emmet, *Rules, Roles and Relations*, 1966.

3. See his *Religion in Secular Society*, 1966; *Contemporary Transformations of Religion*, 1976; and *Religion in Sociological Perspective*, 1982.

15　Reflections on Leaving the Chair

1. I am referring to the 'one-off' short courses of up to ten sessions, not to a three-year Certificate in Religious Studies, which is very different.

2. It was printed in *The Bulletin of John Rylands Library* of the University of Manchester, Vol. 63 No. 2, Spring 1981.

3. Giles Ecclestone, *The Church of England and Politics*, 1980.

4. Rex Ambler and David Haslam, eds., *Agenda for Prophets: Towards a Political Theology for Britain*, 1980.

Appendix

A select list of books and articles up to the spring of 1981 was included in my *Explorations in Theology 9*; this includes additions since then, with the exception of those included in the present book. The sources of these are listed in the Preface.

1981

'William Temple as a Social Theologian', *Theology*, Vol. 84 No. 701.

1982

'Capitalism, Democracy and Christianity' in Michael H. Taylor, ed., *Christians and the Future of Social Democracy*, Ormskirk & Northridge, California.

Article 'Euthanasia' in *Theologische Realenzyklopädie*, Berlin.

'Re-review; Kenneth Kirk's *The Vision of God*' *The Modern Churchman*, New Series, Vol. 25 No. 2.

1983

'Pope John Paul II on Work', *Theology*, Vol. 86 No. 709.

'The Church of England' in Rupert Davies, ed., *The Testing of the Churches 1932–82; a Symposium.*

Church and Society in the Late Twentieth Century: the Economic and Political Task (Scott Holland Lectures).

1984

'A Bishop ahead of his Church: Leslie Hunter, Bishop of Sheffield 1939–62', *Crucible*, April–June 1984.

1985

'The Church and the Free Market Economy', in Terry Brown and Christopher Lind, eds., *Justice as Mission: an Agenda for the Church*, Essays in Appreciation of Marjorie and Cyril Powles, Burlington, Ontario.

'Critics from Without and from Within' in *Church and Society: Essays in honour of Paul Abrecht*, a special number of the *Ecumenical Review*, Vol. 37 No. 1.

'The Clergy, Secularization and Politics' in W. Block, G. Brennan and K. Elzinga, eds., *The Morality of the Market*, Fraser Institute, Vancouver.

1986

Twenty articles in James F. Childress and John Macquarrie, eds., *A New Dictionary of Christian Ethics*.

'Reinhold Niebuhr and the New Right' in Richard Harries, ed., *Reinhold Niebuhr and the Issues of our Time*.

'The Collapse of the S.C.M.', *Theology* Vol. 89, No. 732. 1987.

'The Ethical Legacy of John Maynard Keynes' in D. A. Reece, ed., *The Legacy of Keynes*, New York.

Index